GRAMMAR EXPLORER 3A

Amy Cooper and Samuela Eckstut-Didier

Series Editors: Rob Jenkins and Staci Johnson

Australia • Brazil • Japan • Korea • Mexico • Singapore • Spain • United Kingdom • United States

Grammar Explorer 3A

Amy Cooper and Samuela Eckstut-Didier

Publisher: Sherrise Roehr

Executive Editor: Laura Le Dréan

Managing Editor: Eve Einselen Yu

Senior Development Editor: Kimberly Steiner

Associate Development Editor: Alayna Cohen

Assistant Editor: Vanessa Richards

Senior Technology Product Manager: Scott Rule

Director of Global Marketing: Ian Martin

Marketing Manager: Lindsey Miller

Sr. Director, ELT & World Languages: Michael Burggren

Production Manager: Daisy Sosa

Content Project Manager: Andrea Bobotas

Print Buyer: Mary Beth Hennebury

Cover Designer: 3CD, Chicago

Cover Image: BRIAN J. SKERRY/National Geographic Creative

Compositor: Cenveo Publisher Services

Student Book 3A: 978-1-111-35134-2

National Geographic Learning
20 Channel Center Street
Boston, MA 02210
USA

Cengage Learning is a leading provider of customized learning solutions with office locations around the globe, including Singapore, the United Kingdom, Australia, Mexico, Brazil and Japan.

Visit National Geographic Learning online at **ngl.cengage.com**

Visit our corporate website at **www.cengage.com**

Printed in Mexico
Print Number: 08 Print Year: 2022

CONTENTS

UNIT 3 A Look Into the Future 62

The Future

UNIT 4 Exploration 90

Negative *Yes/No* Questions; Statement and Tag Questions

UNIT 5 Stages of Life 114

Nouns, Articles, and Subject-Verb Agreement

UNIT 6 Wellness 142

Gerunds and Infinitives

UNIT 7 Globe Trotting 174

Modals: Part 1

UNIT 8 Our Mysterious World 206

Modals: Part 2

ACKNOWLEDGMENTS

The authors and publisher would like to thank the following reviewers and contributors:

Gokhan Alkanat, Auburn University at Montgomery, Alabama; **Dorothy S. Avondstondt**, Miami Dade College, Florida; **Heather Barikmo**, The English Language Center at LaGuardia Community College, New York; **Kimberly Becker**, Nashville State Community College, Tennessee; **Lukas Bidelspack**, Corvallis, Oregon; **Grace Bishop**, Houston Community College, Texas; **Mariusz Jacek Bojarczuk**, Bunker Hill Community College, Massachusetts; **Nancy Boyer**, Golden West College, California; **Patricia Brenner**, University of Washington, Washington; **Jessica Buchsbaum**, City College of San Francisco, California; **Gabriella Cambiasso**, Harold Washington College, Illinois; **Tony Carnerie**, English Language Institute, University of California San Diego Extension, California; **Ana M. Cervantes Quequezana**, ICPNA - Instituto Cultural Peruano Norteamericano; **Whitney Clarq-Reis**, Framingham State University; **Julia A. Correia**, Henderson State University, Arkansas; **Katie Crowder**, UNT Department of Linguistics and Technical Communication, Texas; **Lin Cui**, William Rainey Harper College, Illinois; **Nora Dawkins**, Miami Dade College, Florida; **Rachel DeSanto**, English for Academic Purposes, Hillsborough Community College, Florida; **Aurea Diab**, Dillard University, Louisiana; **Marta Dmytrenko-Ahrabian**, English Language Institute, Wayne State University, Michigan; **Susan Dorrington**, Education and Language Acquisition Department, LaGuardia Community College, New York; **Ian Dreilinger**, Center for Multilingual Multicultural Studies, University of Central Florida, Florida; **Jennifer Dujat**, Education and Language Acquisition Department, LaGuardia Community College, New York; **Dr. Jane Duke**, Language & Literature Department, State College of Florida, Florida; **Anna Eddy**, University of Michigan-Flint, Michigan; **Jenifer Edens**, University of Houston, Texas; **Karen Einstein**, Santa Rosa Junior College, California; **Cynthia Etter**, International & English Language Programs, University of Washington, Washington; **Parvanak Fassihi**, SHOWA Boston Institute for Language and Culture, Massachusetts; **Katherine Fouche**, The University of Texas at Austin, Texas; **Richard Furlong**, Education and Language Acquisition Department, LaGuardia Community College, New York; **Glenn S. Gardner**, Glendale College, California; **Sally Gearhart**, Santa Rosa Junior College, California; **Alexis Giannopolulos**, SHOWA Boston Institute for Language and Culture, Massachusetts; **Nora Gold**, Baruch College, The City University of New York, New York; **Ekaterina V. Goussakova**, Seminole State College of Florida; **Lynn Grantz**, Valparaiso University, Indiana; **Tom Griffith**, SHOWA Boston Institute for Language and Culture, Massachusetts; **Christine Guro**, Hawaii English Language Program, University of Hawaii at Manoa, Hawaii; **Jessie Hayden**, Georgia Perimeter College, Georgia; **Barbara Inerfeld**, Program in American Language Studies, Rutgers University, New Jersey; **Gail Kellersberger**, University of Houston-Downtown, Texas; **David Kelley**, SHOWA Boston Institute for Language and Culture, Massachusetts; **Kathleen Kelly**, ESL Department, Passaic County Community College, New Jersey; **Dr. Hyun-Joo Kim**, Education and Language Acquisition Department, LaGuardia Community College, New York; **Linda Koffman**, College of Marin, California; **Lisa Kovacs-Morgan**, English Language Institute, University of California San Diego Extension, California; **Jerrad Langlois**, TESL Program and Office of International Programs, Northeastern Illinois University; **Janet Langon**, Glendale College, California; **Olivia Limbu**, The English Language Center at LaGuardia Community College, New York; **Devora Manier**, Nashville State Community College, Tennessee; **Susan McAlister**, Language and Culture Center, Department of English, University of Houston, Texas; **John McCarthy**, SHOWA Boston Institute for Language and Culture, Massachusetts; **Dr. Myra Medina**, Miami Dade College, Florida; **Dr. Suzanne Medina**, California State University, Dominguez Hills, California; **Nancy Megarity**, ESL & Developmental Writing, Collin College, Texas; **Joseph Montagna**, SHOWA Boston Institute for Language and Culture, Massachusetts; **Richard Moore**, University of Washington; **Monika Mulder**, Portland State University, Oregon; **Patricia Nation**, Miami Dade College, Florida; **Susan Niemeyer**, Los Angeles City College, California; **Charl Norloff**, International English Center, University of Colorado Boulder, Colorado; **Gabriella Nuttall**, Sacramento City College, California; **Dr. Karla Odenwald**, CELOP at Boston University, Massachusetts; **Ali Olson-Pacheco**, English Language Institute, University of California San Diego Extension, California; **Fernanda Ortiz**, Center for English as a Second Language, University of Arizona, Arizona; **Chuck Passentino**, Grossmont College, California; **Stephen Peridore**, College of Southern Nevada, Nevada; **Frank Quebbemann**, Miami Dade College, Florida; **Dr. Anouchka Rachelson**, Miami Dade College, Florida; **Dr. Agnieszka Rakowicz**, Education and Language Acquisition Department, LaGuardia Community College, New York; **Wendy Ramer**, Broward College, Florida; **Esther Robbins**, Prince George's Community College, Maryland; **Helen Roland**, Miami Dade College, Florida; **Debbie Sandstrom**, Tutorium in Intensive English, University of Illinois at Chicago, Illinois; **Maria Schirta**, Hudson County Community College, New Jersey; **Dr. Jennifer Scully**, Education and Language Acquisition Department, LaGuardia Community College, New York; **Jeremy Stubbs**, Tacoma, Washington; **Adrianne Thompson**, Miami Dade College, Florida; **Evelyn Trottier**, Basic and Transitional Studies Program, Seattle Central Community College, Washington; **Karen Vallejo**, University of California, Irvine, California; **Emily Young**, Auburn University at Montgomery, Alabama.

The publisher would also like to thank Heidi Fischer for her writing of Connect the Grammar to Writing in level 3 of this series.

From the Authors: We would like to thank Tom Jefferies for selecting us to work together on this project and Laura Le Dréan for steering it through to completion. We can't thank our editors, Eve Einselen Yu and Kim Steiner, enough for their expertise and perseverance through charts, drafts, and countless e-mails. We also wish to thank Heidi Fischer for her clear models and writing tasks in Connect the Grammar to Writing. In addition, we are grateful for the inspiration of our fellow authors Daphne Mackay and Paul Carne, as well as Daria Ruzicka in the early stages of the project. Their head start on Levels 1 and 2 set the high standards to which we knew we had to aspire.

Dedication: To Gary, for your patience, support, and invaluable native speaker intuitions.
À Robert, pour tous les bons repas et toutes les belles journées.

National Geographic images introduce the unit theme—real world topics that students want to read, write, and talk about.

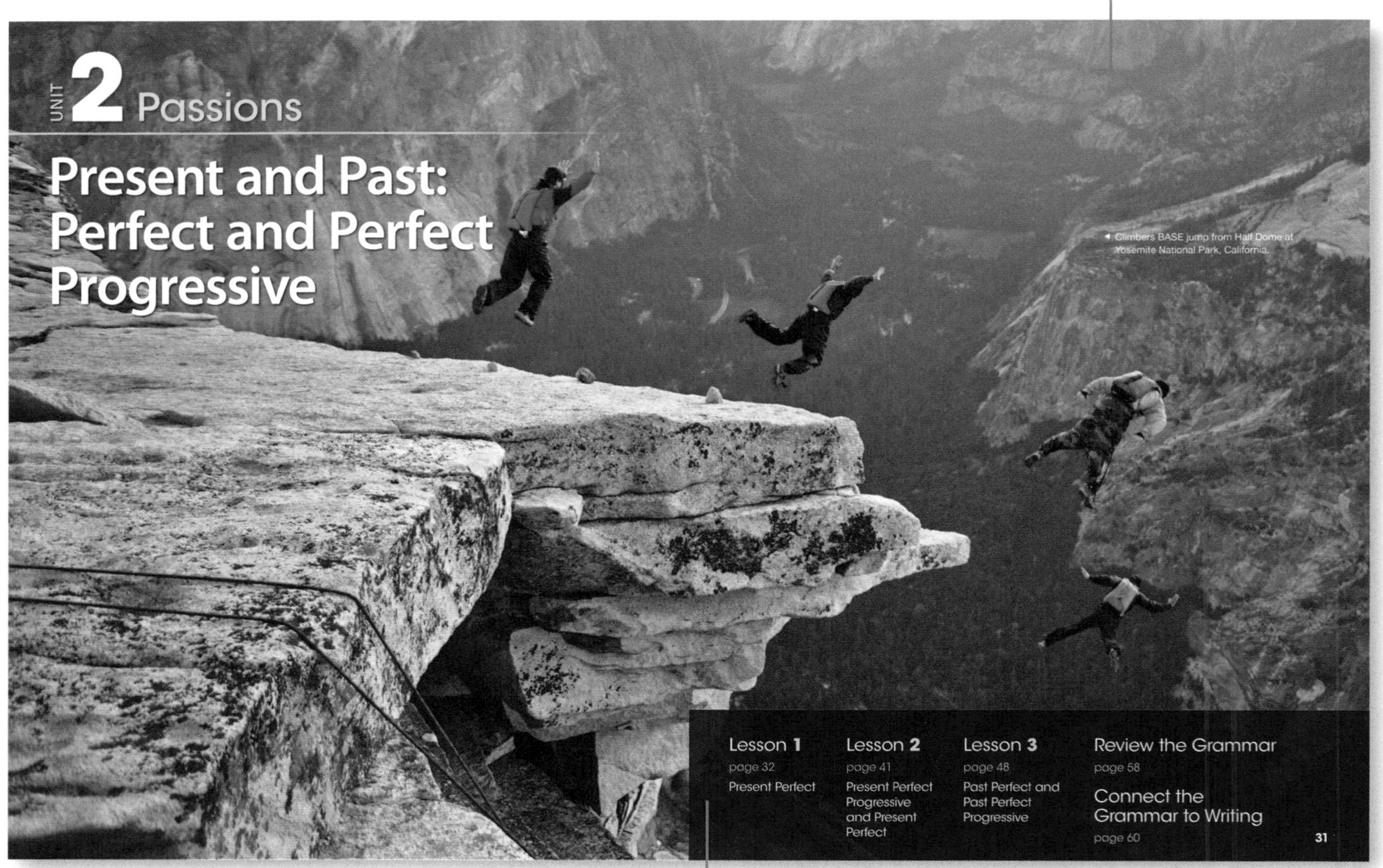

Units are organized in **manageable lessons**, which ensures students **explore, learn, practice,** and **apply** the grammar.

Each lesson begins with the ***Explore*** section, featuring a captivating National Geographic article that introduces the target grammar and builds students' knowledge in a variety of academic disciplines.

LESSON 1 Present Perfect

EXPLORE

1 **READ** the book review of *Polar Obsession*. What is Paul Nicklen's passion?

Paul Nicklen's *Polar Obsession*

For most people, the Arctic and Antarctica are strange places that we know very little about. Paul Nicklen's collection of photographs and stories, *Polar Obsession*, offers an excellent introduction.

Nicklen grew up on an island in Northern Canada, where he learned all about the outdoors from his Inuit[1] neighbors. Ever since that time, he **has loved** animals, cold weather, and adventure.

As a photojournalist, Nicklen **has spent** a lot of time in icy polar waters. He **has followed** sea lions, **dived** with whales, and **studied** polar bears. One of the most exciting parts of the book covers Nicklen's unforgettable encounter with a leopard seal in Antarctica.

As the photographs clearly show, leopard seals are very large—up to 12 feet (4 meters) long and weighing over 1000 pounds (450 kilograms). They have huge, sharp teeth, and they move quickly through the water searching for food such as fish and penguins.

Leopard seals can be dangerous, but this didn't stop Nicklen from trying to photograph one. When a huge seal approached his boat, Nicklen got into the water. He was shaking with fear, but much to his surprise the seal treated him gently. She even tried to feed him! The seal brought him penguins to eat, and he photographed her. Nicklen says it was the most incredible experience that he **has**

In *Polar Obsession*,
He also helps us to und

[1] **Inuit:** indigenous people living

32 PRESENT AND PAST: PERFECT AND P

Present Perfect Progressive and Present Perfect LESSON 2

EXPLORE

1 **READ** the magazine article about Helen Thayer. What advice does she have for other people?

Helen Thayer: A Lifelong Adventurer

Helen Thayer **has** never **let** age stop her. She and her husband, Bill, fulfilled a lifelong dream for their 40th wedding anniversary. They walked 1600 miles

In recent years, Thayer **has been** to travel and bring back stories to sh people to follow goals, plan for su

[1] **nomads:** people who
[2] **inspire:** to make som
[3] **fulfill one's dream:**

The Gobi Desert covers parts of Mongolia and China.

LESSON 3 Past Perfect and Past Perfect Progressive

EXPLORE

1 **READ** the article about Alex Honnold. What big risk did he take to fulfill his dream?

Daring. Defiant. Free.

A new generation of superclimbers is pushing the limits in Yosemite

Every rock climber who has come to Yosemite has a dream. Alex Honnold's dream was to free solo Half Dome, a 2130-foot (649-meter) wall of granite. Free soloing means climbing with only rock shoes and some chalk to help keep the hands dry. Honnold couldn't use a rope or anything else to help him stick to the slippery stone. The few people who **had climbed** Half Dome before **had used** ropes, and it **had taken** them more than a day to do the climb.

On a bright September morning, Honnold was clinging[2] to the face of Half Dome, less than 100 feet (30 meters) from the top. He **had been climbing** for two hours and forty-five minutes, but all of a sudden he stopped. Something potentially disastrous had occurred—he had lost some of his confidence. He **hadn't felt** that way two days before when **he'd been racing** up the same rock *with* a rope. That climb **had gone** well. Today though, Honnold hesitated. He knew that even the slightest doubt could cause a deadly fall, thousands of feet to the valley floor below. He knew he had to get moving, so he chalked his hands, adjusted his feet, and started climbing again. Within minutes, he was at the top.

Bloggers spread the news of Honnold's two-hour-and-fifty-minute free solo, and climbers were amazed. On this warm fall day, 23-year-old Alex Honnold **had** just **set** a new record in one of climbing's biggest challenges.

[1] **granite:** a kind of very hard rock
[2] **cling:** to hold something tightly

Alex Honnold free soloing in Yosemite National Park, California

48 PRESENT AND PAST: PERFECT AND PERFECT PROGRESSIVE

INSIDE A UNIT

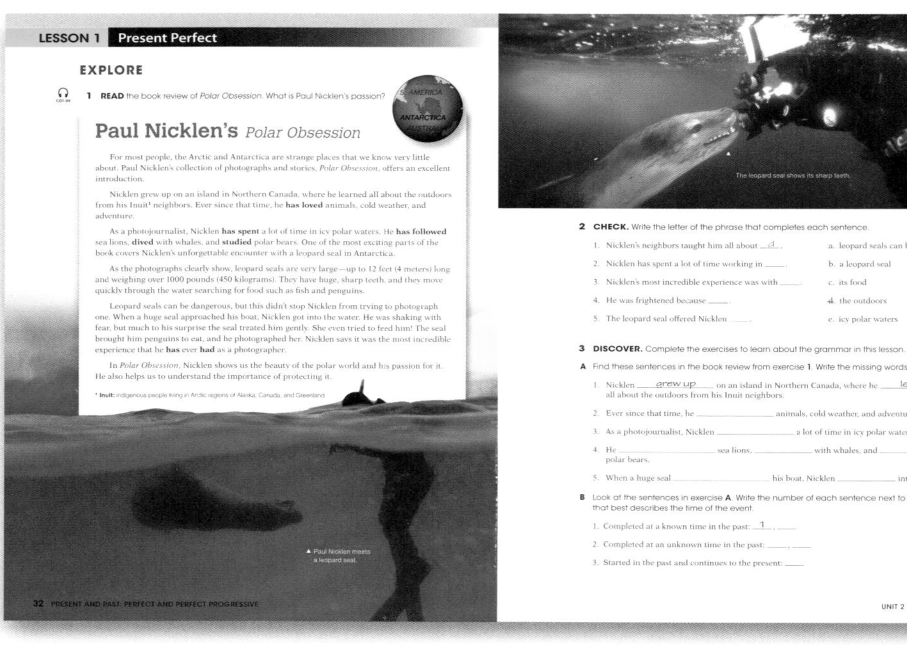

LESSON 1 **Present Perfect**

EXPLORE

1 READ the book review of *Polar Obsession*. What is Paul Nicklen's passion?

Paul Nicklen's *Polar Obsession*

For most people, the Arctic and Antarctica are strange places that we know very little about. Paul Nicklen's collection of photographs and stories, *Polar Obsession*, offers an excellent introduction.

Nicklen grew up on an island in Northern Canada, where he learned all about the outdoors from his Inuit[1] neighbors. Ever since that time, he **has loved** animals, cold weather, and adventure.

As a photojournalist, Nicklen **has spent** a lot of time in icy polar waters. He **has followed** sea lions, **dived** with whales, and **studied** polar bears. One of the most exciting parts of the book covers Nicklen's unforgettable encounter with a leopard seal in Antarctica.

As the photographs clearly show, leopard seals are very large—up to 12 feet (4 meters) long and weighing over 1000 pounds (450 kilograms). They have huge, sharp teeth, and they move quickly through the water searching for food such as fish and penguins.

Leopard seals can be dangerous, but this didn't stop Nicklen from trying to photograph one. When a huge seal approached his boat, Nicklen got into the water. He was shaking with fear, but much to his surprise the seal treated him gently. She even tried to feed him! The seal brought him penguins to eat, and he photographed her. Nicklen says it was the most incredible experience that he **has** ever **had** as a photographer.

In *Polar Obsession*, Nicklen shows us the beauty of the polar world and his passion for it. He also helps us to understand the importance of protecting it.

[1] **Inuit:** indigenous people living in Arctic regions of Alaska, Canada, and Greenland

▲ Paul Nicklen meets a leopard seal.

32 PRESENT AND PAST: PERFECT AND PERFECT PROGRESSIVE

The leopard seal shows its sharp teeth.

2 CHECK. Write the letter of the phrase that completes each sentence.

1. Nicklen's neighbors taught him all about __d__.
2. Nicklen has spent a lot of time working in ____.
3. Nicklen's most incredible experience was with ____.
4. He was frightened because ____.
5. The leopard seal offered Nicklen ____.

a. leopard seals can be dangerous
b. a leopard seal
c. its food
d. the outdoors
e. icy polar waters

3 DISCOVER. Complete the exercises to learn about the grammar in this lesson.

A Find these sentences in the book review from exercise **1**. Write the missing words.

1. Nicklen __grew up__ on an island in Northern Canada, where he __learned__ all about the outdoors from his Inuit neighbors.
2. Ever since that time, he ________ animals, cold weather, and adventure.
3. As a photojournalist, Nicklen ________ a lot of time in icy polar waters.
4. He ________ sea lions, ________ with whales, and ________ polar bears.
5. When a huge seal ________ his boat, Nicklen ________ into the water.

B Look at the sentences in exercise **A**. Write the number of each sentence next to the phrase that best describes the time of the event.

1. Completed at a known time in the past: __1__, ____
2. Completed at an unknown time in the past: ____, ____
3. Started in the past and continues to the present: ____

UNIT 2 LESSON 1 33

In the ***Explore*** section, students discover how the grammar structures are used in the readings and in real academic textbooks.

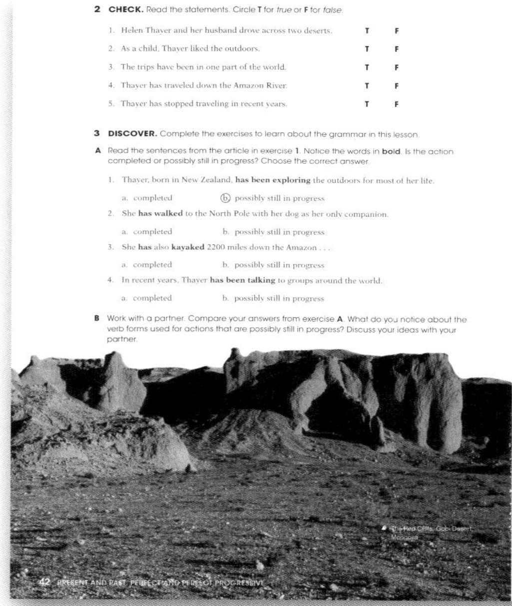

2 CHECK. Read the statements. Circle **T** for *true* or **F** for *false*.

1. Helen Thayer and her husband drove across two deserts.	T	F
2. As a child, Thayer liked the outdoors.	T	F
3. The trips have been in one part of the world.	T	F
4. Thayer has traveled down the Amazon River.	T	F
5. Thayer has stopped traveling in recent years.	T	F

3 DISCOVER. Complete the exercises to learn about the grammar in this lesson.

A Read the sentences from the article in exercise **1**. Notice the words in **bold**. Is the action completed or possibly still in progress? Choose the correct answer.

1. Thayer, born in New Zealand, **has been exploring** the outdoors for most of her life.
   a. completed (b.) possibly still in progress
2. She **has walked** to the North Pole with her dog as her only companion.
   a. completed b. possibly still in progress
3. She **has** also **kayaked** 2200 miles down the Amazon . . .
   a. completed b. possibly still in progress
4. In recent years, Thayer **has been talking** to groups around the world.
   a. completed b. possibly still in progress

B Work with a partner. Compare your answers from exercise **A**. What do you notice about the verb forms used for actions that are possibly still in progress? Discuss your ideas with your partner.

42 PRESENT AND PAST: PERFECT AND PERFECT PROGRESSIVE

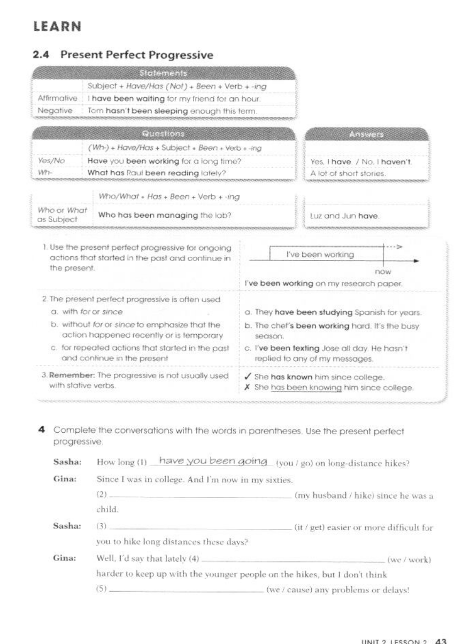

LEARN

2.4 Present Perfect Progressive

Statements	
	Subject + *Have/Has (Not)* + *Been* + Verb + *-ing*
Affirmative	I **have been waiting** for my friend for an hour.
Negative	Tom **hasn't been sleeping** enough this term.

Questions		Answers
	(Wh-) + *Have/Has* + Subject + *Been* + Verb + *-ing*	
Yes/No	**Have** you **been working** for a long time?	Yes, I **have**. / No, I **haven't**.
Wh-	**What has** Raul **been reading** lately?	A lot of short stories.
	Who/What + *Has* + *Been* + Verb + *-ing*	
Who or *What* as Subject	**Who has been managing** the lab?	Luz and Jun **have**.

1. Use the present perfect progressive for ongoing actions that started in the past and continue in the present.	I've been working — now **I've been working** on my research paper.
2. The present perfect progressive is often used a. with *for* or *since* b. without *for* or *since* to emphasize that the action happened recently or is temporary c. for repeated actions that started in the past and continue in the present	 a. They **have been studying** Spanish for years. b. The chef's **been working** hard. It's the busy season. c. **I've been texting** Jose all day. He hasn't replied to any of my messages.
3. **Remember:** The progressive is not usually used with stative verbs.	✓ She **has known** him since college. ✗ She has been knowing him since college.

4 Complete the conversations with the words in parentheses. Use the present perfect progressive.

Sasha: How long (1) __have you been going__ (you / go) on long-distance hikes?

Gina: Since I was in college. And I'm now in my sixties. (2) ________ (my husband / hike) since he was a child.

Sasha: (3) ________ (it / get) easier or more difficult for you to hike long distances these days?

Gina: Well, I'd say that lately (4) ________ (we / work) harder to keep up with the younger people on the hikes, but I don't think (5) ________ (we / cause) any problems or delays!

UNIT 2 LESSON 2 43

The ***Learn*** section features clear grammar charts and explanations followed by controlled practice of the grammar forms.

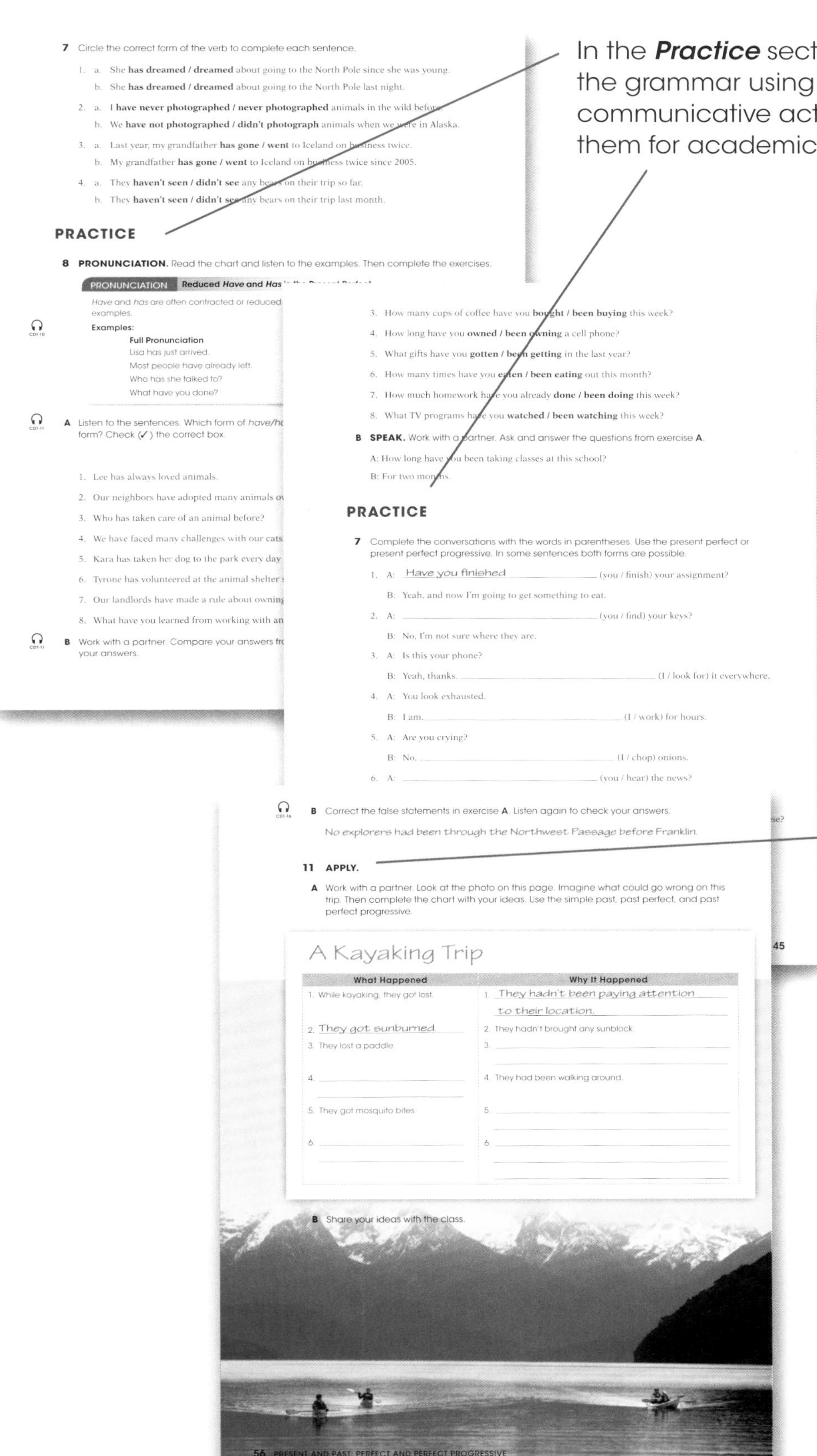

In the ***Practice*** section, students practice the grammar using all four skills through communicative activities that prepare them for academic work.

Students use their new language and critical thinking skills in the ***Apply*** section.

Review the Grammar UNIT 2

Charts 2.1–2.7

1 Complete the paragraph. Use the correct form of each verb in parentheses.

I (1) ___had___ (have) a terrible car accident when I was sixteen. I (2) ______ (lose) a leg. As an athlete, this was especially devastating. I (3) ______ (be) a gymnast from the age of eight, and I (4) ______ (win) three national competitions. It (5) ______ (take) me a lot of time to recover, and I (6) ______ (not think) about competing again. Then, one of my coaches (7) ______ (tell) me about the Paralympics and (8) ______ (suggest) that I train for swimming. I could do that with only one leg. I (9) ______ (always / want) to be in the Olympics. In fact, I (10) ______ (train) for the Olympics at the time of my accident. So I (11) ______ (listen) to my coach and (12) ______ (start) swimming. I (13) ______ (swim) ever since that day and I love it. I (14) ______ (win) several competitions. Lately, I (15) ______ (train) for the next Paralympics. I hope to win a medal!

Charts 2.1, 2.3–2.7

2 EDIT. Read the text by a traveler on safari. Find and correct eight more errors with the simple past, present perfect, past perfect, or past perfect progressive.

Mason's Travels on Safari

It had always been our dream to travel to southern Africa, and we'd ~~make~~ made a lot of plans for our trip. I wanted to take a lot of wildlife photographs, so my friend has recommended that I bring two cameras. When I got to Namibia, I had panicked. One camera had been missing. Luckily, I was finding it later.

The next day, we had started out on our safari with a tour. By the end of our tour, we saw some amazing things. One time, when we stopped to take pictures, we were only a few feet away from a cheetah. Amazing!

We had never bothered the animals at night. How[...] and other noises outside our tent every night. At first, [...] but not by the end of the trip. It was really the most i[...]

Cheetah running, Namibia ▸

Charts 2.1, 2.3–2.4, 2.6

3 LISTEN & SPEAK.

A Circle the correct form of the verb. Then listen to the conversation and check your answers.

CD1-17

1. Liu Yang is the first female astronaut that China **ever sent / has ever sent** into space.
2. She **trained / has trained** to be a pilot at China's Air Force College, and then she **joined / has joined** the Air Force.
3. She **flew / has flown** five different types of aircraft, and she **did / has done** 1680 hours of flight time.
4. She **also participated / has also participated** in military exercises and emergency rescues.
5. Liu started training to be an astronaut. She **has never experienced / had never experienced** anything so challenging.

CD1-18

B Listen to the next part of the conversation. Then work with a partner. Discuss the questions. Then listen again and check your answers.

1. What has Liu Yang done in her life?
2. Had she always wanted to be an astronaut?
3. How have her coworkers described her?
4. How long had she been in the Air Force before becoming an astronaut?

UNIT 2 REVIEW THE GRAMMAR 59

Review the Grammar gives students the opportunity to consolidate the grammar in their reading, writing, listening, and speaking.

Connect the Grammar to Writing

1 READ & NOTICE THE GRAMMAR.

A What is a goal that you have achieved? How did it affect you? Tell a partner your ideas. Then read the narrative.

Achieving a Goal

About a year ago, I was watching the Olympics, and I decided that I wanted to become a runner. I knew I should set an achievable goal, so I decided to train for a 5K race.

My parents were surprised when I told them about my goal, because I had never been interested in running before. In fact, I had never run more than a mile, and I had always been very slow. My friends thought I was joking. Everyone assumed that I would quit after a week.

Fortunately, I proved them all wrong. I did two things to achieve my goal. First, I went online and researched a good training plan. I found a website that helps you plan workouts. You start by walking, and then you gradually start running. After that, I joined a local running group. We ran in the park twice a week, and I made friends who had also decided to run a 5K.

Three months later, I achieved my goal: I ran in my first race. I didn't win, but I ran the whole way, so I was proud of myself. Since then, I have run in several races. I have also started training for a longer run. My next goal is to run in a 10K race. My friends have stopped laughing at me, and a few of them have even asked me to help them start running!

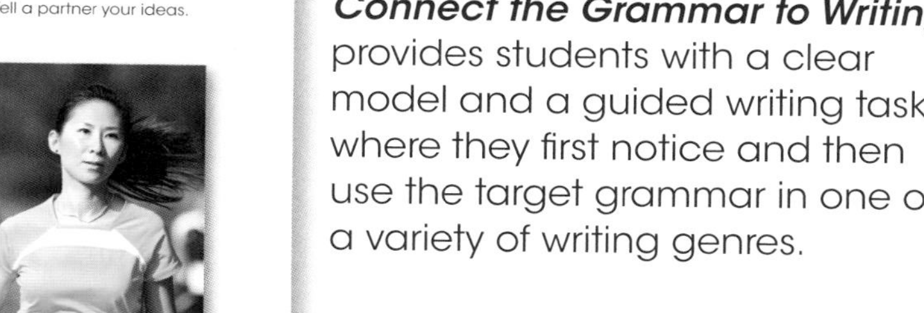

Connect the Grammar to Writing provides students with a clear model and a guided writing task where they first notice and then use the target grammar in one of a variety of writing genres.

GRAMMAR FOCUS

In the narrative in exercise **A**, the writer uses these verb forms:

Simple past	• to tell about the main event of the story (*About a year ago . . . I* ***decided*** *that . . .*)
Past perfect	• to discuss events that happ… (*I* ***had*** *never* ***run*** *more than* …
Present perfect	• with *since* to tell about past… present (*Since then, I* ***have*** …

B Read the narrative in exercise **A** again. Find and circle … past. Underline two past perfect examples, and doubl… examples.

Write a Personal Narrative

C Complete the time line with information from the narrative in exercise **A**. Write the letter of the events in the correct order. Then compare your answers with a partner.

a. Ran in several other races
b. Was never interested in running
c. Joined a running club
d. Parents were surprised
e. Ran in 5K
f. Watched the Olympics
g. Found a good website

b ___ ___ ___ ___ ___ ___

Set a goal to run a 5K — Now

2 BEFORE YOU WRITE.

A Work with a partner. Make a list of goals that you have achieved. Discuss which goals would be the most interesting to write about.

B Create a time line for your personal narrative. Write the events of the story that you want to tell. Use the time line in exercise **1C** as a guide.

3 WRITE two or three paragraphs telling your story. Use your time line in exercise **2B** and the text in exercise **1A** as a guide. Remember to start your story with background information. At the end, tell how your life has changed.

WRITING FOCUS Using *First* and *After that* to Show a Sequence

Notice *first* and *after that* in the narrative in exercise **1A**.

Use these words at the beginning of the sentence to explain the order of events in a text. Place a comma after *first* and *after that*.

First, *I went online and . . .* ***After that,*** *I joined a local running club.*

4 SELF ASSESS. Underline the verb forms in your narrative. Then use the checklist to assess your work.

- ☐ I used the present perfect and the present perfect progressive correctly. [2.1, 2.2, 2.4, 2.5]
- ☐ I used the simple past correctly. [2.3]
- ☐ I used the past perfect and the past perfect progressive correctly. [2.6, 2.7]
- ☐ I used commas correctly with *first* and *after that*. [WRITING FOCUS]

UNIT 1 Family

Present and Past: Simple and Progressive

▶ A grizzly bear with four young cubs near Moraine Creek in Katmai National Park, Southwest Alaska, USA

EXPLORE

1 READ the article about lowland gorillas in northern Congo. What are researchers trying to learn about these animals?

The Family Life of Lowland Gorillas

Scientists know very little about how lowland gorillas behave in the rainforests where they live. However, one thing is clear: their numbers **are** rapidly **declining**.[1] In order to help these animals survive, researchers **are trying** to learn as much as possible about their family relationships as well as their behavior and diet in the wild.

One family that scientists **are** currently **observing** belongs to Kingo. It includes Kingo, his four wives—each with her own baby—and one orphan.[2] The ten gorillas **live** comfortably in a rainforest in northern Congo. Together with a team of trackers,[3] the researchers **follow** the family everywhere. Today, they **are watching** Kingo at lunchtime.

Kingo always **eats** alone; his wives and babies never **go** near him. After he **eats**, he usually **takes** a nap. He **lies back** in the hot shade and instantly **falls** asleep. Then when he **wakes up**, he **leads** his family through the forest in search of more food. The young males **stay** close by his side, and they **copy** every move he **makes**. Kingo's wives **walk** behind him. When he **stops**, they **stop**, and when he **moves**, they **move**.

Kingo's stop today is a pond. Here he **is pulling up** plants, **washing** them in the water, and then **eating** them. This 300-pound (136-kilogram) king of the jungle couldn't be happier right now. The mothers **are resting**, and the young ones **are taking** naps or **playing**. As the researchers can clearly see, this is just one big, happy family.

[1] **decline:** become less
[2] **orphan:** a child whose parents have died
[3] **tracker:** someone who finds animals by following marks in the ground or other signs that show where the animals have been

▲ A family of western lowland gorillas moving through the grass, Odzala National Park, Republic of the Congo

◀ An orphan western lowland gorilla in the forests of Congo

2 CHECK. Read each statement about the article. Circle **T** for *true* or **F** for *false*.

1. The number of lowland gorillas is growing. **T** **(F)**
2. Kingo spends time with his family every day. **T** **F**
3. Kingo's wives don't eat with Kingo. **T** **F**
4. Kingo doesn't usually take a nap after lunch. **T** **F**
5. Lowland gorillas eat plants. **T** **F**

3 DISCOVER. Complete the exercises to learn about the grammar in this lesson.

A Look at these sentences from the article. Circle the answer that is true about the bold verb forms.

1. The ten gorillas **live** comfortably in a rainforest in northern Congo.

   a. describes a temporary situation or one lasting a short period of time

   (b.) describes a permanent situation or one not changing for a long time

2. Kingo always **eats** alone; his wives and children never **go** near him. After he **eats**, he usually **takes** a nap.

   a. describe activities now

   b. describe routines or habits

3. Here he **is pulling up** plants, **washing** them in the water, and then **eating** them. . . . The mothers **are resting**, and the young ones **are taking** naps or **playing**.

   a. describe activities now

   b. describe routines or habits

B Work with a partner. Check (✓) the correct box for each statement. Look at your answers in exercise **A** to help you.

This verb form shows that the action or situation is . . .	**Simple Present** verb (+ *s*)	**Present Progressive** *is/are* + verb + *-ing*
1. permanent.	☑	☐
2. a routine or a habit.	☐	☐
3. in progress now or over a current period of time.	☐	☐

LEARN

1.1 Simple Present and Present Progressive Review

	Simple Present	Present Progressive
Affirmative Statements	I **eat** a healthy diet. Ana **eats** only vegetables.	I**'m eating** an apple now. She**'s eating** a salad.
Negative Statements	We **don't work** on Saturdays. Ali **doesn't work** in a hospital.	We**'re not working** today. Jim**'s not working** now.
Yes/No Questions	**Do** you **eat** breakfast every day? **Does** Jana **study** at the library?	**Are** the children **eating** lunch now? **Is** Jana **studying** now?
Wh- Questions	**Where do** you **read** the news? **How long does** the train **take**?	**What are** you **studying** this semester? **Why is** he **staying** in a hotel this week?
Who or *What* as Subject	**Who lives** in this house? **What helps** a headache?	**Who is taking** math this semester? **What is cooking** in the oven?

1. Use the simple present for: a. routines and habits b. facts and general truths c. permanent actions or situations	a. I **drink** coffee every day. b. The sky often **looks** blue. c. Tomo's parents **live** in a big house.
2. Use the present progressive for actions that are: a. happening now, at the moment of speaking b. happening over a current time period *(today, this week, this month, this year)* c. temporary	a. I can't talk now. I**'m eating** dinner. b. She**'s visiting** her grandmother this week. c. Jared **is living** in a dorm this semester.
3. Do not repeat the verb *be* when the same subject is doing two actions.	Youssef is **singing** and **playing** the guitar in the video.
4. **Be careful!** Do not use *do/does* in questions when *Who* or *What* is the subject.	✓**Who reads** the newspaper? ✗ Who does read the newspaper?

4 Complete the interview with the words in parentheses. Use the simple present or present progressive form of the verbs.

A: How (1) do you find (you / find) the gorillas every day?

B: Every morning (2) I go (I / go) with the trackers to look for them.

A: How long (3) does it take (it / take) to find the gorillas?

B: (4) It usually takes (it / usually / take) a few hours, but sometimes (5) We don't find (we / not find) them for five or six hours.

A: (6) Do the trackers follow (the trackers / follow) Kingo today?

REAL ENGLISH

The adverbs *ever, usually, often,* and *always* are common with the simple present. They usually go before the main verb.

Do you ***ever*** *ride your bike to work?*

What do they ***usually*** *do on weekends?*

Jack doesn't ***always*** *eat breakfast.*

B: No, they aren't. (7) ___They are spending___ (the trackers / spend) time with their families for a few days and (8) ___exploring___ (explore) the area.

A: Where (9) ___do you stay___ (you / stay) this week?

B: (10) ___I stay at___ (I / stay) at a campsite with my guides and trackers.

A: So, tell me, what (11) ___is suprise___ (surprise) you about the gorillas?

B: Good question! I find it interesting that (12) ___gorillas laugh___ (gorillas / laugh).

A: (13) ___Do you follow___ (you / follow) other animal families?

B: Yes. This year (14) ___I do___ (I / do) research on chimp families, too.

A: What (15) ___do make___ (make) gorillas different from chimpanzees?

B: (16) ___Young chimps and gorillas stay___ (young chimps and gorillas / stay) with their mothers. (17) ___chimp fathers usually not stay___ (chimp fathers / usually / not stay) with the family. Gorilla fathers (18) ___rarely leave___ (rarely / leave) their families.

1.2 More Present Progressive

1. Use the present progressive for changes that happen over time.	Her baby **is getting bigger** day by day. Children today **are eating** more sugar.
2. Use the present progressive with *always* to emphasize repeated actions. Sometimes, these actions are not typical or are unwanted.	I'm worried. Julie **is always sleeping**. My car **is always breaking down.**
3. Use the simple present with *always* if the action is normal or expected.	My son **always does** his homework.

5 Complete the paragraph with the words in parentheses. Use the simple present or the present progressive.

The Reed family (1) ___is growing___ (grow) too big for their house. Rose and Jeff Reed now have six children at home, and the kids (2) ______ (get) bigger every day. The challenges for the family (3) ______ (grow), too.

For example, the cost of food (4) ______ (increase). It's hard to feed so many people. Rose and Jeff (5) ______ (always / go) to the grocery store together and (6) ______ (compare) prices, but it's still hard.

Different personalities are another challenge. Melissa Reed says, "I'm the oldest child. I (7) ______ (always / take care of) my younger brothers and sisters. I enjoy all of them most of the time, but my younger brother, Charlie, can be difficult. He (8) ______ (always / get) into trouble. In fact, he (9) ______ (become) impossible. Someone (10) ______ (always / complain) about him."

6 ANALYZE THE GRAMMAR. Work with a partner. Identify the meaning of each verb form you wrote in exercise **5**. Write the number of the item next to the correct meaning.

1. A change over time: __1__, _____, _____, _____, _____
2. An unwanted repeated action: _____, _____
3. A regular or expected action: _____, _____, _____

PRACTICE

7 Complete the paragraphs with the words in parentheses. Use the simple present or the present progressive form of the verbs.

(1) I 'm enjoying (enjoy) my summer here in Japan. I (2) ______________ (stay) with a very nice family, but they (3) ______________ (do) things very differently than my family. Here, they (4) ______________ (take) their shoes off at the entrance to the house and at school. Also, they (5) ______________ (not eat) with forks and spoons; instead, they (6) ______________ (use) chopsticks at every meal. I (7) ______________ (get) better at eating with chopsticks, but I'm still not very good.

My host sister, Sachiko, is my age. She (8) ______________ (speak) English pretty well. Her English is a lot better than my Japanese. My Japanese (9) ______________ (improve) day by day, but Sachiko's younger brother (10) ______________ (often / laugh) at my pronunciation. It (11) ______________ (not bother) me because it is true that I (12) ______________ (often / make) funny mistakes. They make me laugh, too.

8 WRITE & SPEAK.

A Use the words in parentheses to make questions. Use the simple present or the present progressive.

1. (you / eat / with chopsticks at every meal)
   Do you eat with chopsticks at every meal?
2. (your family / remove / their shoes inside the house)
   ____
3. (what / you / get better at)
   ____
4. (anyone in your family / speak / English well)
   ____
5. (what / language / you / speak / at home)
   ____
6. (who / you / live with)
   ____

▶ A view of Mount Fuji from a field of sunflowers, Japan

7. (your English / improve / day by day)

____.

8. (you / ever / laugh / at your mistakes in English)

____.

B Work with a partner. Ask and answer the questions in exercise **A**.

A: *Do you eat with chopsticks at every meal?* B: *No, I don't. How about you?*

9 Complete the exercises.

A Complete each sentence with the verbs in the box. Use *always* and the present progressive.

~~borrow~~	check	complain	lose
make	not return	talk	text

REAL ENGLISH

The present progressive with *always* is a common way to complain about other people's behavior.

My neighbors ***are always playing*** *loud music at night.*

1. My sister ___is always borrowing___ my things and _______________ them.
2. My sons _______________ their phone messages and _______________ their friends.
3. My best friend _______________ about her job. She needs to find a new one.
4. My neighbors _______________ noise late at night. It's hard to fall asleep.
5. My cousin _______________ about her clothes. It drives me crazy!
6. My husband _______________ things. Yesterday it was his car keys!

B **SPEAK** Tell a partner which statements in exercise **A** are true about people you know. Replace the subjects with someone you know.

A: *My brother is always borrowing my things.* B: *Oh, my friend is always doing that, too.*

10 Complete the exercises.

A Complete the sentences according to the information in the chart. Use the verbs in parentheses and the present progressive. Add *not* where necessary.

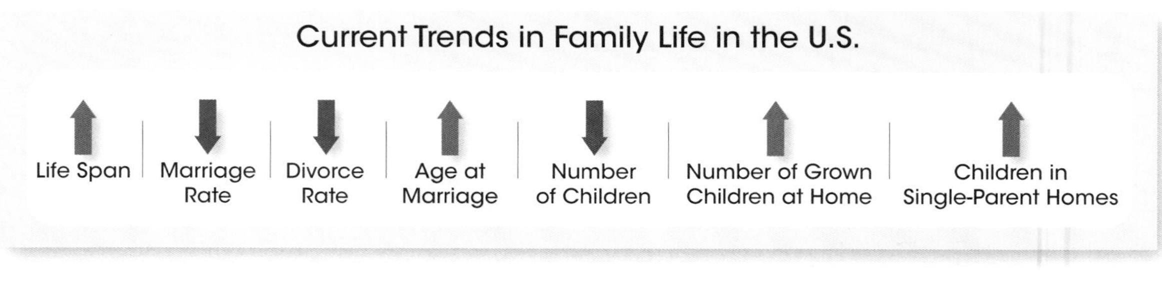

1. People ___are living___ (live) longer.
2. The number of marriages ___is decreasing___ (decrease). The number of marriages __________ (increase).
3. The divorce rate __________ (go) up. It __________ (come) down.
4. Fewer people __________ (get) married at a young age. More people __________ (wait) until their 30s to get married.
5. Most women __________ (have) a lot of children. They __________ (have) fewer children.
6. More grown children __________ (continue) to live with their parents when they become adults.
7. More children __________ (grow) up with only one parent than in the past.

B **SPEAK.** Work with a partner. Read the sentences in exercise **A**. Which trends are true about families in your country? Tell your partner.

A: *In my country, people are living longer. There are more doctors nowadays.*

B: *In mine, most people are not eating healthy food. I don't think they are living longer.*

11 **LISTEN & WRITE.**

CD1-03

A Listen to Julia tell a friend about her family. Match each family member with the correct activity.

1. grandmother ___b___	a. play in an orchestra
2. father _____	b. ~~drive~~
3. brother Alex _____	c. stand next to Alex
4. twin sister _____	d. not get together often
5. brother Lucas _____	e. study in Scotland
6. whole family _____	f. live in New York City

B Write six sentences about Julia and her family. Use the simple present or the present progressive and the information in exercise **A**. Then share your answers as a class.

Julia's grandmother never drives at night.

____

____

____

____

____

____

12 EDIT. Read the paragraph. Find and correct five more errors with the simple present or present progressive.

This week, I ~~visit~~ am visiting my twin sister. We aren't getting together often because we live a couple of hours apart. We talk and text all the time, though, so we don't feel too far apart. We are telling each other our problems and try to help each other out. Another reason we don't see each other very often is because of my sister's job. She is very busy. We often make plans, but she is cancelling always our plans at the last minute. Sometimes this upsets me. It's almost summer, though, so her schedule becomes much less busy. This week, at least, we do a lot together. It's great!

13 APPLY.

A In your notebook, write a paragraph about a family member or a friend. Tell how often you see this person, what you do together, and what the person is doing now. Add other details.

I don't see my older brother very often. He and his wife are very busy. They work full time, and they have a new baby. My sister-in-law is looking for a part-time job . . .

B Work with a partner. Read your partner's paragraph. Then ask him or her at least three follow-up questions.

A: *What kind of job is your sister-in-law looking for?*

B: *She is looking for a job as a nurse.*

EXPLORE

CD1-04

1 READ the article about the changing size of families in Brazil. How and why is the size of families changing?

The Shrinking Families of Brazil

Nowadays, families in Brazil are getting smaller. In the past, Brazilian women often had seven or eight children. Today, however, most women **think** that two children **are** enough. Ask any Brazilian woman, "Why **do you want** only two children? Why not four? Why not have eight like your grandmother did?" The answer **is** always the same: "It'**s** too expensive! It'**s** too much work!"

What **accounts for**[1] this change in Brazilian women's thinking? Why is this happening?

One reason **is** improved education for girls in Brazil. More education usually **means** that women wait longer to have children and have fewer of them. In Brazil, TV soap operas (*novelas*) **are** also a big influence. No one can deny[2] the popularity of these programs. People all over the country watch them every evening. In the average *novela*, 90 percent of the female characters **have** just one child or no children at all.

There **are** signs of this trend all over the country. As one business executive in Rio de Janeiro points out, "Look at the apartments. They'**re** designed for a maximum of four people. Two bedrooms. In the supermarkets, even the labels on frozen foods—always for four people." Clearly, many of today's Brazilian women **are not thinking** about having big families anymore.

[1] **account for:** cause or be the explanation for something
[2] **deny:** to say something is not true

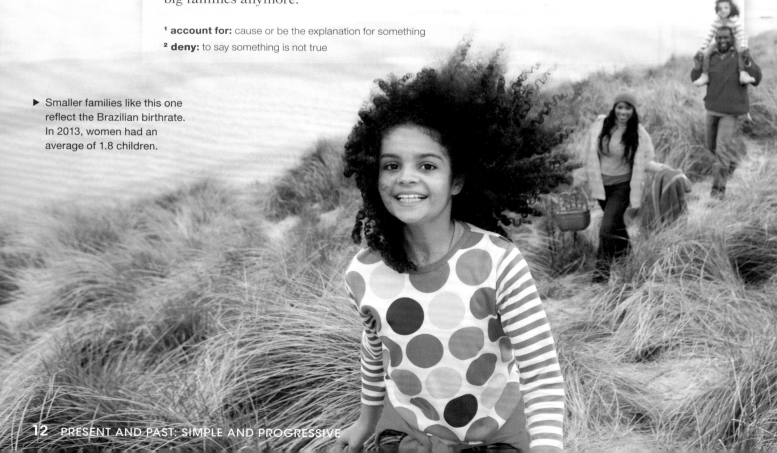

▶ Smaller families like this one reflect the Brazilian birthrate. In 2013, women had an average of 1.8 children.

▼ In the past, Brazilian families were larger.

2 CHECK. Correct the error in each sentence to make it true according to the article in exercise **1**.

1. Brazilian women today ~~want~~ don't want big families.
2. In Brazil today, women are having more children than their grandmothers did.
3. There is only one reason for smaller families in Brazil.
4. Most of the women in Brazilian soap operas have a lot of children.

3 DISCOVER. Complete the exercises to learn about the grammar in this lesson.

A Read the statements about the article in exercise **1**. Then underline the verb or verb phrase that agrees with each bold subject. Notice the different verb forms.

1. **The couple** is thinking about having more children.
2. **Most people** think that two children are enough.
3. **My mother** is looking at family photos.
4. **My sister** looks happy in the photo.
5. **Some large families** are having trouble finding big apartments.
6. **Most apartments** have only two bedrooms.

B Work with a partner. Read the statements below. Then decide which statement is true for each sentence in exercise **A**. Write the number of the sentence next to the correct statement.

1. The meaning of the verb is active; it expresses physical or mental action. __1__, ____
2. The meaning of the verb is not active; it expresses a state or condition. ____, ____, ____, ____

LEARN

1.3 Stative Verbs

1. Stative verbs* usually express states or conditions. Stative verbs are not usually used in the progressive.	✓ The baby **wants** the bottle now. ✗ The baby is wanting the bottle now.
2. Many stative verbs fall in the following categories:	
a. **Description:** *appear, be, look, look like, resemble, seem, sound*	a. Your niece **looks like** you.
b. **Feelings:** *dislike, hate, like, love, miss*	b. I **love** the picture of the whole family.
c. **Senses:** *feel, hear, see, smell, taste*	c. I **hear** a phone ringing. Is it yours?
d. **Possession:** *belong, have, own*	d. That book **belongs** to Sofia.
e. **Desires:** *hope, prefer, want*	e. **Do** you **prefer** coffee or tea?
f. **Mental states:** *agree, believe, know, think, understand*	f. He **understands** the assignment.
g. **Measurements:** *cost, weigh*	g. How much **does** the red hat **cost?**

* *Stative verbs* are sometimes called *non-action verbs*. See page **A1** for a list of stative verbs.

4 Look at the underlined verbs. Write **A** if it is an action verb and **S** if it is a stative verb.

1. _____ We are a very musical family.
2. _____ I play the piano.
3. _____ My older sister owns five guitars.
4. _____ My younger brother sings beautifully.
5. _____ He has a wonderful voice.
6. _____ My parents love to listen to us.
7. _____ Sometimes they dance to our music.
8. _____ My grandparents know a lot about classical music.

5 Complete the questions and answers with the subjects and stative verbs in parentheses.

1. A: Do most people have (most people / have) large or small families nowadays?

   B: Usually small ones. __________ (many families / have) only one child.

2. A: __________ (most people / own) their own homes these days?

   B: No, __________ (most people / not own) their own homes. They rent.

3. A: __________ (it / cost) a lot to own a home?

   B: Yes. __________ (it / cost) a lot of money.

4. A: What __________ (you / think) is the ideal number of children to have?

   B: Two. __________ (I / hope) to have one boy and one girl someday.

5. A: ______________________ (you / know) anyone with more than four brothers and sisters?

   B: No. ______________________ (it / seem) that everyone I know has only one brother or sister.

6. A: ______________________ (you / look like) anyone else in your family?

   B: Yes. ______________________ (I / resemble) my older brother a lot.

6 **SPEAK.** Work with a partner. Ask and answer the questions from exercise **5**. Use your own answers, not the answers in the book.

A: *Do most people in your country have large or small families nowadays?*

B: *Most families have two or three children.*

1.4 Stative Verbs: Stative and Active Meanings

Stative Meaning	Active Meaning
feel sick (state of body) **have** a car (own/possess) **see** something (perceive visually) **taste** good (flavor) **weigh** 120 lbs (state of body)	**feel** the soft material (touch) **have** a good time (experience) **see** a movie (watch); **see** a doctor (visit) **taste** the food (take a bite) **weigh** the apples (put on scale)

1. Some stative verbs have both stative and active meanings.*	Stative: The flowers **smell** wonderful! Active: **Smell** this perfume. Do you like it?
2. When the meaning is active, it is possible to use the progressive form of some stative verbs.	Stative: He doesn't **see** well. He wears glasses. Active: He**'s seeing** a doctor monthly. He has a back problem. Stative: I **think** those people are nice. (*believe*) Active: I**'m thinking** of going to Mexico. (*considering*)
3. Use the simple present or the present progressive for verbs that describe physical conditions.	How **do** you **feel?** = How **are** you **feeling?** My foot **hurts.** = My foot **is hurting.** My back **aches.** = My back **is aching.**

*See page **A1** for examples of stative verbs that also have active meanings.

7 Circle the correct form of the verb in each sentence.

1. a. My sister's eyes are blue, and she **has / is having** brown hair.
   b. Linda's in the kitchen. She **has / is having** breakfast.
2. a. I **think / am thinking** Jon is her brother, but I'm not sure.
   b. I **think / am thinking** of going to the beach on Sunday.
3. a. Al should eat more. He only **weighs / is weighing** 120 pounds (55 kilograms).
   b. The store clerk **weighs / is weighing** the apples. Then, he'll tell us the price.

4. a. Henry **isn't / isn't being** very friendly today. I wonder if he's angry.
   b. The test **is / is being** difficult. You need to study very hard for it.
5. a. Jana **doesn't see / isn't seeing** well. She has to wear glasses when she drives.
   b. Farah **sees / is seeing** her accountant today. She needs help with her taxes.
6. a. Yoko **looks / is looking** at the beautiful sunset.
   b. Yoko **looks / is looking** wonderful. Her dress is beautiful.
7. a. I **smell / am smelling** the milk. I think it's sour.
   b. What are you cooking? It **smells / is smelling** delicious!
8. a. The storm **comes / is coming**. Look at the dark clouds.
   b. Jaime **comes / is coming** from Mexico. He was born in Puebla.

REAL ENGLISH

Sometimes, *being* + adjective is used to describe temporary changes in someone's personality or behavior.

*My son **is being bad.** He's usually good.*
*The teacher **isn't being fair.***

PRACTICE

8 Complete the conversations with the words in parentheses. Use the simple present or present progressive form of the verbs.

1. A: Why ___are you tasting___ (you / taste) the soup, Mom?
   B: ________________ (it / not smell) right. I want to make sure it's OK.
2. A: ________________ (you / have) time to talk right now?
   B: Not really. ________________ (I / be) busy at the moment.
3. A: Why ________________ (you / look) so serious? What ________________ (you / think) about?
   B: All the things ________________ (we / need) to do for the family reunion.
4. A: What's wrong? ________________ (you / seem) sad.
   B: ________________ (I / miss) my family.

9 Complete the paragraphs with the stative verbs in parentheses. Use the simple present or present progressive form of the verbs.

I (1) ___like___ (like) a TV show called *Modern Family*. My favorite character is Gloria. She (2) ________________ (be) funny, and I (3) ________________ (love) her accent. She (4) ________________ (come) from Colombia and (5) ________________ (have) a son, Manny, from a previous marriage. Gloria's husband on the show is a much older man named Jay.

Jay, Gloria, and Manny (6) ______________ (not always / agree) with each other. In fact, I (7) ______________ (watch) the program right now, and Gloria and Jay (8) ______________ (have) an argument. Jay (9) ______________ (be) stubborn, and Gloria is complaining about Jay's selfish behavior. She (10) ______________ (sound) very angry. Manny (11) ______________ (seem) like the only adult. It's very funny.

Gloria's son, Manny, (12) ______________ (not resemble) her at all, and he (13) ______________ (have) different ideas about everything, but Gloria (14) ______________ (love) him very much. Jay makes a lot of money and they (15) ______________ (own) a beautiful home, but you never actually (16) ______________ (see) him at work in the show. This can only happen on television!

CD1-05

10 Complete the article about emperor penguins with the verbs in the box. Use the simple present or the present progressive. Use the present progressive when possible. Then listen and check your answers.

be	have	know	not be	not have
not need	resemble	see	~~seem~~	weigh

Some aspects of family life among Antarctica's emperor penguins (1) ____*seem*____ strange to people. For example, the female lays one egg, and then she leaves. She (2) ______________ a bad mother. She simply needs to find food, and she is depending on the male to keep the egg warm. In about two months, the female returns and the egg hatches.

The chick (3) ______________ its parents, but it (4) ______________ black and white feathers. It (5) ______________ grey ones. Also, it (6) ______________ much smaller, and it (7) ______________ much less than the average 75-pound adult. The parents teach the chick how to take care of itself, but there's one thing the chick (8) ______________ to learn: how to swim! When a penguin (9) ______________ water, it (10) ______________ exactly what to do. Emperor penguins are excellent swimmers!

▼ A penguin protects its chick by resting the chick on its feet.

11 APPLY.

A In your notebook, write a short paragraph about a family you know. Use at least five stative verbs that can have active meanings. Use chart 1.4 and the list on page **A1** to help you.

B Read your description to the class. Ask your classmates follow-up questions.

A: *How old is Manny?* B: *I'm not sure. I think he's eleven or twelve.*

A: *Do Carla and James have any children?* B: *Yes, they have a son and two daughters.*

EXPLORE

CD1-06

1 READ the newspaper article about twins and look at the photos. What do you think happens at a Twins Days Festival?

Notes from the Twins Days Festival

Jim Lodge, *The Sunset Times*

The opening day of the Twins Days Festival was an exciting one. Over 2000 sets of twins **arrived** for three full days of fun. Everyone **was looking** forward to all the scheduled events—picnics, talent shows, parades, and contests.

I found that there was a serious side to the festival, too. A lot of scientific research **was going on**. One afternoon, while I **was walking** around, I **stopped** by a research tent. Inside, technicians **were photographing** sets of twins, **collecting** their fingerprints, and **scanning** their irises.[1] They **were using** the latest face-recognition software to try to tell the twins apart. As one scientist explained, "Although identical twins may look the same to you and me, a digital imaging system can spot tiny differences in freckles,[2] skin pores,[3] or the curve of their eyebrows."

Some twins **were** a challenge for the researchers. For example, it **was** hard to tell Dave and Don Wolf apart because their beards **covered** half of their faces. I **looked** very carefully at the brothers, but I **didn't see** any difference at all. They **seemed** absolutely identical to me. But I **had** the very same reaction to almost every set of twins at the festival. It was like seeing double all the time!

[1] **iris:** round colored part of a person's eye
[2] **freckle:** a small light brown spot on someone's skin
[3] **pore:** a tiny hole in the skin

▼ A gathering of identical twins.

▲ Identical twins Dave and Don Wolf

2 CHECK. Answer the questions. Write complete sentences.

1. How many sets of twins were at the festival?

   Over 2000 sets of twins were at the festival.

2. What were some of the festival events?

   ____

3. Who was doing serious work at the festival?

   ____

4. Why were Dave and Don Wolf a challenge for the researchers?

   ____

3 DISCOVER. Complete the exercises to learn about the grammar in this lesson.

A Look at these sentences from the newspaper article in exercise **1**. Underline all of the verb forms.

1. One afternoon, while I was walking around, I stopped by a research tent.
2. Inside, technicians were photographing sets of twins, collecting their fingerprints, and scanning their irises.
3. I looked very carefully at the brothers, but I didn't see any difference at all.

B Work with a partner. Look at the sentences in exercise **A** and the verb forms you underlined. Then check (✓) the correct box for each statement below.

This verb form shows that an action or situation . . .	**Simple Past** verb + *-ed* / *didn't* + base form	**Past Progressive** *was/were* (*not*) + verb + *-ing*
1. continued for a period of time.	☐	☐
2. started and finished without interruption.	☐	☐
3. interrupted another action.	☐	☐

LEARN

1.5 Simple Past and Past Progressive Review

	Simple Past	Past Progressive
Affirmative Statements	Jim **left** the party at 8:00 last night. Jun and Kim **stayed** until 10:00.	Jim **was driving** home at 8:15. Jun and Kim **were talking** at 8:15.
Negative Statements	Javier **didn't go** to class yesterday. He **didn't feel** well.	Sue **wasn't taking** notes. We **weren't texting** during the class.
Yes/No Questions	**Did** Jan **read** the news this morning? **Did** you **eat** lunch yesterday?	**Was** Tim **reading** at age five? **Were** you **eating** lunch at 1:00?
Wh- Questions	**Where did** you **go** last night?	**What were** you **doing** at 8:00 last night?
Who or What as Subject	**Who went** to the movie after class?	**Who wasn't paying** attention in class?

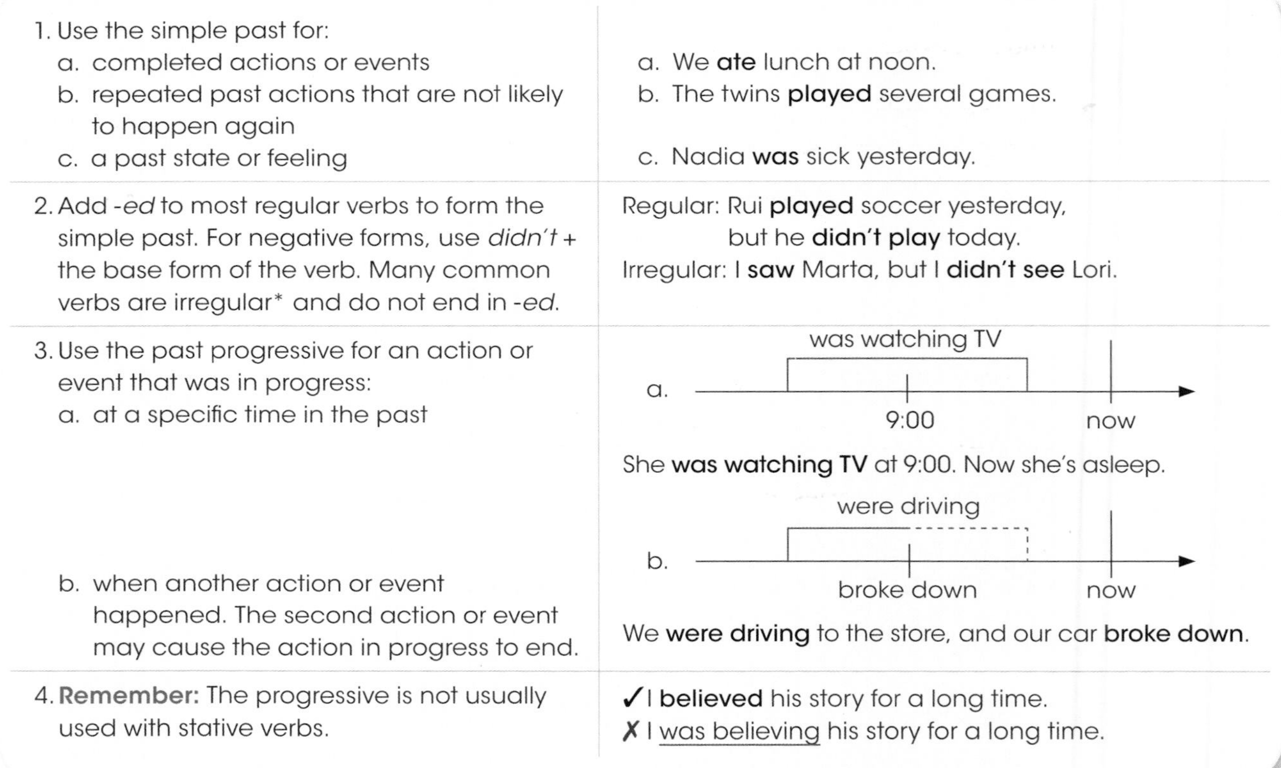

1. Use the simple past for: a. completed actions or events b. repeated past actions that are not likely to happen again c. a past state or feeling	a. We **ate** lunch at noon. b. The twins **played** several games. c. Nadia **was** sick yesterday.
2. Add *-ed* to most regular verbs to form the simple past. For negative forms, use *didn't* + the base form of the verb. Many common verbs are irregular* and do not end in *-ed.*	Regular: Rui **played** soccer yesterday, but he **didn't play** today. Irregular: I **saw** Marta, but I **didn't see** Lori.
3. Use the past progressive for an action or event that was in progress: a. at a specific time in the past b. when another action or event happened. The second action or event may cause the action in progress to end.	a. (was watching TV; 9:00; now) She **was watching TV** at 9:00. Now she's asleep. b. (were driving; broke down; now) We **were driving** to the store, and our car **broke down**.
4. **Remember:** The progressive is not usually used with stative verbs.	✓ I **believed** his story for a long time. ✗ I was believing his story for a long time.

* See pages **A1-A2** for a list of spelling rules for the *-ed* and *-ing* forms of verbs.
** See page **A3** for a list of irregular verb forms.

4 Complete the exercises.

A Complete the stories about twins. Use the simple past or the past progressive.

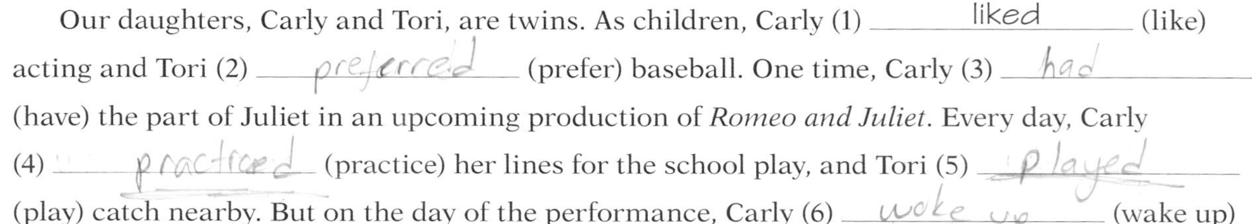

Story 1

Our daughters, Carly and Tori, are twins. As children, Carly (1) ___liked___ (like) acting and Tori (2) ___preferred___ (prefer) baseball. One time, Carly (3) ___had___ (have) the part of Juliet in an upcoming production of *Romeo and Juliet*. Every day, Carly (4) ___practiced___ (practice) her lines for the school play, and Tori (5) ___played___ (play) catch nearby. But on the day of the performance, Carly (6) ___woke up___ (wake up) sick. Luckily, Tori (7) knew (know) all of Carly's lines. On the night of the play, Carly (8) stayed (stay) in bed at home, and Tori (9) performed (perform) the part of Juliet instead of Carly. No one at school ever (10) found (find) out!

Story 2

My wife and I have twin daughters, and I'm a twin, too. As a child, I (11) didn't enjoy (not enjoy) sports like my twin, Ray, did. I (12) like (like) books. One summer day around noon, I (13) was reading (read) alone on the porch, and Ray (14) was playing (play) baseball in the yard with his friends. One of his friends (15) threw (throw) the ball to him, but at that moment Ray (16) wasn't looking (not look). So it (17) hit (hit) him hard in the arm. Strangely, at the same time, I (18) felt (feel) a sharp pain in my arm. It (19) was (be) a very unusual experience.

B Use the words and phrases to write simple past or past progressive questions about the stories in exercise **A**.

1. Why did Carly stay (Carly / stay) in bed on the night of the play?
2. Why ______ (Tori / perform) in the play?
3. Which twin ______ (read) alone on the porch?
4. What ______ (happen) to Ray?
5. Why ______ (Sam / feel) a pain in his arm?
6. Of the two stories, which one ______ (you / prefer)?

C **SPEAK.** Work with a partner. Take turns asking and answering the questions in exercise **B**.

A: *Why did Carly stay in bed on the night of the play?* B: *Because she was sick.*

1.6 Past Time Clauses with *When* and *While*

Time Clause First	Time Clause Second
While Rob was eating lunch, the phone rang. (While Rob was eating lunch = Time Clause; the phone rang = Main Clause)	Dave was hiking when he hurt his foot. (Dave was hiking = Main Clause; when he hurt his foot = Time Clause)

1. Use a *when* or *while* clause + a main clause to show the relationship between two past actions or events. Use a comma after the time clause when it comes first in the sentence.	was walking home / started to rain / now I was walking home **when it started to rain.** **While I was walking home**, it started to rain.
2. Use *when* or *while* + the past progressive for an action or event that was in progress when another action happened. Use *when* + the simple past in the time clause to show an interrupted action.	**While the boy was running**, he dropped his book. **When the boy was running**, he dropped his book. ✓ The boy was running **when he dropped his book.** ✗ The boy was running while he dropped his book.

1.6 Past Time Clauses with *When* and *While* (cont.)

3. To show that one action or event happened before another, use a *when* time clause for the action that happened first. Use the simple past in both clauses.	**When** the phone **rang,** Lili **answered** it. First Event / Second Event
4. To show that two actions were in progress at the same time in the past, use *while* in the time clause. Use the past progressive in both clauses.	 **While** Li **was studying,** we **were watching** TV.

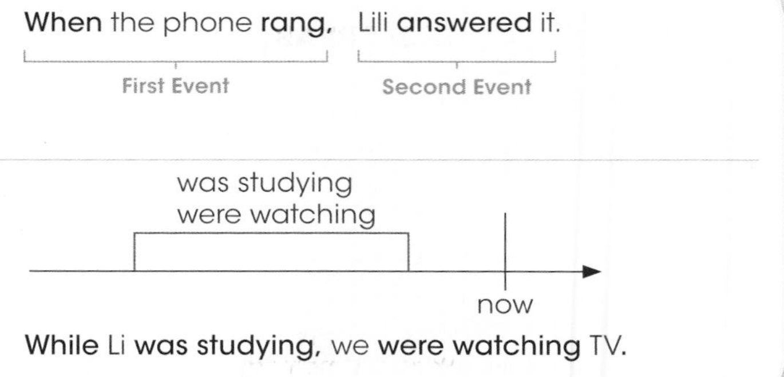

5 Circle the correct words to complete the tourist's notes about an elephant family.

We (1) **saw / were seeing** a family of elephants when we (2) **drove / were driving** down a road in Tanzania. We stopped to watch them. Some of the elephants (3) **drank / were drinking** water while others were eating grass. (4) **When / While** I raised my hand to say "hello," one of the elephants (5) **lifted / was lifting** its trunk as though to greet me. It made me laugh.

A little later, one big female elephant (6) **lead / was leading** her family across the river (7) **when / while** one of her babies slipped. It was OK, of course. Later, while another young elephant (8) **played / was playing** near us, it (9) **fell / was falling** in the water and (10) **got / was getting** us very wet. We (11) **decided / were deciding** to head back to the camp (12) **when / while** it started to rain. We were already wet enough!

▼ An elephant herd at a river bank in Sri Lanka

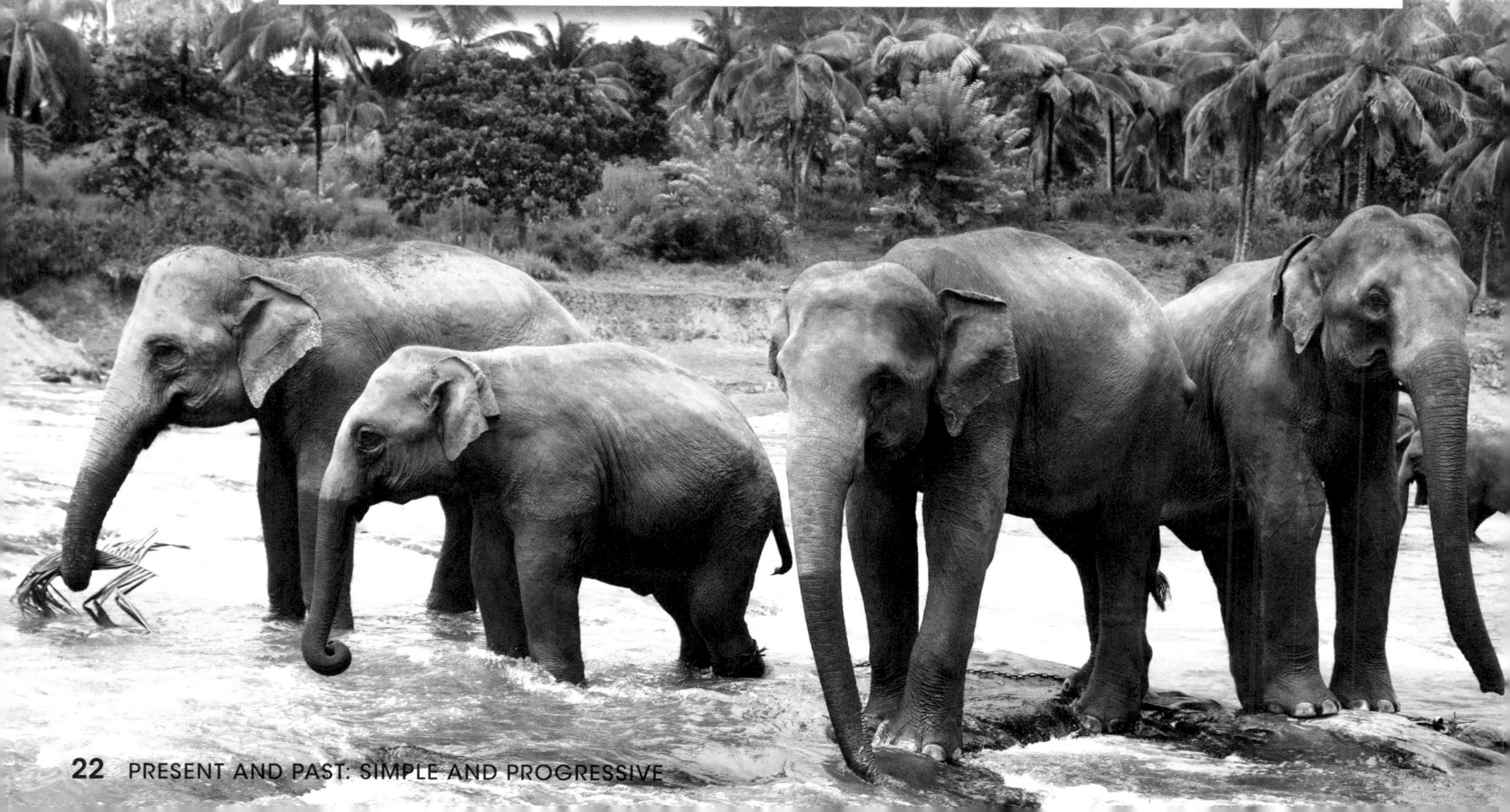

PRACTICE

6 WRITE & SPEAK.

A Work with a partner. Look at the time line and discuss the events in Julio's family history.

Julio's Grandparents				Julio's Father, Jiro			Julio's Parents, Jiro & Susan	
saved money	emigrated to Peru	met & married	Jiro born	turned six	worked, went to high school	met Susan	got married in college	had Julio after college
Japan		Sugar Plantation in Peru		Lima, Peru				

B Read each pair of sentences. Then combine the sentences into one sentence with a past time clause. Use the simple past and the past progressive. Add a comma when necessary. For some sentences, more than one answer may be possible.

1. Julio's grandparents lived in Japan. They didn't know each other.

   When *Julio's grandparents were living in Japan, they didn't know each other*.

2. They saved enough money. They each emigrated to Peru.

   They each emigrated to Peru when *they saved enough money*.

3. Julio's grandparents worked on a sugar plantation in Peru. They met.

   ______________ when ______________.

4. Julio's father, Jiro, was born. They lived on the sugar plantation.

   ______________ while ______________.

5. Jiro turned six. His family moved to Lima so he could go to school.

   When ______________.

6. Jiro worked in the family store. He went to high school.

   ______________ while ______________.

7. Jiro saw Susan at school. He introduced himself.

   When ______________.

8. Jiro and Susan attended college in Lima. They got married.

   When ______________.

C In your notebook, write five questions about the information in exercise **B**. Use the simple past and the past progressive with time clauses.

When Julio's grandparents were living in Japan, did they know each other?

D Work with a partner. Ask and answer your questions from exercise **C** on page 23.

A: *When Julio's grandparents were living in Japan, did they know each other?*

B: *No, they didn't. They met in Peru.*

7 LISTEN.

CD1-07

A Read the phrases about Bella's family history. Then listen to her talk about a secret in her family. Who does each phrase relate to? Check (✓) the correct box(es).

Story of Bella's Family Secret	Bella	Bella's Mother	Maria	Marina
1. found a copy of the family tree	✓	☐	☐	☐
2. told Bella about the secret	☐	☐	☐	☐
3. wanted to go to America	☐	☐	☐	☐
4. looked alike	☐	☐	☐	☐
5. did not move to America	☐	☐	☐	☐
6. was Bella's grandmother	☐	☐	☐	☐

CD1-07

B Work with a partner. Write the missing words to complete the story about Bella's family secret. Then listen again and check your answers.

One day, I (1) ___was cleaning___ out a desk drawer (2) ___when___ I found a copy of my family tree. While I (3) ______________ at it, my mother (4) ______________ into the room. (5) ______________ she saw it, she (6) ______________ quiet. That's when she (7) ______________ me the family secret.

It turns out that Grandma's name wasn't really (8) ______________. Her real name was (9) ______________. Many years ago back in Russia, my grandmother's sister planned to marry an American (10) ______________ she turned 20. But while she (11) ______________ to go to America, she started to cry. She (12) ______________ to go anymore, but her sister, Marina, (13) ______________. The two sisters (14) ______________ alike, so when Maria's passport and boat ticket (15) ______________, Marina took them and (16) ______________ all the way from Russia to America.

(17) ________________ my mother was growing up, no one, not even my grandfather, (18) ________________ the secret. Of course, they (19) ________________ shocked when they (20) ________________ out. I certainly (21) ________________!

8 EDIT.

A Read the phone conversation between Erica and her mother. Find and correct seven more errors with the simple past and the past progressive.

Erica: Hello?

Mother: Hello, Erica? Were you asleep? ~~Was I waking~~ Did I wake you up?

Erica: Yeah. I slept. I didn't sleep well last night, so I decided to take a nap.

Mother: Oh, I'm sorry. I just was wanting to say hello.

Erica: Well, I had the strangest dream when the phone rang. I talked to Aunt Jelena. We were sitting in her living room. While we were talking, a bear suddenly was appearing. It was terrifying! When the bear came toward us, we were running outside. That's when I heard the phone.

Mother: That sounds like a scary dream!

Erica: It was. It was a very strange dream. I'm glad I was waking up.

B Complete the chart with information about Erica's dream in exercise **A**.

Erica's Dream	Notes
1. Where was Erica in her dream?	In Aunt Jelena's living room.
2. What was she doing?	
3. What happened?	
4. What did they do when the bear came toward them?	
5. How did she feel when she woke up?	

9 APPLY.

A In your notebook, make a chart like the one in exercise **8B**. Write 5–6 questions for a partner about a strange dream or experience. Then ask your partner your questions. Write his or her answers in the chart.

A: *Where were you?* B: *I was on a boat in the Mediterranean.*

A: *What were you doing?* B: *I was on vacation with friends. We were taking pictures.*

B Write a paragraph about your partner's dream.

My partner had a dream about a vacation. She went away with two friends from college. They were celebrating their graduation. In her dream, they were taking pictures . . .

Charts 1.1–1.7

1 Complete the paragraphs with the correct forms of the words in parentheses. Use the simple present, present progressive, simple past, or past progressive. Add *not* where necessary.

I'm an only child. (1) I ___don't have___ (have) any brothers or sisters. A lot of people (2) ____________ (feel) sorry for me when I tell them that, but I (3) ____________ (know) why. They (4) ____________ (believe) certain things to be true about all only children, but they're wrong. For example, many people (5) ____________ (think) that all only children are lonely, but I (6) ____________ (be) lonely as a child. I (7) ____________ (go) to my friends' houses and (8) ____________ (play) with the kids in my apartment building. Also, not all only children are spoiled. While I (9) ____________ (grow up), my parents (10) ____________ (give) me a lot of love and attention, but I (11) ____________ (get) everything I asked for.

It's really not bad to grow up without siblings. Nowadays, more and more couples (12) ____________ (decide) to have only one child. One reason is that it (13) ____________ (cost) a lot of money to raise children. Also, many couples (14) ____________ (wait) until their thirties to start a family. My husband and I (15) ____________ (have) only one child, and we (16) ____________ (plan) to have more. One child is just fine.

Charts 1.1, 1.2, 1.3, 1.5, 1.6

2 **EDIT.** Read the e-mail from Max's father to Anna, a family member. Find and correct eight more errors with present and past (simple and progressive) verb forms.

Hi Anna,

How ~~do things go~~ are things going? Everything is great with Emily, Max, and me. Max grows day by day. He's four months old now. He is getting big! Emily is working part time now. She was going back to work last month, so she's always really tired. It's too bad babies aren't sleeping through the night. Max wakes up two or three times a night. I'm lucky. I'm never waking up. Emily does.

I need my sleep. I'm working long hours these days. On top of that, my boss is always complaining about something. The other day, at 6:00 p.m., while I walked out the door to go home, he said, "Do you leave already?" These comments upset me, so now I think about changing jobs. Anyway, enough about me. What do you do nowadays? Write soon!

Love,
Carlos

Charts 1.1–1.6

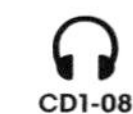

3 LISTEN.

A Read the sentences about sibling relationships. Then listen to the interview and circle **T** for *true* or **F** for *false*.

1. Gender doesn't play a role in sibling differences. **T** **F**
2. Family relationships are different all over the world. **T** **F**
3. Parents often say that their children don't fight. **T** **F**
4. Children in the research study didn't fight very often. **T** **F**
5. When children are fighting about a toy, they are really fighting about something that is more important to them. **T** **F**

B Listen again and circle the word or phrase you hear in the interview.

1. Sometimes we **love / loved** them to death; other times we **don't / didn't**.
2. Our siblings **know / knew** us differently from the way our adult friends **know / knew** us because our siblings **know / knew** us when we were children.
3. The relationship **is / was** constantly changing.
4. **I'm not talking / I don't talk** about sibling relationships all over the world.
5. And my brother is ten years older than I am, so we **don't fight / didn't fight**.
6. . . . but in fact, the research studies **show / showed** that children between the ages of three and seven **fight / fought** about 3.5 times per hour.

Charts 1.1, 1.3, 1.6

4 SPEAK & WRITE.

A Work in a group of three or four students. Ask and answer questions using the phrases in the box. When a student in your group answers *yes* to one of the questions, get more details by asking follow-up questions.

comes from a large family	has a set of twins in the family
is an only child	enjoyed swimming as a child
is the youngest	played a sport while he/she was growing up
resembles a family member	won a competition while he/she was growing up

A: *Do you come from a large family?*

B: *Yes, I have a lot of relatives.*

A: *Oh really? Where do they live?*

B Write four or five sentences about your classmates based on your conversations from exercise **A**. Share your information with the class.

Andrea comes from a very large family. She has more than 20 cousins.

Misha won a pie-eating contest when he was 14 years old.

Connect the Grammar to Writing

1 READ & NOTICE THE GRAMMAR.

A Why do many adult children in their 20s and 30s live with their parents? Tell a partner your ideas. Then read the text.

Moving Back Home

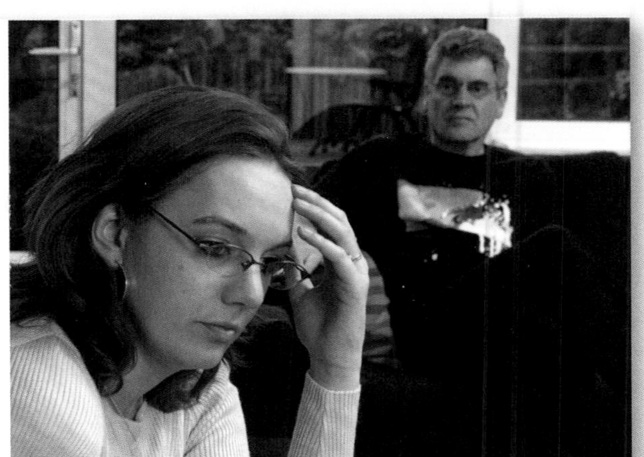

The number of children who return home in adulthood to live with their parents is increasing. In the past, grown children left home as soon as they could afford it. For example, my father left his parents' house when he went to college. Then, he got a job and his own apartment. He never returned.

Today life is different. Many young adults cannot find jobs, so they return home. Plus, they want to save money. My sister and her husband, for example, are living at our parents' house to save money for a house.

This new trend is affecting both the parents and their children. Sometimes their children get too comfortable and think that their parents can support them forever. Often parents face economic challenges because of this and have to postpone retirement. It seems that young adults these days are taking longer to grow up.

GRAMMAR FOCUS

In this text, the writer uses simple and progressive verb forms in the following ways.

Present progressive
- to tell about current trends in society (*The number of children . . .* ***is increasing****.*)
- to tell about temporary situations (*My sister and her husband . . .* ***are living*** *. . .*)

Simple present
- to give facts (*. . . , so they* ***return*** *home.*)
- with stative verbs (*It* ***seems*** *. . .*)

Simple past
- to give examples from the past (*Then, he* ***got*** *a job . . .*)

B Read the text in exercise **A** again. Find one more example of each verb form and identify its use. Complete the chart. Then work with a partner and compare your answers.

Verb Form	Example	Use
Present progressive		
Simple present		
Simple past		

C Complete the chart with information from the text in exercise **A**. Discuss your answers with a partner.

Short Essay Question	*Why do many children in their 20s and 30s still live with their parents?*
In the Past	
Today	
Final Thoughts	

2 BEFORE YOU WRITE.

A Work with a partner. Brainstorm more ways families are changing in the United States (or in your culture). Use exercise **10A** on page 10 for ideas. Write at least five questions that ask about these changes.

Why are people getting married at an older age?

B Choose one of your questions from exercise **A** to respond to. Make a chart like the one in exercise **1C** and write your question in the top row. Add notes to help you organize your ideas for your response.

3 WRITE a response to your question from exercise **2B**. Write three paragraphs. Use your notes from exercise **1C** and the text in exercise **1A** to help you.

WRITING FOCUS Using *For Example* to Give Supporting Ideas

Notice *for example* in the text in exercise **1A**.

When *for example* starts a sentence, use a comma after it.

__For example,__ my father left his parents' house . . .

When *for example* is in the middle of a sentence, use a comma before and after it.

My sister and her husband, __for example__, are living at our parents' house.

4 SELF ASSESS. Read your response. Underline the verb forms in your response. Then use the checklist to assess your work.

- ☐ I used the simple present and simple past correctly. [1.1, 1.4]
- ☐ I used the present progressive and past progressive correctly. [1.1, 1.2, 1.4]
- ☐ I used the simple present with stative verbs. [1.3]
- ☐ I used commas correctly when using *for example*. [WRITING FOCUS]

UNIT 2 Passions

Present and Past: Perfect and Perfect Progressive

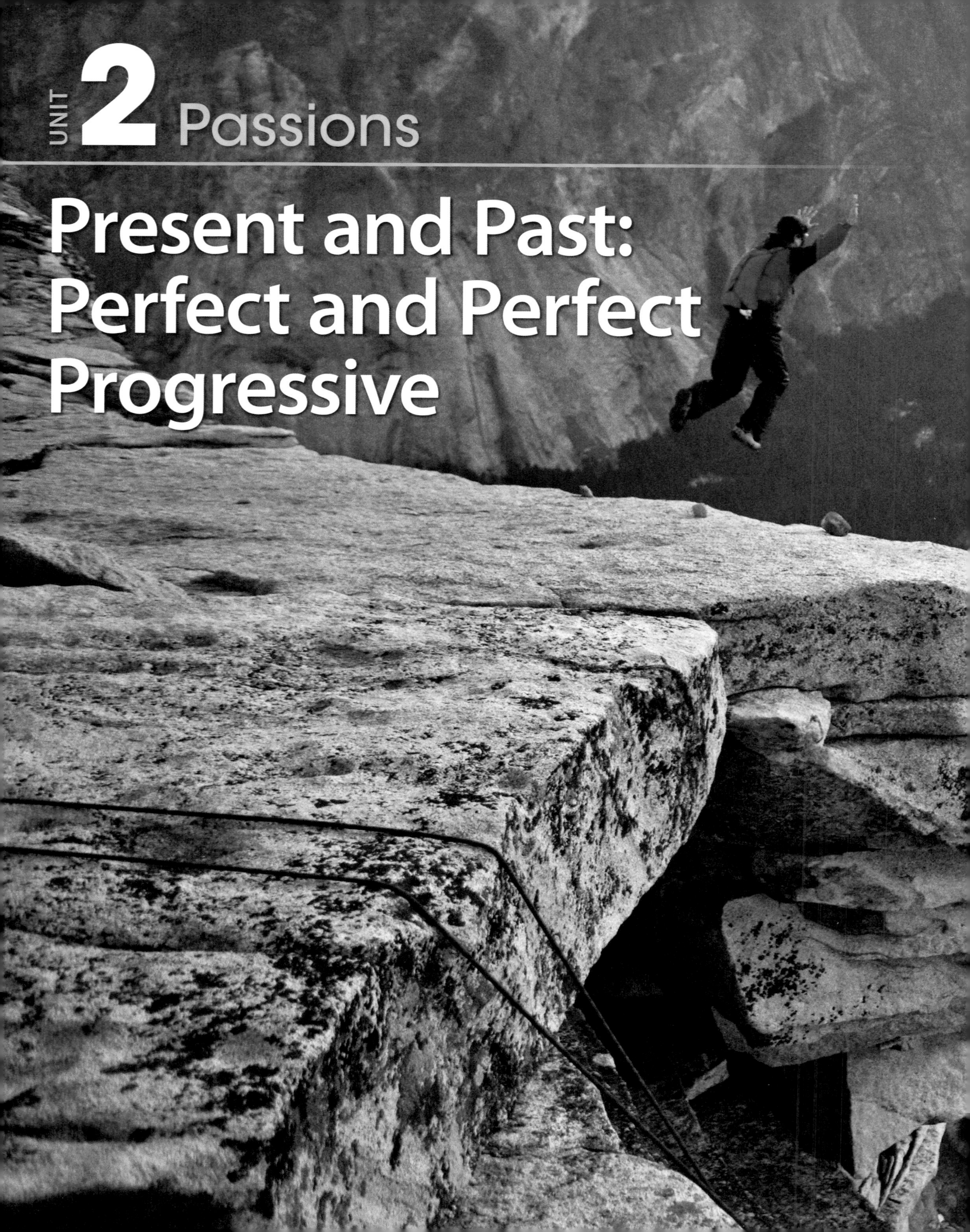

Climbers BASE jump from Half Dome at Yosemite National Park, California.

LESSON 1 Present Perfect

EXPLORE

CD1-09

1 READ the book review of *Polar Obsession*. What is Paul Nicklen's passion?

Paul Nicklen's *Polar Obsession*

For most people, the Arctic and Antarctica are strange places that we know very little about. Paul Nicklen's collection of photographs and stories, *Polar Obsession*, offers an excellent introduction.

Nicklen grew up on an island in Northern Canada, where he learned all about the outdoors from his Inuit[1] neighbors. Ever since that time, he **has loved** animals, cold weather, and adventure.

As a photojournalist, Nicklen **has spent** a lot of time in icy polar waters. He **has followed** sea lions, **dived** with whales, and **studied** polar bears. One of the most exciting parts of the book covers Nicklen's unforgettable encounter with a leopard seal in Antarctica.

As the photographs clearly show, leopard seals are very large—up to 12 feet (4 meters) long and weighing over 1000 pounds (450 kilograms). They have huge, sharp teeth, and they move quickly through the water searching for food such as fish and penguins.

Leopard seals can be dangerous, but this didn't stop Nicklen from trying to photograph one. When a huge seal approached his boat, Nicklen got into the water. He was shaking with fear, but much to his surprise the seal treated him gently. She even tried to feed him! The seal brought him penguins to eat, and he photographed her. Nicklen says it was the most incredible experience that he **has** ever **had** as a photographer.

In *Polar Obsession*, Nicklen shows us the beauty of the polar world and his passion for it. He also helps us to understand the importance of protecting it.

[1] **Inuit:** indigenous people living in Arctic regions of Alaska, Canada, and Greenland

▲ Paul Nicklen meets a leopard seal.

The leopard seal shows its sharp teeth.

2 CHECK. Write the letter of the phrase that completes each sentence.

1. Nicklen's neighbors taught him all about __d__.
2. Nicklen has spent a lot of time working in __b__.
3. Nicklen's most incredible experience was with __e__.
4. He was frightened because __a__.
5. The leopard seal offered Nicklen __c__.

a. leopard seals can be dangerous
b. a leopard seal
c. its food
d. the outdoors
e. icy polar waters

3 DISCOVER. Complete the exercises to learn about the grammar in this lesson.

A Find these sentences in the book review from exercise **1**. Write the missing words.

1. Nicklen __grew up__ on an island in Northern Canada, where he __learned__ all about the outdoors from his Inuit neighbors.
2. Ever since that time, he __worked__ animals, cold weather, and adventure.
3. As a photojournalist, Nicklen __has spent__ a lot of time in icy polar waters.
4. He ______________ sea lions, ____________ with whales, and ______________ polar bears.
5. When a huge seal ______________ his boat, Nicklen ____________ into the water.

B Look at the sentences in exercise **A**. Write the number of each sentence next to the phrase that best describes the time of the event.

1. Completed at a known time in the past: __1__, ____
2. Completed at an unknown time in the past: ____, ____
3. Started in the past and continues to the present: ____

LEARN

2.1 Present Perfect

Statements	
	Subject + *Have/Has (Not)* + Past Participle
Affirmative	I **have visited** many countries.
Negative	Tom **hasn't seen** the photos of my trip.

Questions		Answers
	(Wh-) + *Have/Has* + Subject + Past Participle	
Yes/No	**Have** you **visited** the Arctic? **Has** Paul **taken** many photos?	No, I **haven't**. Yes, he **has**.
Wh-	**What have** you **heard?** **Who has** he **met?**	Nothing. Why? An explorer.
	Who/What + *Has* + Past Participle	
Who or *What* as Subject	**Who has completed** the assignment? **What has happened?**	Only one student **(has)**. Nothing, yet.

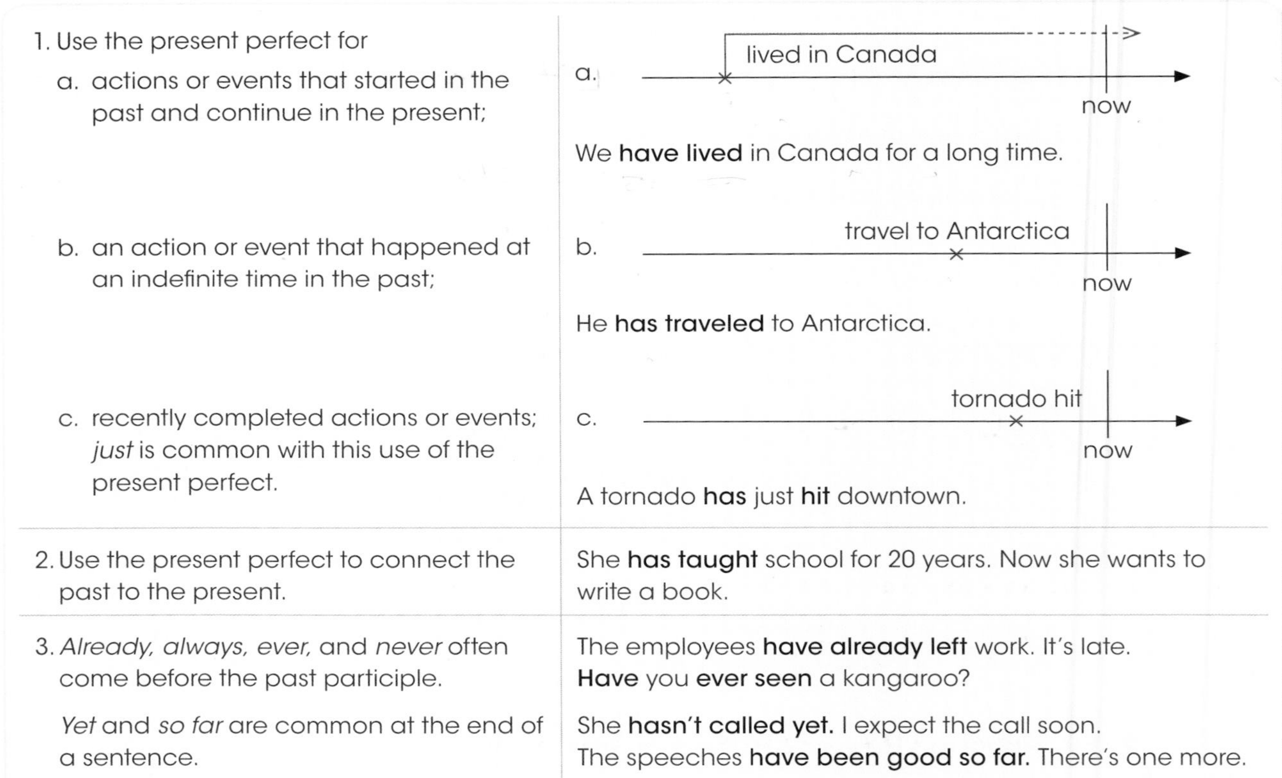

1. Use the present perfect for a. actions or events that started in the past and continue in the present;	a. lived in Canada — now We **have lived** in Canada for a long time.
b. an action or event that happened at an indefinite time in the past;	b. travel to Antarctica — now He **has traveled** to Antarctica.
c. recently completed actions or events; *just* is common with this use of the present perfect.	c. tornado hit — now A tornado **has** just **hit** downtown.
2. Use the present perfect to connect the past to the present.	She **has taught** school for 20 years. Now she wants to write a book.
3. *Already, always, ever,* and *never* often come before the past participle. *Yet* and *so far* are common at the end of a sentence.	The employees **have already left** work. It's late. **Have** you **ever seen** a kangaroo? She **hasn't called yet.** I expect the call soon. The speeches **have been good so far.** There's one more.

4 Complete the conversations with the words in parentheses. Use the present perfect.

Conversation 1

Bev: How is your class going?

Ken: Great. (1) I've learned (I / learn) a lot about the Arctic and polar explorers.

Bev: That sounds interesting. (2) ______________ (you / see) that book by Paul Nicklen?

Ken: No, (3) ______________. Who is he? (4) ______________ (I / never / hear) of him.

Bev: He's a photographer. (5) ______________ (he / live) and (6) ______________ (work) in polar climates for many years. (7) ______________ (he / take) amazing photos of all kinds of animals.

> **REAL ENGLISH**
>
> Do not repeat *have/has* between present perfect verbs connected by *and*.
>
> *He* ***has followed*** *sea lions and* ***studied*** *polar bears.*

Conversation 2

Lee: (8) ______________ (Mr. Chin / just / cancel) today's class.

Jen: Really? (9) ______________ (he / reschedule) it yet?

Lee: No, not yet. But I heard the class might be on Saturday.

Jen: Is that possible? (10) ______________ (you / ever / have) a class on a Saturday?

5 **ANALYZE THE GRAMMAR.** Work with a partner. Look at each answer you wrote in exercise **4**. Then write the number of each answer next to the correct description below. Refer to chart 2.1.

1. Started in the past and continues to the present: ____, ____
2. Happened at an indefinite time in the past: 1, ____, ____, ____, ____, ____
3. Happened recently: ____, ____

2.2 Present Perfect with *For* and *Since*

Use *for* or *since* with actions or events that started in the past and continue to the present.	graduated (May) — worked at store — now/December
a. Use *for* + an amount of time (number of days, months, . . .).	a. Jo has worked at this store **for six months**.
b. Use *since* + a specific past time (exact date, time, month, . . .).	b. He hasn't been a student **since May**.
c. Use a past time clause with *since*.	c. I've known him **since he graduated**.

6 Complete the sentences. Use the present perfect form of the verb in parentheses. Then write *since* or *for*.

1. People in many countries enjoy ice swimming. It became popular several decades ago.

   People ___have enjoyed___ (enjoy) ice swimming ___for___ several decades.

2. The first Canadian Polar Bear Swim was in 1920. It is still an annual event.

   The Canadian Polar Bear Swim ___have been___ (be) an annual event ___since___ 1920.

3. Our town had its first New Year's Day swim in 2010. Our town still has this swim.

   Our town ___had been___ (have) a New Year's Day swim ___for___ many years.

4. I wanted to swim with the Polar Bears when I was 13. I'm 23 and I still want to do it.

   I ______________ (want) to swim with the Polar Bears ______________ ten years.

5. The only sport my brother does is winter swimming. He ______________ (not play) any other sport ______________ he was a teenager.

6. My father doesn't participate anymore. His last winter swim was four years ago.

   My father ______________ (not participate) ______________ four years.

7. My cousin always jumps into the water first. He did this last year and the year before.

   My cousin ______________ (always / jump) into the water first ______________ he joined the Polar Bears.

8. We all love winter swimming. We loved our first experience, and we still love it.

   We ______________ (love) winter swimming ______________ we first tried it.

2.3 Present Perfect and Simple Past

1. The present perfect is used for a. actions or events that started in the past and continue to the present; b. completed actions or events with a connection to the present.	a. Mary is our math teacher. She **has taught** here for five years. b. The children **have read** the rules. They're ready to play the game now.
2. The simple past is used for completed actions or events.	She **taught math** ten years ago. Now she works in finance.
3. With the present perfect, the exact time of the action or event is not given. With the simple past, the exact time of the past action or event is given or understood.	✓ They **have gone** to Morocco. ✗ They have gone to Morocco last month. ✓ They **went** to Morocco **last month**. ✓ **Did** you **sleep** well?
4. Use the present perfect with a time period that has not ended yet. Use the simple past with a completed past time period.	**I've called** her twice **this morning**. (It's still morning. I may call her again.) I **called** her twice **yesterday**.

7 Circle the correct form of the verb to complete each sentence.

1. a. She **has dreamed / dreamed** about going to the North Pole since she was young.
   b. She **has dreamed / dreamed** about going to the North Pole last night.
2. a. I **have never photographed / never photographed** animals in the wild before.
   b. We **have not photographed / didn't photograph** animals when we were in Alaska.
3. a. Last year, my grandfather **has gone / went** to Iceland on business twice.
   b. My grandfather **has gone / went** to Iceland on business twice since 2005.
4. a. They **haven't seen / didn't see** any bears on their trip so far.
   b. They **haven't seen / didn't see** any bears on their trip last month.

PRACTICE

8 **PRONUNCIATION.** Read the chart and listen to the examples. Then complete the exercises.

PRONUNCIATION **Reduced *Have* and *Has* in the Present Perfect**

Have and *has* are often contracted or reduced in the present perfect. Repeat these examples.

CD1-10

Examples:

Full Pronunciation	**Reduced Pronunciation**
Lisa has just arrived.	*Lisəz just arrived.*
Most people have already left.	*Most peopləv already left.*
Who has she talked to?	*Whoz she talked to?*
What have you done?	*Whatəv you done?*

CD1-11

A Listen to the sentences. Which form of *have/has* do you hear, the full form or the reduced form? Check (✓) the correct box.

	Full	**Reduced**
1. Lee has always loved animals.	☐	☑
2. Our neighbors have adopted many animals over the years.	☑	☐
3. Who has taken care of an animal before?	☐	☑
4. We have faced many challenges with our cats.	☐	☑
5. Kara has taken her dog to the park every day for years.	☑	☐
6. Tyrone has volunteered at the animal shelter since 2012.	☑	☐
7. Our landlords have made a rule about owning pets.	☑	☐
8. What have you learned from working with animals?	☑	☐

CD1-11

B Work with a partner. Compare your answers from exercise **A**. Then listen again and check your answers.

▲ Eye of a green tree python snake, common to Australia

9 Complete the exercises.

A Complete the interview with the words in parentheses. Use the present perfect or simple past.

Sara: How long (1) ___have you been___ (you / be) a snake catcher, Tim?

Tim: (2) __________ (I / have) this job for over ten years.

Sara: When (3) __________ (you / become) interested in snakes?

Tim: When (4) __________ (I / be) a kid, and (5) __________ (snakes / fascinate) me ever since then. When (6) __________ (I / be) in middle school, (7) __________ (I / not read) much about any other subject. During my high school years, (8) __________ (I / often / volunteer) at the local zoo, and then in college (9) __________ (I / major) in herpetology—the study of reptiles.

Sara: And after college (10) __________ (you / spend) a few years in Thailand. Isn't that right?

Tim: Yes, I was working with Thai snake experts. (11) __________ (I / really enjoy) my time with them.

Sara: (12) __________ (you / ever / experience) any life-threatening situations since you started working with snakes?

Tim: (13) __________ (I / work) with many poisonous snakes over the years, but (14) __________ (only one / bite) me. That was scary! Since that time, (15) __________ (I / pay more attention) to the snakes' behavior.

Sara: Why do you love your job?

Tim: (16) Because __________ (I / be) able to live my childhood dream.

CD1-12

B Listen and check your answers. Then practice the conversation with a partner. Notice your pronunciation.

10 EDIT. Read the e-mail. Find and correct eight more errors with the present perfect and simple past.

Dear Ms. Ramos,

I am writing to apply for the position of staff photographer that I have seen on your website. I believe that my experience has prepared me well for this job.

Photography is my passion. I loved photography ever since I was a child. That is when I have gotten my first camera. The thrill of taking pictures never gone away, but my interests have changed over the years. While I was growing up, I liked to photograph people; however, as an adult, I have took more pictures of nature than people.

I lived in Hawaii since 2013, and I have traveled all over the islands to photograph rare birds and plants. I've learned a lot, and my technique has improved in the last few years. My photos has never appeared in a magazine or book, but several have been on display at a local gallery since several months. I would be happy to share my portfolio on request.

I have heared a lot about your magazine, and it would be a pleasure to work for you. I look forward to talking to you about this opportunity.

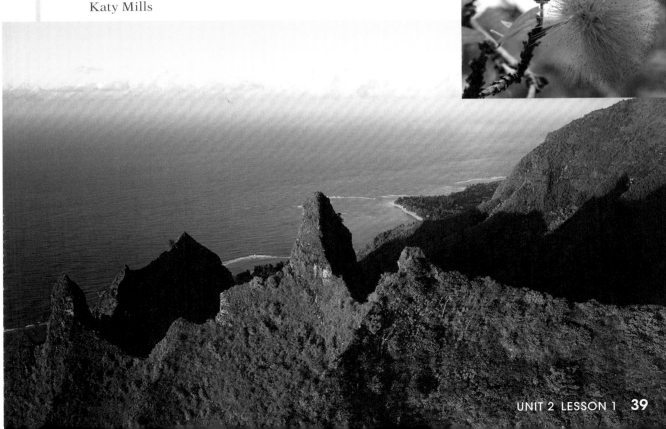

Sincerely,

Katy Mills

11 WRITE & SPEAK.

A Use the words to write questions. Use the present perfect or simple past.

1. what activities / you / always / love / to do

   What activities have you always loved to do?

2. what activities / you / enjoy / when you were younger

   ____

3. you / visit / any interesting places / when you were a child

   ____

4. you / visit any interesting places / recently

   ____

5. what dreams for the future / you / have / as a child

   ____

6. what / goals / you / achieved / in the last few years

   ____

B Work with a partner. Ask and answer the questions in exercise **A**.

A: *What activities have you always loved to do?*

B: *I've always loved listening to music.*

12 APPLY.

A What is your passion? What kind of job would allow you to follow your passion? Imagine that you are applying for your ideal job. Write an e-mail and apply for that job. Use ideas from the e-mail in exercise **10** on page 39 to help you. Use the simple past and present perfect.

B Read a partner's e-mail. Ask and answer questions about each other's passion.

A: *So, you've been playing the flute ever since you were a child. I didn't know that.*

B: *Yeah. I've always loved it.*

A: *Have you always wanted to play in an orchestra?*

B: *No. At first, I wanted to be a music teacher.*

EXPLORE

CD1-13

1 READ the magazine article about Helen Thayer. What advice does she have for other people?

Helen Thayer: A Lifelong Adventurer

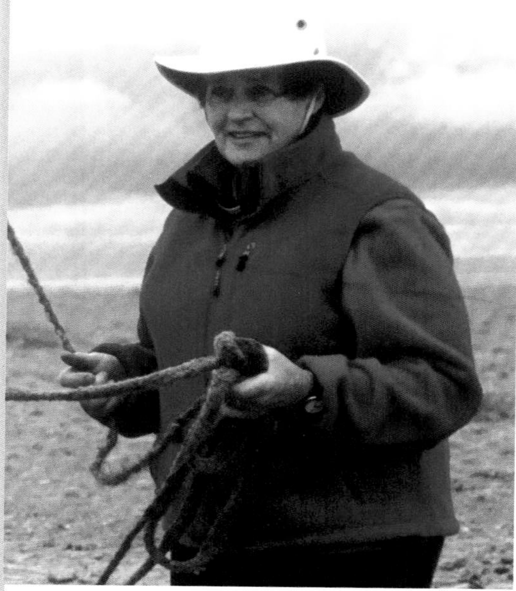

Helen Thayer **has** never **let** age stop her. She and her husband, Bill, fulfilled a lifelong dream for their 40th wedding anniversary. They walked 1600 miles (2575 kilometers) in intense heat across the Gobi Desert. There they met Mongolian nomads[1] and learned about their culture. To celebrate 50 years of marriage, the Thayers walked almost 900 miles (1448 kilometers) across the Sahara Desert to study the customs of the people who live there. Now in her seventies, Thayer keeps on planning trips for the future.

Thayer, born in New Zealand, **has been exploring** the outdoors for most of her life. Since childhood, she **has traveled** widely in harsh climates and across rough lands. She **has walked** to the North Pole with her dog as her only companion. She **has** also **kayaked** 2200 miles (3541 kilometers) down the Amazon, and **done** several mountain climbs. These trips **haven't been** easy, but they**'ve been** very satisfying.

In recent years, Thayer **has been talking** to groups around the world. She **has continued** to travel and bring back stories to share with both children and adults. Thayer hopes to inspire[2] people to follow their passions and fulfill their dreams.[3] What is her advice? Set goals, plan for success, and never give up.

[1] **nomads:** people who move from place to place instead of living in one place
[2] **inspire:** to make someone want to do something
[3] **fulfill one's dream:** to manage to do what you hoped you would do

▶ The Gobi Desert covers parts of Mongolia and China

2 CHECK. Read the statements. Circle **T** for *true* or **F** for *false*.

1. Helen Thayer and her husband drove across two deserts.	**T**	**F**
2. As a child, Thayer liked the outdoors.	**T**	**F**
3. The trips have been in one part of the world.	**T**	**F**
4. Thayer has traveled down the Amazon River.	**T**	**F**
5. Thayer has stopped traveling in recent years.	**T**	**F**

3 DISCOVER. Complete the exercises to learn about the grammar in this lesson.

A Read the sentences from the article in exercise **1**. Notice the words in **bold**. Is the action completed or possibly still in progress? Choose the correct answer.

1. Thayer, born in New Zealand, **has been exploring** the outdoors for most of her life.

   a. completed (b.) possibly still in progress

2. She **has walked** to the North Pole with her dog as her only companion.

   a. completed b. possibly still in progress

3. She **has** also **kayaked** 2200 miles down the Amazon . . .

   a. completed b. possibly still in progress

4. In recent years, Thayer **has been talking** to groups around the world.

   a. completed b. possibly still in progress

B Work with a partner. Compare your answers from exercise **A**. What do you notice about the verb forms used for actions that are possibly still in progress? Discuss your ideas with your partner.

▲ The Red Cliffs, Gobi Desert, Mongolia

LEARN

2.4 Present Perfect Progressive

Statements	
	Subject + *Have/Has (Not)* + *Been* + Verb + *-ing*
Affirmative	I **have been waiting** for my friend for an hour.
Negative	Tom **hasn't been sleeping** enough this term.

Questions		Answers
	(Wh-) + *Have/Has* + Subject + *Been* + Verb + *-ing*	
Yes/No	**Have** you **been working** for a long time?	Yes, I **have**. / No, I **haven't**.
Wh-	**What has** Raul **been reading** lately?	A lot of short stories.

	Who/What + *Has* + *Been* + Verb + *-ing*	
Who or *What* as Subject	**Who has been managing** the lab?	Luz and Jun **have**.

1. Use the present perfect progressive for ongoing actions that started in the past and continue in the present.	I've been working — now I**'ve been working** on my research paper.
2. The present perfect progressive is often used a. with *for* or *since* b. without *for* or *since* to emphasize that the action happened recently or is temporary c. for repeated actions that started in the past and continue in the present	a. They **have been studying** Spanish for years. b. The chef**'s been working** hard. It's the busy season. c. I**'ve been texting** Jose all day. He hasn't replied to any of my messages.
3. **Remember:** The progressive is not usually used with stative verbs.	✓ She **has known** him since college. ✗ She has been knowing him since college.

4 Complete the conversations with the words in parentheses. Use the present perfect progressive.

Sasha: How long (1) have you been going (you / go) on long-distance hikes?

Gina: Since I was in college. And I'm now in my sixties. (2) ____________ (my husband / hike) since he was a child.

Sasha: (3) ____________ (it / get) easier or more difficult for you to hike long distances these days?

Gina: Well, I'd say that lately (4) ____________ (we / work) harder to keep up with the younger people on the hikes, but I don't think (5) ____________ (we / cause) any problems or delays!

Jack: (6) ______________________ (you / enjoy) yourselves on the trip so far?

Katya: Oh, yes. (7) ______________________ (we / have) a wonderful time.

Jack: So what (8) ______________________ (you / do) during your stay here in town?

Katya: Well, (9) ______________________ (we / visit) museums and (10)______________________ (take) tours of the major sights.

2.5 Present Perfect Progressive and Present Perfect

1. The present perfect is used for completed actions. The present perfect progressive is used for continuous actions that are not complete.	I've **read** the chapter. I'm ready to discuss it. Jill **has made** five phone calls. I've **been reading** the chapter. I'm almost finished. Jill **has been making** phone calls for two hours.
2. The present perfect and present perfect progressive have similar meanings with some verbs that express routines, such as *live, work,* and *teach.*	Tony **has lived** in New York for ten years. He **has been living** in New York for ten years.
3. The present perfect is often used to express the idea of *how many* or *how much.* The present perfect progressive is often used to express the idea of *how long.*	How many cookies **has** he **eaten**? He **has eaten** five cookies. How long **have** you **been playing** the piano? We **have been playing** for a long time.
4. **Remember:** The progressive is not usually used with stative verbs.	✓ I **have loved** that movie since I was a child. ✗ I have been loving that movie since I was a child.

5 Read the sentences. Circle **Y** for *yes* or **N** for *no* to answer the questions.

1.	a. Tony has set high goals for himself.	Is he still setting goals?	Y	N
	b. Nick has been setting high goals for himself.	Is he still setting goals?	Y	N
2.	a. We've been counting votes for hours.	Are they counting now?	Y	N
	b. We've counted the votes.	Are they counting now?	Y	N
3.	a. Dana has lost 35 pounds.	Is she still losing the 35 pounds?	Y	N
	b. Dana has been losing weight.	Is she still losing weight?	Y	N
4.	a. I've been working in a store this summer.	Is he still working?	Y	N
	b. I've worked in the store for 25 years.	Is he still working?	Y	N

6 Complete the exercises.

A Circle the best answer to complete each question.

1. How long have you **taken / been taking** classes at this school?
2. How many friends have you **made / been making** since you started studying here?

3. How many cups of coffee have you **bought / been buying** this week?

4. How long have you **owned / been owning** a cell phone?

5. What gifts have you **gotten / been getting** in the last year?

6. How many times have you **eaten / been eating** out this month?

7. How much homework have you already **done / been doing** this week?

8. What TV programs have you **watched / been watching** this week? both

B **SPEAK.** Work with a partner. Ask and answer the questions from exercise **A**.

A: How long have you been taking classes at this school?

B: For two months.

PRACTICE

7 Complete the conversations with the words in parentheses. Use the present perfect or present perfect progressive. In some sentences both forms are possible.

1. A: Have you finished (you / finish) your assignment?

   B: Yeah, and now I'm going to get something to eat.

2. A: Have you heard (you / find) your keys?

   B: No, I'm not sure where they are.

3. A: Is this your phone?

   B: Yeah, thanks. I been looking for (I / look for) it everywhere.

4. A: You look exhausted.

   B: I am. I have been working (I / work) for hours.

5. A: Are you crying?

   B: No, I have been chopping (I / chop) onions.

6. A: Have you heard (you / hear) the news?

   B: No, what happened?

7. A: How long has Pat been studying (Pat / study) Chinese?

   B: He has taken / has been taken (he / take) classes for about a year now,

   and learned / has been learning (he / learn) a lot.

8. A: Has Julio taken (Julio / take) his final exam?

   B: Not yet, but he had been studying (he / study) all week.

8 LISTEN, WRITE & SPEAK. Look at the photo and read the caption. What is chef Barton Seaver's passion?

CD1-14

A Read the sentences about Barton Seaver. Then listen to the interview with him. Circle **T** for *true* and **F** for *false.*

1. Barton Seaver hasn't been eating seafood for very long. **T** **F**
2. His family and childhood have influenced his career choices. **T** **F**
3. Seaver hasn't been focusing on his seafood restaurants recently. **T** **F**
4. Seaver has developed a list of popular fish to eat. **T** **F**
5. In his opinion, people have been eating too many vegetables. **T** **F**
6. Seaver hasn't written about oceans or seafood for a long time. **T** **F**

▲ Barton Seaver, chef and advocate for the oceans, believes that the choices we make directly affect the ocean and all the life it supports.

B Look at the false sentences from exercise **A**. Write a true sentence for each.

1. Barton Seaver has been eating seafood since he was a child.
2. ______
3. ______
4. ______
5. ______
6. ______

CD1-14

C Work in a group. Discuss the questions. Listen again if necessary.

1. Why did Barton Seaver create a list of substitute fish for people to eat?
2. What do you think he has been talking about in his lectures?
3. What is an aspect of eating/food production that you have heard about or feel is important?

9 Complete the exercises.

A Look at the checklist. Hank and Jake must complete these tasks by the end of next week to graduate from cooking school. Who is closer to graduating, Hank or Jake?

Tasks	Hank	Jake
1. Plan a daily menu	✓	✓
2. Take an online course on food science	✓	
3. Write a paper on food safety	✓	
4. Plan a food budget for one week	✓	✓
5. Serve a four-course holiday meal		

B Complete the paragraph with the words in parentheses. Use the present perfect or present perfect progressive. Add *not* where necessary.

(1) Both Hank and Jake have planned (plan) a daily menu. (2) Jake hasn't complete (complete) the online food science course yet because he was sick for two weeks. The professor is letting him make up the final exam next week. (3) Hank has already taken (already / take) the course, so (4) he has been helping (help) Jake study for the exam. (5) Hank has already turned in (already / turn in) his food safety paper. (6) Jake has been working (work) hard on his food safety paper, but (7) he hasn't finished (finish) it yet. (8) They have been planing (plan) the food budget and the menu for the holiday meal together for a few weeks. (9) They haven't been served (serve) the holiday meal yet, but they plan to serve it next Thursday. Both hope to graduate in December.

10 **APPLY.**

A Write a paragraph about a short or long-term goal you have for the future, such as passing a test or graduating from college. Write at least three things you have or have not done or been doing to achieve your goal.

My goal is to get an A in my history class. I've been doing my homework every night and participating a lot in class. I've finished all my assignments on time. I haven't started my research paper yet, but I've been thinking about different topics.

B Share your goals with a group. Ask your classmates follow-up questions.

A: *Have you gotten As on your tests?*

B: *I've gotten one A and one B, but it was 89 percent, so that's a pretty high B.*

EXPLORE

CD1-15

1 READ the article about Alex Honnold. What big risk did he take to fulfill his dream?

Daring. Defiant. Free.

A new generation of superclimbers is pushing the limits in Yosemite

Every rock climber who has come to Yosemite has a dream. Alex Honnold's dream was to free solo Half Dome, a 2130-foot (649-meter) wall of granite[1]. Free soloing means climbing with only rock shoes and some chalk to help keep the hands dry. Honnold couldn't use a rope or anything else to help him stick to the slippery stone. The few people who **had climbed** Half Dome before **had used** ropes, and it **had taken** them more than a day to do the climb.

On a bright September morning, Honnold was clinging[2] to the face of Half Dome, less than 100 feet (30 meters) from the top. He **had been climbing** for two hours and forty-five minutes, but all of a sudden he stopped. Something potentially disastrous **had occurred**—he **had lost** some of his confidence. He **hadn't felt** that way two days before when **he'd been racing** up the same rock *with* a rope. That climb **had gone** well. Today though, Honnold hesitated. He knew that even the slightest doubt could cause a deadly fall, thousands of feet to the valley floor below. He knew he had to get moving, so he chalked his hands, adjusted his feet, and started climbing again. Within minutes, he was at the top.

Bloggers spread the news of Honnold's two-hour-and-fifty-minute free solo, and climbers were amazed. On this warm fall day, 23-year-old Alex Honnold **had** just **set** a new record in one of climbing's biggest challenges.

[1] **granite:** a kind of very hard rock
[2] **cling:** to hold something tightly

◄ Alex Honnold free soloing in Yosemite National Park, California

2 CHECK. Circle the correct answer to complete each statement.

1. When you free solo, you climb without **shoes / rope**.
2. Alex Honnold's free solo of Half Dome **was / wasn't** successful.
3. Honnold lost his **confidence / rope** for a moment on his way up Half Dome.
4. **No / Some** climbers before Honnold climbed Half Dome in under three hours.

3 DISCOVER. Complete the exercises to learn about the grammar in this lesson.

A Work with a partner. Read the sentences about the article. Write *1* above the underlined action or situation that happened first. Write *2* above the one that happened second.

1. Honnold <u>climbed</u> (2) Half Dome without a rope. Others <u>had climbed</u> (1) it with a rope.
2. He <u>had been</u> confident until he <u>got near the top</u>.
3. This time <u>was different</u> from the last time. The last time he <u>had used a rope</u>.
4. He <u>climbed the fastest</u>. Nobody <u>had ever climbed so quickly</u>.

B Look at the sentences in exercise **A** again. Did the sentences with *had* + past participle happen first or second? Discuss your answer with a partner and then your class.

LEARN

2.6 Past Perfect

Statements	
	Subject + *Had (Not)* + Past Participle
Affirmative	Lisa **had finished** her assignment by the due date.
Negative	Tim **hadn't revised** his essay before class.

Questions		Answers
	(Wh-) + *Had* + Subject + Past Participle	
Yes/No	**Had** you **been** to Tokyo before your trip?	Yes, I **had**. / No, I **hadn't**.
Wh-	**Where had** Raul **lived** before he came here?	Japan.

	Who/What + *Had (Not)* + Past Participle	
Who or *What* as Subject	**Who had left** the party when you arrived?	Most people **had**.

1. The past perfect is used to show that one action or event happened before another past action, event, or time.	finished dinner — ordered dessert — now We **had finished** dinner, so we **ordered** dessert.
2. Use the past perfect for the action or event that happened first. Use the simple past for the one that happened second.	When I **arrived,** (Second Event) the first band **had already played.** (First Event)
3. The past perfect is not necessary when the context is clear. Words like *before* and *after* make the order of events clear.	She **had left** home **before** he arrived. She **left** home **before** he arrived.
4. *Already, always, ever, just,* and *never* usually go before the past participle.	**Had** you **ever noticed** that sign before? She **had never eaten** a kiwi until her trip.
5. *By* + a time or *by the time* + subject + simple past are often used with the past perfect. *By* means *before* or *not later than.*	**By 5:00 p.m.,** it had rained two inches. **By the time we finished dinner**, the rain had stopped.

4 Complete the conversation with the words in parentheses. Use the simple past or past perfect. In some sentences both forms are correct. Use contractions where possible.

Deb: So tell me, why (1) ___did you take___ (you / take) the train from Moscow to Beijing?

Joe: Because it was my dream to ride the Trans-Siberian Railway. It was something (2) ___I'd always wanted___ (I / always / want) to do.

Deb: How long (3) ______________ (the trip / take)?

Joe: Seven days. By the time the train arrived at Beijing's main train station, (4) ______________ (I / travel) 4735 miles.

Deb: (5) ____________________ (you / ever / be) on such a long ride?

Joe: No, never. The longest train ride (6) ____________________ (I / ever / take) was only six hours long.

Deb: What (7) ____________________ (you / do) during those seven days? Did you ever get bored?

Joe: No, not at all. It was fun on the train, and I had many conversations. By the time the journey was over, (8) ____________________ (I / make) many new friends. In fact, one of them (9) ____________________ (go) to my high school. (10) ____________________ (I / never / meet) her before!

2.7 Past Perfect Progressive

Statements	
	Subject + *Had (Not)* + *Been* + Verb + *-ing*
Affirmative	Nick **had been skiing** for years when he first skied the Alps.
Negative	We **hadn't been climbing** since 2008.

Questions		Answers
	(Wh-) + *Had* + Subject + *Been* + Verb + *-ing*	
Yes/No	**Had** Linda **been waiting** for a long time?	Yes, she **had**. / No, she **hadn't**.
Wh-	**How long had** you **been waiting** before he arrived?	Ten minutes.
	Who/What + *Had (Not)* + *Been* + Verb + *-ing*	
Who or *What* as Subject	**What had been causing** that noise?	A broken car alarm.

1. Use the past perfect progressive a. when an action or event was happening for a period of time until (or just before) another action, event, or time	a. She **had been climbing** for half an hour when she suddenly got a pain in her leg.
b. to talk about how long something happened	b. We**'d been trying** to win the contest **for five years**.
2. **Be careful!** Use the past perfect to talk about how many times something happened.	We**'d tried** to win the contest **five times**.

5 Complete the exercises.

A Complete the sentences with the words in parentheses. Use the past perfect progressive. Then compare your answers with a partner.

1. By the time Sylvia was 18, she ___had been hiking___ (hike) for several years.
2. Two German hikers ________________ (follow) a difficult trail when they lost their way.
3. The Danish hikers ________________ (prepare) dinner when a bear approached their campsite.
4. Two young hikers were getting ready to go home. They ________________ (not camp) for very long when they lost interest.
5. The rescue workers ________________ (stay) at the park office before they moved into a house nearby the park.
6. Yesterday, George rescued a hiker who ________________ (wait) for help for over 12 hours.
7. Some hikers were worried. They ________________ (head) back to the camp when they heard thunder, and they had to look for shelter.
8. They ________________ (not think) about the weather until the sky turned very dark.

B Complete the questions about the people in exercise **A**.

1. How long ___had___ Sylvia ___been hiking___ by the time she was 18?
2. What kind of trail ________ the German hikers ________________ when they lost their way?
3. What ________ the Danish hikers ________________ when the bear approached?
4. How long ________ the two young hikers ________________ when they lost interest?
5. Where ________ the rescue workers ________________ before they moved?
6. How long ________ the hiker ________________ for help?
7. Where ________ the hikers ________________ when they heard thunder?
8. ________ the hikers ________________ about the weather before?

C **SPEAK.** Work with a partner. Ask and answer the questions in exercise **B**. Find the answers in exercise **A**.

A: *How long had Sylvia been hiking by the time she was 18?* B: *For several years.*

PRACTICE

6 WRITE & SPEAK.

A Complete the questions with the words in parentheses. Use the simple past or past perfect.

1. What ___had you learned___ (you / learn) to do by the age of ten?
2. What ___did you learn___ (you / learn) to do in your teens?
3. How many languages ______________ (you / study) by the time you were fifteen years old?
4. How many languages ______________ (you / learn) as a child?
5. What things ______________ (you / never / do) when you were a child?
6. What things ______________ (you / never / do) until recently?
7. How many places ______________ (your parents / live) by the time you were born?
8. Where ______________ (you / live) when you were growing up?

B Work with a partner. Ask and answer the questions in exercise **A** with information about yourself. Answer with the simple past or past perfect.

A: *What had you learned to do by the age of ten?*

B: *I had learned to catch fish by then.*

7 SPEAK & WRITE.

A Work with a partner. Read the time line about an athlete who paid the ultimate price for his passion. What was his passion? Discuss your answer with your partner.

Dan Osman: A Passionate Life

1963	Born in Reno, Nevada
1975	Starts rock climbing
1981	Moves to California and starts free solo climbing at Yosemite
1989	Gets bored with climbing and tries jumping from cliffs
1990s	Appears in the Masters of Stone videos
1995	Meets Andrew Todhunter, who starts to write a book about him
11/22/98	Makes a successful 925-foot jump off a cliff at Yosemite
11/23/98	Fails trying to make a 1000-foot jump at Yosemite; dies at age 35
1999	Todhunter's book about Osman is published

B Use information from the time line in exercise **A** on page 53 and the words in parentheses to complete the sentences. Use the past perfect. Add *not* where necessary.

1. Dan Osman ___hadn't been___ (be) a rock climber before the age of twelve.
2. Osman ________________ (climb) free solo until he moved to California.
3. By 1989, he ________________ (become) bored with climbing.
4. In 1989, Osman ________________ (appear) in the Masters of Stone videos yet.
5. Andrew Todhunter didn't start his book about Osman until he ________________ (meet) him.
6. When Osman died, Todhunter ________________ (finish) the book yet.
7. Before his death, Osman ________________ (already / jump) from many cliffs.
8. He ________________ (complete) a jump of almost 1000 feet not long before his fatal jump.

C Write questions in your notebook about the sentences in exercise **B**. Then ask and answer the questions with a partner.

A: *Had Osman done any climbing before the age of twelve?*

B: *No, he hadn't. He did his first climb when he was twelve.*

8 Complete the story with the verbs in the box. Use the past perfect or the past perfect progressive. Add *not* where necessary.

~~go~~	eat	notice	plan	rest	ride	sleep	want

Ginny was about to start a mountain biking trip. She was excited because she (1) ___hadn't gone___ mountain biking alone before. She (2) ________________ to go on a biking trip for a long time, and (3) ________________ for this trip for five months.

On the day of her trip, Ginny had a lot of energy because she (4) ________________ well the night before. She started smoothly. She (5) ________________ for several hours when she got a flat tire. Fortunately, she had a spare tire. A bit later, she was hungry because she (6) ________________ anything since her mid-morning snack, so she stopped and ate a sandwich. Later, she decided to rest, so she rode back to a pond because she (7) ________________ that it was shady there. She (8) ________________ for long before she felt ready to get up and finish her ride.

REAL ENGLISH

The past perfect is often used to give a reason or explain an event that happened before another event in the past.

*I didn't recognize her because she **had changed** her hairstyle.*

▲ An image of the Canadian Arctic around 1834

9 READ & SPEAK.

A Read the paragraph about an expedition to the Canadian Arctic. Find and underline the simple past, past perfect, and past perfect progressive verb forms.

> By the mid-nineteenth century, Europeans had been trying to find a quick way to travel to Asia for hundreds of years. They had been looking for a waterway through the icy Canadian Arctic since the sixteenth century; however, no one had ever found it. Then in 1845, Sir John Franklin tried. He set out on the risky journey with an expedition of 128 men. Two years passed by, but Franklin did not return. What had happened to him and his men? Had their ship sunk? Had they gotten lost? A rescue team went to find out.

B Work with a partner. Read the questions about the text in exercise **A**. Discuss the answers with your partner and then your class.

1. What had the Europeans been trying to find since the sixteenth century?
2. Why do you think they wanted to find it?
3. What did Sir John Franklin do?
4. What do you think happened to Franklin and his men?

10 LISTEN.

CD1-16

A Listen to the interview with an author who wrote a book about the search for Franklin and his crew. Then read the sentences. Circle **T** for *true* or **F** for *false*.

1. The Northwest Passage was a popular route. Many explorers had been through before Franklin.	**T**	**(F)**
2. One rescue team found proof that Franklin had died.	**T**	**F**
3. A rescue team found a detailed message about the difficulties Franklin and his men had faced.	**T**	**F**
4. Franklin's men had abandoned their ships.	**T**	**F**
5. The men died from several different things, including starvation and disease.	**T**	**F**

CD1-16

B Correct the false statements in exercise **A**. Listen again to check your answers.

No explorers had been through the Northwest Passage before Franklin.

11 APPLY.

A Work with a partner. Look at the photo on this page. Imagine what could go wrong on this trip. Then complete the chart with your ideas. Use the simple past, past perfect, and past perfect progressive.

A Kayaking Trip

What Happened	Why It Happened
1. While kayaking, they got lost.	1. They hadn't been paying attention to their location.
2. They got sunburned.	2. They hadn't brought any sunblock.
3. They lost a paddle.	3. ______
4. ______	4. They had been walking around.
5. They got mosquito bites.	5. ______
6. ______	6. ______

B Share your ideas with the class.

C Work in a group. Imagine what went wrong on the camping trip in the photo or any trip you know about. Follow the instructions below.

1. Discuss what happened and why.
2. Complete the chart below with the five most interesting ideas from your discussion. Use the chart from exercise **A** as a guide.
3. Share your answers with the class.

What Happened	Why It Happened
1.	1.
2.	2.
3.	3.
4.	4.
5.	5.

Review the Grammar UNIT 2

Charts 2.1–2.7

1 Complete the paragraph. Use the correct form of each verb in parentheses.

I (1) ___had___ (have) a terrible car accident when I was sixteen. I (2) __________ (lose) a leg. As an athlete, this was especially devastating. I (3) __________ (be) a gymnast from the age of eight, and I (4) __________ (win) three national competitions. It (5) __________ (take) me a lot of time to recover, and I (6) __________ (not think) about competing again. Then, one of my coaches (7) __________ (tell) me about the Paralympics and (8) __________ (suggest) that I train for swimming. I could do that with only one leg. I (9) __________ (always / want) to be in the Olympics. In fact, I (10) __________ (train) for the Olympics at the time of my accident. So I (11) __________ (listen) to my coach and (12) __________ (start) swimming. I (13) __________ (swim) ever since that day and I love it. I (14) __________ (win) several competitions. Lately, I (15) __________ (train) for the next Paralympics. I hope to win a medal!

Charts 2.1, 2.3–2.7

2 **EDIT.** Read the text by a traveler on safari. Find and correct nine more errors with the simple past, present perfect, present perfect progressive, past perfect, or past perfect progressive.

Mason's Travels on Safari

It had always been our dream to travel to southern Africa, and we'd ~~make~~ made a lot of plans for our trip. I wanted to take a lot of wildlife photographs, so my friend has recommended that I bring two cameras. When I got to Namibia, I had panicked. One camera had been missing. Luckily, I was finding it later.

The next day, we had started out on our safari with a tour. By the end of our tour, we saw some amazing things. One time, when we stopped to take pictures, we were only a few feet away from a cheetah. Amazing!

We had never bothered the animals at night. However, we heard their various calls and other noises outside our tent every night. At first, I had been afraid of the sounds, but not by the end of the trip. It was really the most incredible trip I've ever been taking.

Cheetah running, Namibia ▶

Charts 2.1, 2.3–2.4, 2.6

CD1-17

3 LISTEN & SPEAK.

A Circle the correct form of the verb. Then listen to the conversation and check your answers.

1. Liu Yang is the first female astronaut that China **ever sent / has ever sent** into space.
2. She **trained / has trained** to be a pilot at China's Air Force College, and then she **joined / has joined** the Air Force.
3. She **flew / has flown** five different types of aircraft, and she **did / has done** 1680 hours of flight time.
4. She **also participated / has also participated** in military exercises and emergency rescues.
5. Liu started training to be an astronaut. She **has never experienced / had never experienced** anything so challenging.

CD1-18

B Listen to the next part of the conversation. Then work with a partner. Discuss the questions. Then listen again and check your answers.

1. What has Liu Yang done in her life?
2. Had she always wanted to be an astronaut?
3. How have her coworkers described her?
4. How long had she been in the Air Force before becoming an astronaut?

Connect the Grammar to Writing

1 READ & NOTICE THE GRAMMAR.

A What is a goal that you have achieved? How did it affect you? Tell a partner your ideas. Then read the narrative.

Achieving a Goal

About a year ago, I was watching the Olympics, and I decided that I wanted to become a runner. I knew I should set an achievable goal, so I decided to train for a 5K race.

My parents were surprised when I told them about my goal, because I had never been interested in running before. In fact, I had never run more than a mile, and I had always been very slow. My friends thought I was joking. Everyone assumed that I would quit after a week.

Fortunately, I proved them all wrong. I did two things to achieve my goal. First, I went online and researched a good training plan. I found a website that helps you plan workouts. You start by walking, and then you gradually start running. After that, I joined a local running group. We ran in the park twice a week, and I made friends who had also decided to run a 5K.

Three months later, I achieved my goal: I ran in my first race. I didn't win, but I ran the whole way, so I was proud of myself. Since then, I have run in several races. I have also started training for a longer run. My next goal is to run in a 10K race. My friends have stopped laughing at me, and a few of them have even asked me to help them start running!

GRAMMAR FOCUS

In the narrative in exercise **A**, the writer uses these verb forms:

Simple past	• to tell about the main event of the story *(About a year ago . . . I **decided** that . . .)*
Past perfect	• to discuss events that happened before the main story *(I **had** never **run** more than a mile . . .)*
Present perfect	• with *since* to tell about past events that continue to the present *(**Since** then, I **have run** in several races.)*

B Read the narrative in exercise **A** again. Find and circle two more examples of the simple past. Underline two past perfect examples, and double underline two present perfect examples.

C Complete the time line with information from the narrative in exercise **A**. Write the letter of the events in the correct order. Then compare your answers with a partner.

a. Ran in several other races
b. Was never interested in running
c. Joined a running club
d. Parents were surprised
e. Ran in 5K
f. Watched the Olympics
g. Found a good website

b ___ ___ ___ ___ ___ ___

Set a goal to run a 5K — Now

2 BEFORE YOU WRITE.

A Work with a partner. Make a list of goals that you have achieved. Discuss which goals would be the most interesting to write about.

B Create a time line for your personal narrative. Write the events of the story that you want to tell. Use the time line in exercise **1C** as a guide.

3 **WRITE** two or three paragraphs telling your story. Use your time line in exercise **2B** and the text in exercise **1A** as a guide. Remember to start your story with background information. At the end, tell how your life has changed.

WRITING FOCUS Using *First* and *After that* to Show a Sequence

Notice *first* and *after that* in the narrative in exercise **1A**.

Use these words at the beginning of the sentence to explain the order of events in a text. Place a comma after *first* and *after that*.

First, I went online and . . . *After that, I joined a local running club.*

4 **SELF ASSESS.** Underline the verb forms in your narrative. Then use the checklist to assess your work.

- ☐ I used the present perfect and the present perfect progressive correctly. [2.1, 2.2, 2.4, 2.5]
- ☐ I used the simple past correctly. [2.3]
- ☐ I used the past perfect and the past perfect progressive correctly. [2.6, 2.7]
- ☐ I used commas correctly with *first* and *after that*. [WRITING FOCUS]

UNIT 3 A Look Into the Future

The Future

▲ Supertrees act as vertical gardens, generating solar power and collecting rainwater, Supertree Glove, Singapore.

EXPLORE

CD1-19

1 READ the conversation about robots. What amazing things will robots do in the future?

Will robots be our friends one day?
HSM Open University
CLICK TO PLAY
Unit 3 Robots: The New Generation
Course: Artificial Intelligence
Professor L. Lacy

Paulo: Wasn't Professor Lacy's online lecture last week amazing?

Kate: I haven't watched it yet. What did he say?

Paulo: He talked about a new generation of robots. Apparently they**'ll seem** almost human.

Kate: That's interesting, but why do scientists want to make them look real?

Paulo: Well, many of the new robots **will do** tasks for people at home. They **will** also **be** in schools and offices. Scientists are making robots look more human so people **will be** comfortable around them.

Kate: Hmm. What kind of tasks **are** the robots **going to do**?

Paulo: According to Professor Lacy, they**'ll cook, fold laundry, go shopping,** and even **babysit** children.

Kate: Don't you think the idea is a little creepy? I think a lot of people **won't want** robots in their homes.

Paulo: Maybe not. But scientists are working hard so robots **won't be** scary looking. These robots **are** even **going to be** responsive to our thoughts and feelings, and they**'re going to look** friendly.

Kate: I still think robots that look and act like humans **will make** people feel uncomfortable. And what about children? **Will** they **develop** normally if they have robots for babysitters?

Paulo: Good question. Nobody knows how robots **will affect** people and their relationships, but scientists are researching those issues.

Kate: Really? I want to hear more, but my class **starts** in five minutes. **Are** you **going** to the study session on Friday?

Paulo: No, but **I'll e-mail** you. Let's get together soon.

▲ "Actroid" is a human-looking robot made by a Japanese robotics company.

2 CHECK. Read the statements. Circle **T** for *true* or **F** for *false*.

1. In the future, robots will look and act more like people. **T** **F**
2. The new robots won't prepare food. **T** **F**
3. Some robots are going to take care of people. **T** **F**
4. Everyone will want a robot helper at home. **T** **F**
5. Scientists are studying the effects of robots on humans. **T** **F**

3 DISCOVER. Complete the exercises to learn about the grammar in this lesson.

A Find these sentences in the conversation in exercise **1**. Write the missing words.

1. What kind of tasks ___are___ the robots ___going to do___?
2. Really? I want to hear more, but my class __________ in five minutes.
3. __________ you __________ to the study session on Friday?
4. No, but I __________ you later so we can get together.

B How many different verb forms are used in exercise **A** to talk about the future? _____

LEARN

3.1 Review of *Will* and *Be Going To*

	Will	*Be Going To*
Affirmative Statements	Patty **will be** a doctor someday.	Tim **is going to teach** high school.
Negative Statements	Ty **won't eat** that. He doesn't like fish.	Mari **isn't going to eat** with us.
Yes/No Questions	**Will** you **visit** us soon? We miss you.	**Are** you **going to visit** your sister this weekend?
Wh- Questions	**Who will** I **know** at the party?	**What are** you **going to do** on your birthday?
Who or *What* as Subject	**Who will bring** a cake?	**Who is going to watch** the game on Friday?

1. Use *will* and *be going to* for predictions. **Be careful!** Use *be going to* only when you are certain about something in the future because of evidence or information you have now.	I think the movie **will be** very popular. I think the movie **is going to be** popular. ✓ The score is five to zero. We**'re going to win** the game! ✗ The score is five to zero. We will win the game!
2. Use *be going to* for plans or intentions. (An intention is something you decide to do.)	We **are going to see** that new movie this weekend. Sue went to get her tools. She**'s going to fix** the door.
3. Use *will* for a. sudden decisions (made at the time of speaking) b. offers c. promises d. requests	 a. Amy's not home? I**'ll call** back later. b. Do you want some tea? I**'ll get** you some. c. I **won't be** late. I promise. d. **Will** you **give** the teacher the message?
4. Use *won't* for refusals.	My parents **won't lend** him any more money.

4 Complete the exercises.

A Complete the sentences with the words in parentheses. Use *will* or the correct form of *be going to* depending on the meaning (prediction, intention, etc.). Both *will* and *be going to* are possible in some sentences.

1. I think ___robots will scare___ (robots / scare) people if they look and act too human.
   prediction
2. ___I going to make___ (I / make) copies of my notes for a few other students.
   intention
3. ___I will make___ (I / make) you a copy of my notes if you like.
   offer
4. ___Are you going to explain___ (you / explain) the connection between robotics and students' everyday lives?
   intention
5. ___Will you explain___ (you / explain) the connection between robotics and students' everyday lives?
   request
6. I'm afraid there's no time to discuss your question now. ___we will talk___ (we / talk) about it next week.
   promise

7. I'm afraid there's no time to discuss your question now. ______________ (you / remind) me about it next class?

8. I have an appointment with my professor. ______________ (I / talk) to her about my test grade.

9. We want Mr. Lu to cancel the exam, but ______________ (he / not do) it.

10. ______________ (robots / be) common in everyday life in the future?

11. ______________ (you / help) me cook dinner tonight?

12. This room is a mess! ______________ (I / help) you clean up.

B SPEAK. Work with a partner. Compare your answers from exercise **A**.

3.2 Review of Present Progressive and Simple Present for the Future

1. Use the present progressive for definite plans. The plan is often in the near future, or the details of the plan (such as time or place) are known.	I'**m meeting** friends for dinner on Saturday. We'**re eating** at Grimaldi's.
2. When the present progressive refers to the future, we often use a future time expression. The present progressive refers to *now* when it does not have a time expression and does not refer to the future.	Future: My parents **are leaving** Sunday. Now: My parents **are leaving.**
3. Use the simple present for future events that have a fixed or regular schedule.	The plane **leaves** at 8:30 Monday night. I'll be at the airport by 7:00.

5 Complete the conversations with the words in parentheses. Use the present progressive or simple present. More than one answer is sometimes correct. Then work with a partner and compare your answers.

REAL ENGLISH

The simple present is often used for scheduled future events with these verbs: *start, finish, begin, end, arrive, come, leave, open,* and *close.*

Stores at the mall ***open*** *at 11:00.*
The bus ***leaves*** *at 10:30.*

Conversation 1

A: What (1) ______________ (you / do) after class?

B: (2) ______________ (I / go) to New York. In fact, I'm in a hurry. It's 3:30 and (3) ______________ (my train / leave) at five o'clock.

A: (4) ______________ (you / go) alone?

B: No. (5) ______________ (I / go) with a few friends.

A: When (6) ______________ (you / come) back?

B: (7) ______________ (the train / get in) around 9:00 on Sunday night.

A: Do you want me to meet you at the train station?

B: No, that's OK. (8) ______________________ (my friends and I / share) a taxi.

Conversation 2

A: (9) ______________________ (you / work) tomorrow?

B: No, it's my day off.

A: (10) ______________________ (you / go) to the student government meeting tomorrow afternoon? (11) ______________________ (it / begin) at 2:00.

B: I'd love to, but (12) ______________________ (I / play) tennis with a friend in the morning. Then, (13) ______________________ (we / meet) another friend for lunch.

Conversation 3

A: (14) ______________________ (everyone / go) to the new *Star Wars* movie this weekend?

B: Yeah. Do you want to come?

A: Sure. What time (15) ______________________ (it / start)?

B: Around 7:00, I think. (16) ______________________ (we / meet) in front of the theater at 6:30.

A: OK. Great. I'll see you then.

PRACTICE

REAL ENGLISH

With the verbs *go* and *come*, the present progressive is used more often than *be going to*.

*We **are going** to the movies tonight.*
*Cecilia **is coming** with us.*

CD1-20

6 Circle the correct answers to complete the conversation. Then listen and check your answers.

Kesha: Steve, hi! Hey, (1) **are you going / do you go** to the Robotics Club party at Chris and Pat's place next Saturday?

Steve: I don't know yet. (2) **I'm playing / I'll play** basketball that afternoon.

Kesha: (3) **You're having / You'll have** plenty of time. The party (4) **is / will be** at 8:00.

Steve: Chris and Pat's house is really far away. The bus (5) **is taking / will take** a long time.

Kesha: (6) **I'm going to borrow / I'll borrow** my brother's car. I've already asked him, and he said OK. So, (7) **I'm going to drive / I'll drive** you.

Steve: Great. Thanks. . . . Hey, watch out! That guy on the bike (8) **is going to / will** hit you!

Kesha: Wow! Thanks. I didn't see him!

7 **ANALYZE THE GRAMMAR.** Work with a partner. For each item in exercise **6**, decide how the future form is used. Circle the correct letter.

1. a. plan	b. prediction	c. offer
2. a. plan	b. prediction	c. sudden decision
3. a. intention	b. prediction	c. schedule

4. a. prediction b. offer c. schedule

5. a. plan b. prediction c. offer

6. a. intention b. offer c. request

7. a. plan b. prediction c. offer

8. a. prediction b. offer c. sudden decision

8 SPEAK. Work with a partner. Ask and answer questions about your plans. Use the words in the box.

after class	tonight	tomorrow	this weekend

A: *Are you going home after class?*

B: *No, I'm going to the school play. Do you want to come?*

9 LISTEN.

CD1-21

A You will hear some people talking at a Robotics Club party. Choose the correct response to each statement or question you hear.

1. _____ it.
   a. I'll get b. I get
2. Thanks. It's freezing out there. I think _____ snow tonight.
   a. it'll b. it's going to
3. Do you want some? _____ pour you a cup. offer
   a. I'm going to b. I'll
4. That's right. _____ help me set up the exhibits?
   a. Will you b. Are you going to
5. That's great! _____ it at the tech fair next week?
   a. Are you showing b. Will you show
6. OK, _____ quiet about it from now on. I promise.
   a. I'm going to keep b. I'll keep
7. I'm really busy tomorrow, but I can try. What time _____? intention
   a. are you meeting b. will you meet
8. Sorry, but the last bus _____. I don't want to miss it.
   a. will leave at 10:30 b. leaves at 10:30

CD1-22

B Work with a partner. Compare your answers from exercise **A**. Then listen to the complete conversations and check your answers.

10 LISTEN & WRITE.

CD1-23

A Listen and check (✓) the topics that Sasha talks about.

Sasha's immediate future

- [ ] Start high school next year
- [x] Graduate from high school next year
- [ ] Do some research on engineering programs
- [ ] Begin an engineering program
- [ ] Plan to read about robot projects this year
- [ ] Work on robot projects this year

HERB and other robots

- [ ] Be a help in people's homes
- [ ] Drive cars
- [ ] Take care of children
- [ ] Take care of the elderly

Sasha's robot

- [ ] Respond to human questions
- [ ] Respond to human needs
- [ ] Understand what people say
- [ ] Not understand what people say
- [ ] Have an amazing name
- [ ] Be amazing

CD1-23

B Listen again. Then write at least six sentences about what Sasha said. Use *will/won't, be (not) going to,* and the present progressive. Use each subject in the box at least once.

Sasha	Sasha's robot	HERB and other robots

1. Sasha is graduating from high school next year.
2. __________
3. __________
4. __________
5. __________
6. __________

C Work with a partner. Share your sentences from exercise **B**.

11 APPLY.

APPLY. Work in groups. Discuss your goals, plans, and predictions for the future. Discuss the topics below or your own ideas.

- The kind of work you want or hope to do in the future
- The things you are going to do in order to help you achieve your goals
- Some things you will probably do in your future job
- The feelings you will probably have about your work

I want to be a clothing designer someday. I'm going to take classes in design this summer.

EXPLORE

CD1-24

1 READ the article about the clothes of the future. Which item of clothing do you think is most useful?

Clever Clothes

These days we want clothes to make us look good and to protect us from the weather. However, scientists say that things are going to change. Thanks to technological advances, soon we will be wearing clever clothes such as the following.

▲ This jacket sleeve contains control buttons for a cell phone.

- **Cell Phone Jackets:** These jackets will power a cell phone **when we push a button on the sleeve.**[1]
- **Health-Monitoring Shirts:** These shirts will check our heart rate and blood pressure and will collect other important health information **while we go about our daily lives**. They will inform us of any possible problems.
- **GPS[2] Clothes for Kids:** These clothes have built-in GPS tracking systems. They will allow parents to watch their children on the computer and know where they are at all times.
- **Military "First-Aid"[3] Uniforms:** These uniforms will allow soldiers to turn the sleeve or leg of their clothing into casts[4] if they break a bone. This way, soldiers will be able to treat injuries **as soon as they happen**.

Scientists are developing all kinds of intelligent textiles in their labs. However, we won't see many clever clothes in stores **until researchers learn how to make them comfortable to wear. When that happens**, there will probably be a clothing revolution! Experts say that clever clothes will change not only the fashion industry but also the way we think. We will still want clothes to look good, but we will also want them to work for us.

[1] **sleeve:** the part of a piece of clothing that covers the arm or part of the arm
[2] **GPS (Global Positioning System):** a system that uses satellites to show exact locations on Earth
[3] **first aid:** medical treatment given as soon as possible after a person is injured
[4] **cast:** a hard covering used to prevent a broken bone from moving while it heals

2 CHECK. Work with a partner. Discuss the answers to these questions. Then share your answers with the class.

1. According to the article, what do we expect our clothes to do for us now?
2. What are two items of clever clothing that have a health purpose? Describe them.
3. What is one disadvantage of clever clothes?
4. What do we want our clothes to do for us in the future?

3 DISCOVER. Complete the exercises to learn about the grammar in this lesson.

A Read the sentences based on the article from exercise **1** on page 71. Circle the time word or phrase in each sentence.

1. Jackets will power a cell phone when we push a button on the sleeve.
2. Shirts will check our heart rate while we are wearing them.
3. This way, soldiers will be able to treat injuries as soon as they happen.
4. We won't see clever clothes in stores until they are more comfortable to wear.
5. When that happens, there will probably be a clothing revolution.

B Look at the time words you circled in exercise **A** and write them in the chart. Complete the chart with the subject and verb that follows each time word.

Time Word/Phrase	Subject	Verb
1. when	we	push
2.		
3.		
4.		
5.		

C What form are the verbs in the chart in exercise **B**: past, present, or future?

◄ Professor Takao Someya displays wearable electrical circuits. They can monitor blood temperature, blood pressure, and electrical impulses from the heart.

LEARN

3.3 Future Time Clauses

Time Clause First
Before I turn in my essay, I'm going to ask someone to read it.
(Time Clause) (Main Clause)

Time Clause Second
I'll read your essay before you turn it in.
(Main Clause) (Time Clause)

1. A future time clause tells when the future action in the main clause will happen. The time clause can come first or second. **Remember:** Use a comma after a time clause when it comes first in the sentence.	**After we do the dishes,** I'll serve dessert. I will wake up **before the alarm goes off.** **When we arrive,** we'll call your office.
2. A future time clause = a time word/phrase + subject + simple present form of a verb.	Will you call **as soon as you arrive?**
3. **Be careful!** Use a future form only in the main clause. Use a present form in the time clause.	✓ I'm going to take the trash out after the rain **stops**. ✗ I'm going to take the trash out after the rain will stop.
4. The present perfect can also be used in a future time clause. It emphasizes the completion of the action in the time clause.	I won't send the e-mail **until you have read it.** (have read = Present Perfect)

4 Complete the exercises.

A Complete each prediction with the correct form of the verbs in parentheses. For future forms, both *will* or *be going to* are possible. Add a comma when necessary.

1. When scientists ______________ (develop) clever clothes with cell phone controls people ______________ (not wear) ordinary clothes.
2. People ______________ (purchase) clever clothes online before they ______________ (see) them in stores.
3. In the future, clever car seats ______________ (warn) a driver before he or she ______________ (fall) asleep at the wheel.
4. Stores ______________ (sell) GPS clothing before they ______________ (offer) health-monitoring clothing.
5. Before people ______________ (have) robots as friends they ______________ (use) robots to help around the house.
6. When robots ______________ (become) affordable everyone ______________ (want) one.

B Read the predictions in exercise **A**. Tell a partner which you think will or will not come true.

A: *I don't believe number 6 is true. I won't want a robot when they become affordable.*

B: *Really? I think people are going to rush to the stores to get them.*

3.4 Future Time Clauses: *After, As Soon As, Before, Once, Until, When,* and *While*

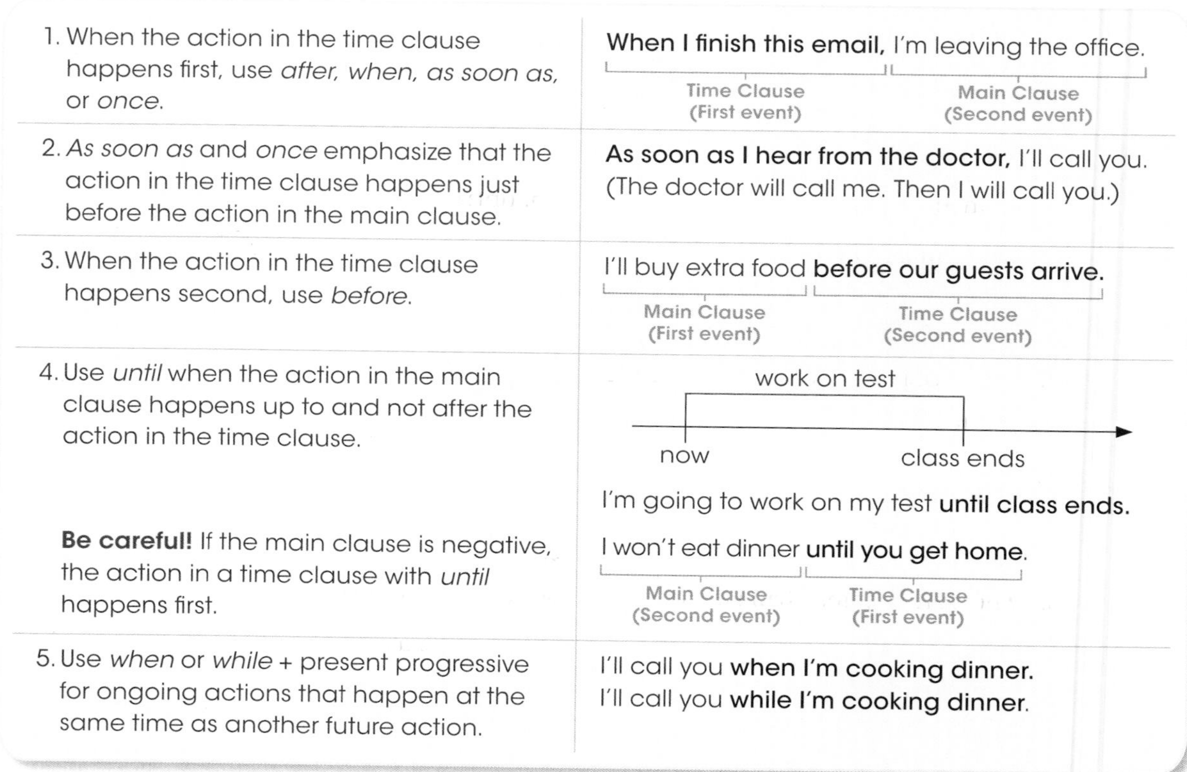

1. When the action in the time clause happens first, use *after, when, as soon as,* or *once.*	**When I finish this email,** I'm leaving the office. Time Clause (First event) / Main Clause (Second event)
2. *As soon as* and *once* emphasize that the action in the time clause happens just before the action in the main clause.	**As soon as I hear from the doctor,** I'll call you. (The doctor will call me. Then I will call you.)
3. When the action in the time clause happens second, use *before.*	I'll buy extra food **before our guests arrive.** Main Clause (First event) / Time Clause (Second event)
4. Use *until* when the action in the main clause happens up to and not after the action in the time clause.	work on test now — class ends I'm going to work on my test **until class ends.**
Be careful! If the main clause is negative, the action in a time clause with *until* happens first.	I won't eat dinner **until you get home.** Main Clause (Second event) / Time Clause (First event)
5. Use *when* or *while* + present progressive for ongoing actions that happen at the same time as another future action.	I'll call you **when I'm cooking dinner.** I'll call you **while I'm cooking dinner.**

5 Read each sentence. Circle the time clause and underline the main clause. Then write *1* above the action that will happen first and write *2* above the action that will happen second.

1. Ron will receive a bionic arm, as soon as it is ready.
2. Ron isn't going to be able to hold anything until he gets his bionic arm.
3. Before he has the new arm, he will learn as much as possible about bionics.
4. As soon as Ron gets the arm, he is going to try to use it.
5. When Ron thinks about moving his fingers, his brain will send messages to his hand.
6. The fingers in his bionic arm will move after they receive the messages from his brain.
7. Until he gets his bionic arm, Ron is going to need help with his everyday tasks.
8. He will be very happy once he is able to do everyday tasks again.

6 Complete the sentences about a home computer system that will change the way we live. Circle the letter of each correct answer.

1. The lights will come on _____ you get home.

   a. until　　　b. as soon as

2. While you _____, the home system is going to cook your dinner.

   a. are watching TV　　　b. are going to watch TV

3. Chairs will change their shape _____ different family members sit in them.

   a. until　　　b. when

4. Music will start playing _____ you enter the house.

   a. once　　　b. until

5. You will be able to turn on the oven _____ you are driving home.

   a. after　　　b. while

6. Your computer will create products for you _____ you give it instructions.

   a. when　　　b. before

7. While you _____ a bath, the home system will prepare your clothes.

   a. will take　　　b. are taking

8. The home system will stay on _____ you leave the house.

   a. until　　　b. as soon as

PRACTICE

7 Combine each pair of sentences into one sentence with a time clause. Use the time words in parentheses. Add a comma when necessary.

1. First: The car manufacturer is going to test its new self-driving car.
   Second: The manufacturer is going to sell the new car.

   (after) The car manufacturer is going to sell its new self-driving car after it tests it.

2. First: A car in front of you will stop.
   Second: Your self-driving car will stop automatically. as soon as a car in front of you stop

   (as soon as) ______________________________

3. First: Your self-driving car will warn you.
   Second: You will make a wrong turn.

   (before) Your self driving car will worm you before you make a wrong turn

4. First: People won't feel relaxed.
   Second: Engineers will make these cars safe.

   (until) Until engineers make these cars safe, people wont feel relaxed

5. First: You will find a parking space.
   Second: Your car will park itself.

   (once) Your car will park itself once you find a parking space

6. First: People will name their destination.
   Second: Their cars will start up and drive there.

   (when) Some people name their cars with start up and drive there

7. First: Engineers are going to build more automated highways.
   Second: People will take more trips by car.

   (as soon as) As seen as engineers build more automated highways People will take more trips by car

8. First: People are not going to buy self-driving cars.
   Second: Self-driving cars are going to become affordable.

   (until) People are not going to buy self-driving cars until become affordable

8 WRITE & SPEAK.

A Complete the sentences with your own ideas about the future. Add a comma when necessary.

1. I'll go out and buy something nice for myself after I get my first paycheck.
2. Before I buy new shoes I will not go outside.
3. I'm going to read a book when I have more time.
4. I won't wait you until morning.
5. Once this course is over I will take rest.
6. I will look for a job as soon as possible.

B Share your sentences with a partner. Ask follow-up questions for more information.

A: *I'll go out and buy something nice for myself after I pass all my exams.*

B: *When will you finish your exams?*

A: *December 15.*

9 EDIT. Read the paragraph. Find and correct five more errors with future time clauses.

When Ari graduates from college next month, he ~~starts~~ is going to start working as a designer for a car company. It's a great job, but he's a little worried about it. When he will go to work on the first day, everything about the job will be new. Also, as soon as he begins, his long summer vacations ~~are over~~ will be over. Ari will miss all that free time, but after he works for a couple of weeks, he loves his new job. He will learn a lot, and he definitely ~~doesn't~~ won't complain when he ~~will~~ get his first paycheck.

10 LISTEN & WRITE.

CD1-25

A Listen to Ari talk about the first day at his new job. What are his worries? Take notes in your notebook. Then share what you heard with a partner.

won't remember everyone's name

A: *He's worried that he won't remember everyone's name.*

B: *Yes, I heard that, too.*

B Work with a partner. Compare your notes from exercise **A**.

C Ari needs encouragement. Write a main clause or a time clause to complete each sentence. Use your own ideas. Add a comma when necessary.

1. Don't worry! You'll learn everyone's name after a few weeks.
2. ______________________ you'll feel great.
3. You'll learn all the information ______________________.
4. While you are learning about the job ______________________.
5. When you get your first paycheck ______________________.

11 APPLY.

CD1-26

A Listen to Janet talk about her plans to study abroad. What are her fears? Take notes in your notebook. Then share your notes with a partner.

B Imagine that you are Janet's friend. Write a paragraph to encourage her to go abroad. Use time clauses in at least five sentences. Use the ideas in exercise **10** to help you.

LESSON 3 Future: Progressive, Perfect, and Perfect Progressive

EXPLORE

CD1-27

1 READ the web article about jobs in the future. Which job would you like to read more about?

Jobs for the Future

In the future, people around the world **will be facing** big challenges. They **will be dealing with** a growing population, the depletion[1] of energy sources, pollution, and climate change. However, there is a positive side. The search for solutions may lead to a variety of new jobs. Here are some examples.

Vertical farmers: By 2045, the global population **will have reached** nine billion. Most people **will be living** in cities. How will there be enough food for everyone? One possible answer is vertical farming—or using tall buildings to grow food in urban areas. Vertical farms will use much less space than traditional farms. Farmers will deliver food locally, so they won't use a lot of fuel for transportation.

Floating city designers: Climate scientists predict that by mid-century, many coastal[2] people **will have lost** their homes due to rising sea levels. One solution may be floating cities. These are offshore[3] communities of homes, offices, and recreational space. They will protect homes from flooding and create more living space. Their main sources of energy will be water and solar power.

Clean car engineers: In the future, more and more people **will be asking** auto manufacturers to make cars that will not pollute the air with harmful gases. Engineers will need to design cars that can run without using fossil fuels such as coal, oil, or gasoline.

In the coming years, these new jobs **are going to be growing** in importance. The future of our planet very much depends on them.

[1] **depletion:** the reduction of something by using too much of it

[2] **coastal:** describes things that are on land near the sea

[3] **offshore:** located in the sea, near the coast

▶ Design for a vertical farm

◀ Design for a floating city

2 CHECK. Match the problems on the left with the possible solutions on the right.

1. overpopulated cities a
2. the loss of some energy sources b, _____
3. the loss of homes _____
4. polluted air _____
5. not enough food _____

a. vertical farms
b. floating cities
c. clean cars

3 DISCOVER. Complete the exercises to learn about the grammar in this lesson.

A Find these sentences in the article in exercise **1**. Write the missing words.

1. In the future, people around the world will be facing big challenges.
2. By 2045, the global population _____ nine billion.
3. Most people _____ in cities.
4. Many coastal people _____ their homes due to rising sea levels.

B Write the words from exercise **A** next to the correct pattern.

1. *will be* + verb + *-ing*: will be facing, _____
2. *will have* + past participle: _____, _____

C Which pattern from exercise **B** expresses each idea below? Write the number on the line.

1. This verb form expresses something that will be in progress at a future time. _____
2. This verb form expresses something that happened before a time in the future. _____

LEARN

3.5 Future Progressive

Statements	
	Subject + *Will (Not)* + *Be* + *Verb* + *-ing*
Affirmative	I **will be sitting** on a beach this time next week.
Negative	We **won't be staying** at a hotel on our vacation.

Questions		Answers
	Will + Subject + *Be* + Verb + *-ing*	
Yes/No	**Will** you **be working** on your vacation?	Yes, I **will**. No, I **won't**.
Wh-	**What will** you **be doing** tomorrow at noon?	I'm not sure.
	Who/What + *Will* + *Be* + Verb + *-ing*	
Who or What as Subject	**Who will be studying** for exams Saturday?	Joe and Miriam.

1. The future progressive is used to describe actions that will be in progress at a certain time in the future.	studying now 9:00 A: Can I call you around 9:00? B: No, I'm sorry. I**'ll be studying** then.
2. Use the future progressive for an action or event that you expect to happen. This action or event may lead to others.	People **will be asking** for cleaner cars, so car companies **will be making** them.
3. The future progressive can also be formed with *be going to*.	I**'m going to be sitting** on a beach this time next week.

4 Complete the conversations with the words in parentheses. Use the future progressive.

1. A: Jim, do you and Pam want to get some lunch around 1:00?

   B: Sorry, we can't. (1) *We're going to be meeting* (we / be going to / meet) with the engineers until 2:00.

   A: Then how about tomorrow at 1:00?

   B: That sounds good. (2) ______________ (we / will / not do) anything then.

2. A: So, when do you think my car will be ready?

   B: Shortly. (3) ______________ (I / be going to / test) it in a few minutes. If all goes well, (4) ______________ (you / will / drive) home soon.

   A: Great. (5) ______________ (I / will / shop) at the store across the street. Can you call my cell when it's ready?

3. A: What (6) ________________________________ (Julio and Ramon / will / do) tomorrow at 4:00?

   B: The same as today. (7) ________________________________ (they / be going to / work) on their design project.

   A: (8) ________________________________ (you / will / help) them?

   B: Yes, (9) ________________________________ (I / be going to / write) a report about the project.

4. A: Excuse me. When (10) ________________________________ (the plane / will / take off)?

   B: In just a few minutes. Please sit down and fasten your seat belt.

   A: I'd like something to drink, please.

   B: (11) ________________________________ (I / will / come) around with drinks once we are in the air.

3.6 Future Perfect and Future Perfect Progressive

Future Perfect	
	Subject + *Will (Not) Have* + Past Participle
Affirmative	By tomorrow, everyone **will have heard** about your job offer.
Negative	I **won't have finished** the work by the time you need it.

Future Perfect Progressive	
	Subject + *Will (Not) Have Been* + Verb + *-ing*
Affirmative	When I finally turn the essay in, I **will have been working** on it for a month.
Negative	They **won't have been working** on the project long when the new boss arrives.

1. The future perfect is used for
   a. an action or series of actions that will be complete before a specific time in the future
   b. a situation that continues for a period of time until and possibly after a particular time in the future

a. 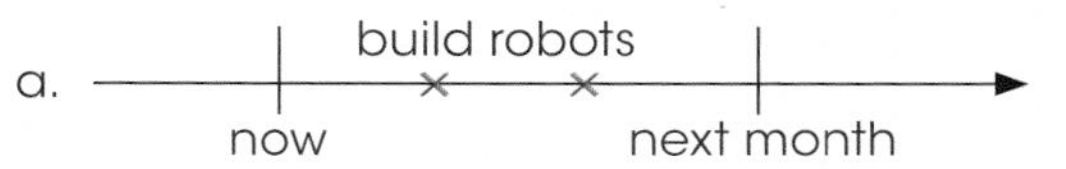

We **will have built** the robots by next month.

b. 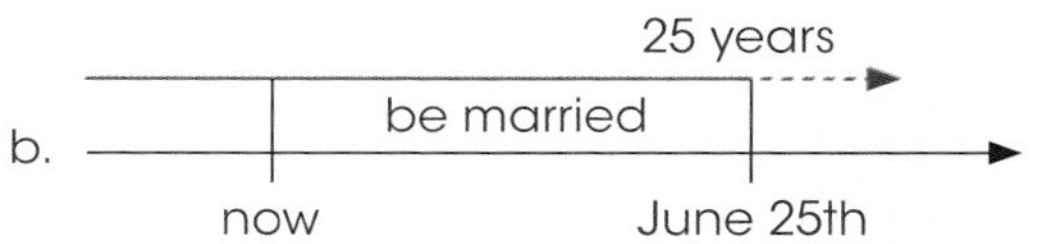

On June 25th, we **will have been married** for 25 years.

2. The future perfect progressive is used for actions or situations that will be in progress until a particular time in the future. They may continue after the future time.

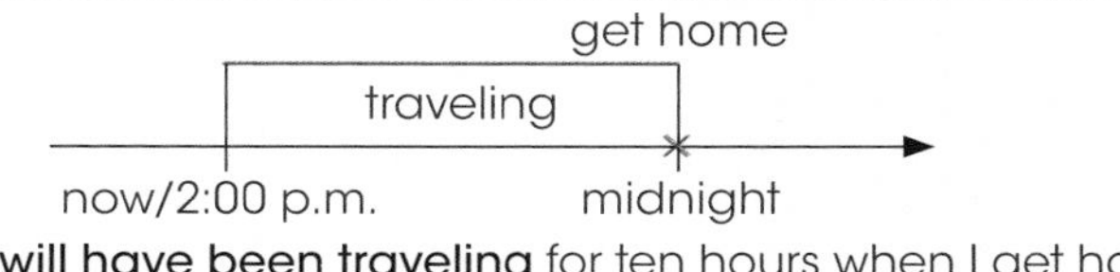

I **will have been traveling** for ten hours when I get home.

3. *By* and *by the time* + clause are often used with the future perfect and the future perfect progressive.

By 2018, my daughter **will have finished** college.
By the time we get home, we **will have been driving** for two days.

5 Complete the sentences with the future perfect.

1. Rosa wrote one report yesterday. She is writing another report today and will write another one tomorrow. By the end of the week, she ___will have written___ three reports.

2. Tom built his first home in 2004 and then two more over the next ten years. He plans to build one more next year. By the end of next year, he ______________________ four homes.

3. Dr. Magano saw six patients in the morning and seven this afternoon. She is going to see two more patients in the evening. By the end of the day, she ______________________ 15 patients.

4. The photographer took over 500 pictures this morning. She is still at work. She ______________________ between 800 and 1000 photos by the end of the workday.

5. The building engineer has made seven designs and wants to make several more before next week's meeting. He ______________________ at least ten designs by the time of the meeting.

6. The guitarist is performing on Friday and Saturday evenings. He will perform again on Sunday afternoon. He ______________________ three times by Sunday night.

6 Complete the sentences with the future perfect progressive.

1. Yu-Ming started translating books at age 30. He is retiring next year at age 65. By the time he retires, he ___will have been translating___ books for over 30 years.

2. The flight attendants started serving food at 10:00 and will continue serving until shortly before landing at 12:30. Before the plane lands, the flight attendants ______________________ food for just over two hours.

3. Santana started playing baseball three years ago. At the end of the season, he ______________________ baseball for over three years.

4. Dale began to work at the restaurant six months ago. He plans to stay in the job for another six months. By the time he leaves, Dale ______________________ at the restaurant for a year.

5. Flora started to watch a movie at 6:00. It's a three-hour movie, and she wants to watch the whole thing. At 8:00, Flora ______________________ the movie for two hours.

6. The bike race began on May 15. Hari's team will ride for two weeks. By May 22, the team ______________________ for one week.

PRACTICE

7 WRITE & SPEAK.

A Kayden Lee is a worker on Floating City Island. Today is Wednesday. Look at his schedule for Thursday and Friday. Then complete the paragraph about his schedule for Thursday. Use the words from his schedule and the future progressive, the future perfect, or the future perfect progressive. Add *not* when necessary.

Early Thursday morning, Kayden (1) ___will be attending___ a staff meeting. At 8:30, he (2) ______________ the solar panels. By 10:30, (3) he ______________ the trash, but he (4) ______________ the repairs yet. When he finally finishes the repairs, he (5) ______________ for eight and a half hours already. At 4:30, he (6) ______________ the ferry boat to the mainland. By 6:00, he (7) ______________ supplies for the next workday. At 7:00, he (8) ______________ to Floating City Island.

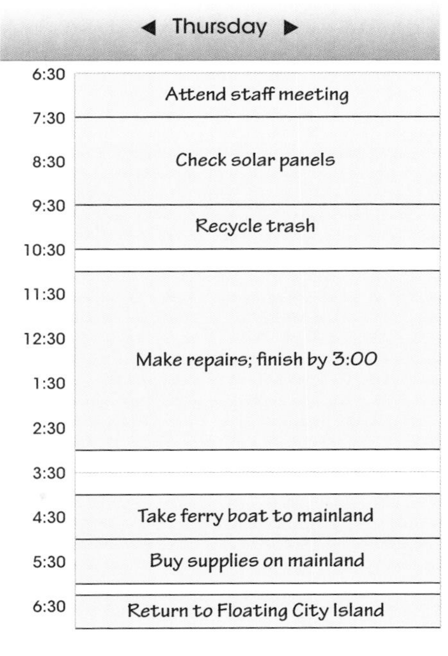

Thursday
6:30
Attend staff meeting
7:30
8:30
Check solar panels
9:30
Recycle trash
10:30
11:30
12:30
Make repairs; finish by 3:00
1:30
2:30
3:30
4:30
Take ferry boat to mainland
5:30
Buy supplies on mainland
6:30
Return to Floating City Island

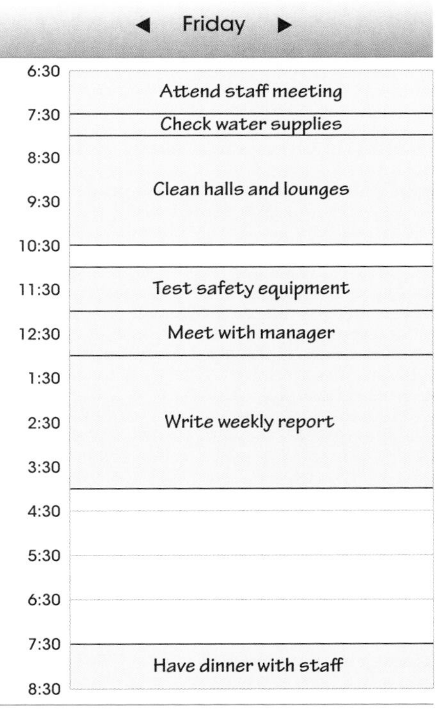

Friday
6:30
Attend staff meeting
7:30
Check water supplies
8:30
Clean halls and lounges
9:30
10:30
11:30
Test safety equipment
12:30
Meet with manager
1:30
2:30
Write weekly report
3:30
4:30
5:30
6:30
7:30
Have dinner with staff
8:30

B Write a paragraph about Kayden's schedule for Friday. Use the future progressive, future perfect, and future perfect progressive at least once each. Use the paragraph in exercise **A** as a model.

C Work with a partner. Compare your paragraphs from exercise **B**.

8 WRITE & SPEAK.

> **REAL ENGLISH**
>
> The future progressive is often used to ask about someone's plans or make a request in a more polite way.
>
> *Will you **be getting** the tickets for the concert?*

A Change the questions to polite requests. Use the future progressive.

1. **Boss:** Who is going to take notes at the meeting?

   Who will be taking notes at the meeting?

2. **Auto Mechanic:** Are you picking up your car today?

   ____

3. **Student:** Are you going to return the homework next week?

   ____

4. **Teacher:** When are you going to hand in your project?

   ____

5. **Passenger:** Are you going to stop at the next bus stop?

   ____

B Work with a partner. Read each polite request in exercise **A**. With your partner, decide who the speaker is talking to. Then write another polite request for each situation. Role-play one short conversation for the class.

Boss ⟶ Employee

A: *How many days will you be taking off?*   B: *Just three.*

9 WRITE & LISTEN.

A By the year 2050, how will the workplace be different? Use the prompts to write affirmative or negative statements that express your own ideas. Use the future progressive, future perfect, or the future perfect progressive.

1. large numbers of people / work / in offices / in the years to come

   Large numbers of people won't be working in offices in the years to come.

2. fewer people / use / company office space

   ____

3. over the next few decades / more workers / have / video conferences

____

4. desktop computers and phones / disappear / from offices / by the middle of the century

____

5. almost everyone / communicate / with mobile phones and wireless computers / for years

____

6. by 2050 / many companies / rethink / office space

____

7. some offices / replace / office walls with electronic walls / by 2050

____

8. people / not share / information in the same ways they do now

____

CD1-28

B Listen to an office designer talk about the workplace of the future. Put a check (✓) before the statements you wrote in exercise **A** that the designer agrees with.

10 APPLY.

A In your notebook, write three responses to each question with the words and phrases in the boxes and your own ideas. Use each time phrase once. You can include ideas about your work, your studies, and your personal goals.

1. What do you think you are going to be doing . . . ?

at 8 o'clock tomorrow night	this time next year	ten years from now

This time next year, I'm going to be looking for a job.

2. What do you hope you will have done . . . ?

by the end of this course	five years from now	by retirement

By the end of this course, I hope I will have learned many useful new words.

3. What activity will you have been doing for a long time . . . ?

when you graduate	by the time you're 40	when you are 60

When I graduate, I will have been studying Chinese for almost six years.

B Work in a group. Discuss your answers to the questions in exercise **A**.

A: *What do you think you are going to be doing this time next year?*

B: *I'm going to be looking for a job, I think.*

Charts 3.1–3.4

1 Circle the correct words to complete the advertisement.

The future is now.

Get your degree in the comfort of your own home!

Your college application is ready, and you (1) **send / are going to send** it to the admissions office this afternoon. Then, you (2) **are waiting / are going to wait** for a reply. It (3) **will take / will be taking** time. (4) **After / While** you are waiting, you (5) **worry / will be worrying**. You'll think to yourself, "(6) **Will I be getting in / Will I get in**, or (7) **are they rejecting / are they going to reject** me?" You (8) **aren't receiving / won't receive** the answer for a few months.

That's not the only worry. When you (9) **go / will go** away to college, your friends and family (10) **will be / will have been** far away. You (11) **miss / are going to miss** them every day.

There's a way to avoid all this: Get your degree online! Yes, that's right. Online learning isn't something for the *future*. (12) **It happens / It's happening** right *now*. Contact us now. Classes (13) **begin / will begin** next Monday and every Monday after that. Don't wait. You (14) **aren't / won't be** sorry.

Charts 3.1–3.6

2 SPEAK, WRITE & LISTEN.

A Look at the information in the chart about three people's career paths. What are their plans and goals? Discuss them with a partner.

Hiro and Jamal are both going to do internships.

Time Period	Alex	Jamal	Hiro
By end of May	Send application	Send application	Start application
June to December	Take online classes in design and economics	Do internship	Do internship
January	Find a job	Start grad school	Start grad school
In 2 years	Work as urban designer	Get master's degree	Start job search
In 10 years	Start own company	Run urban planning company	Work as urban engineer
In 15 years	Sell company for a profit	Work on many helpful projects	Start own company

B In your notebook, write sentences about each person's career plans. Use the words below and the information from the chart in exercise **A**. Use the future progressive, the future perfect, and the future perfect progressive. Add *not* when necessary. More than one form is sometimes correct.

1. Hiro / send in his application / by the end of May

   Hiro won't have sent in his application by the end of May.

2. Jamal / do an internship / in August
3. Alex / finish his online classes / by January
4. Hiro / start a job search / later this year
5. Alex / work as an urban designer / in two years
6. Hiro / start his own company / in ten years

CD1-29

C Look at the chart in exercise **A** again. Then listen to the conversation. Circle the name of the person Sarah is talking to.

a. Alex   b. Jamal   c. Hiro

D In your notebook, write six sentences about the information from the conversation in exercise **C**. Use the phrases from the box and the future forms from this unit. Add *not* when necessary.

get a part-time job	make contacts	work on application
get some experience	take a year off	write full time

He will have made some good contacts by November.

Charts 3.1–3.6

3 EDIT. Read the blog. Find and correct eight more errors with future forms.

It's going to work

I finally have a plan for the future. ~~It is going to have worked~~ like this. Next week, I'm starting my application for graduate school. I'm studying urban planning. At the end of the month, I will sending in the application. While I'm going to wait for a response, I'm going to do an internship. That will be between June and December. Hopefully, I'll start classes in January. By the time I will graduate in two years, I'll take a variety of courses. They will prepare me for the job market, and hopefully in ten years I'll be working as an urban engineer for several years. In fifteen years, I will have been starting my own company. At least, that's the plan right now.

Charts 3.1–3.6

4 SPEAK. Work with a partner. Discuss a plan you have for the future. It can be a plan about your studies, your job, or your family life.

Next year, my husband and I are going to buy a house.

Connect the Grammar to Writing

1 READ & NOTICE THE GRAMMAR.

A What do you want cars to do in the future? Tell a partner your ideas. Then read the text.

The Car of the *Future*

For many people in the world, having a car is a basic necessity, but it is a dangerous one. The World Health Organization estimates that 1.2 million people die each year in traffic accidents. Right now, the technology for self-driving cars exists, but not many people are taking it seriously. I hope that they will very soon. I strongly believe that self-driving cars are going to help us greatly in the future for two reasons: safety and productivity.

I believe that the cars of the future will be much safer because humans won't be driving them. Self-driving cars will take bad drivers, such as irresponsible teenagers and drunk drivers, off the road. They will also eliminate human error such as falling asleep at the wheel. In a generation or two, I think traffic fatalities[1] will have become a thing of the past.

Self-driving cars will also make the time we spend on the road more productive. For example, while we're sitting in traffic, we can read or study. This will help us to use our time more effectively. We will be more relaxed and happier, too.

Some people think that self-driving cars will never become popular, but I disagree. Once people realize how many lives can be saved by this technology, and how much more free time they will have, they will no longer want to drive themselves. When self-driving cars become available, everyone is going to want one.

[1] **fatality:** a death resulting from an accident, disease, natural disaster, or war

GRAMMAR FOCUS

In the text, the writer uses future forms and time clauses to make predictions and talk about future actions or events.

The writer uses *be going to* and *will* to make predictions.

I strongly believe that self-driving cars ***are going to help*** *us . . . ; . . . cars of the future* ***will be*** *much safer . . .*

The writer uses future time clauses to talk about when future actions or events will happen.

When self-driving cars become available, *everyone is going to want one.*

The writer uses the future perfect to talk about future actions or events that will be completed before a specific time in the future.

In a generation or two, . . . traffic fatalities ***will have become*** *. . . .*

B Read the text in exercise **A** again. Find one more example of each of the following: *will, be going to,* and a future time clause. Then work with a partner and compare your answers.

C Complete the chart with the writer's ideas from the text in exercise **A**. Then work with a partner and compare your answers.

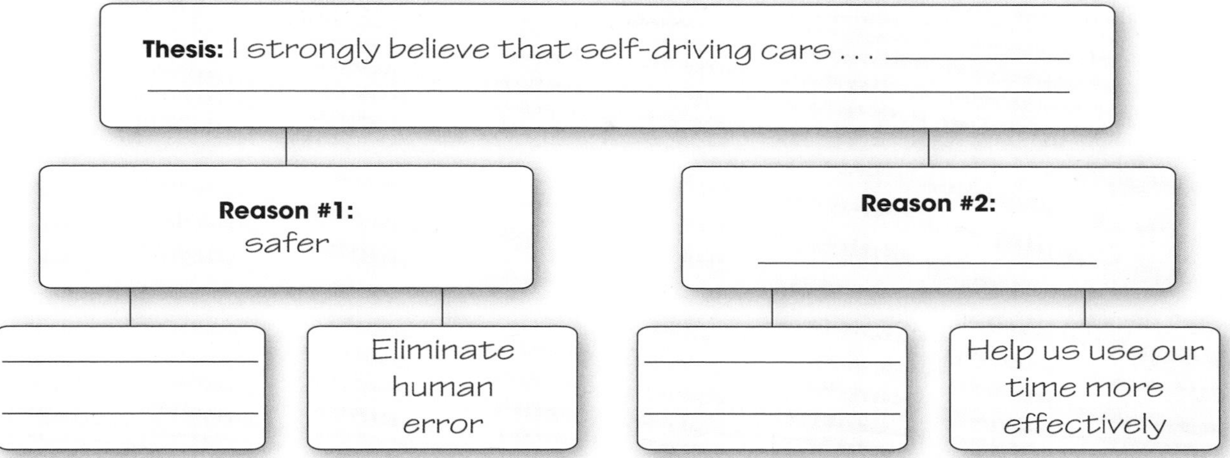

2 BEFORE YOU WRITE.

A Choose a current form of technology, such as cell phones. What are your predictions about this topic? Brainstorm a list of your ideas. Then share your ideas with a partner.

B In your notebook, make a chart like the one in exercise **1C**. Write a thesis statement and at least two reasons with examples to support it.

WRITING FOCUS Using *Believe, Think,* and *Hope*

Notice how *believe, think,* and *hope* are used in the text in exercise **1A**.

Use *believe* and *think* to express opinions.

*I **strongly believe** that self-driving cars are going to help us greatly . . .*

*Some people **think** that self-driving cars will never become popular . . .*

Use *hope* to express a wish or desire.

*I **hope** that they will (take them seriously) very soon.*

3 WRITE your predictions and opinion about your topic. Write two or three paragraphs. Use your chart from exercise **2B** and the text in exercise **1A** to help you.

4 SELF ASSESS. Read your text again and underline the future forms. Then use the checklist to assess your work.

- ☐ I used the future with *will* and *be going to* correctly. [3.1]
- ☐ I used the simple present in future time clauses. [3.3]
- ☐ I used the future perfect correctly. [3.6]
- ☐ I used *believe, think,* and *hope* to express opinions or wishes. [WRITING FOCUS]

UNIT 4 Exploration

Negative *Yes/No* Questions; Statement and Tag Questions

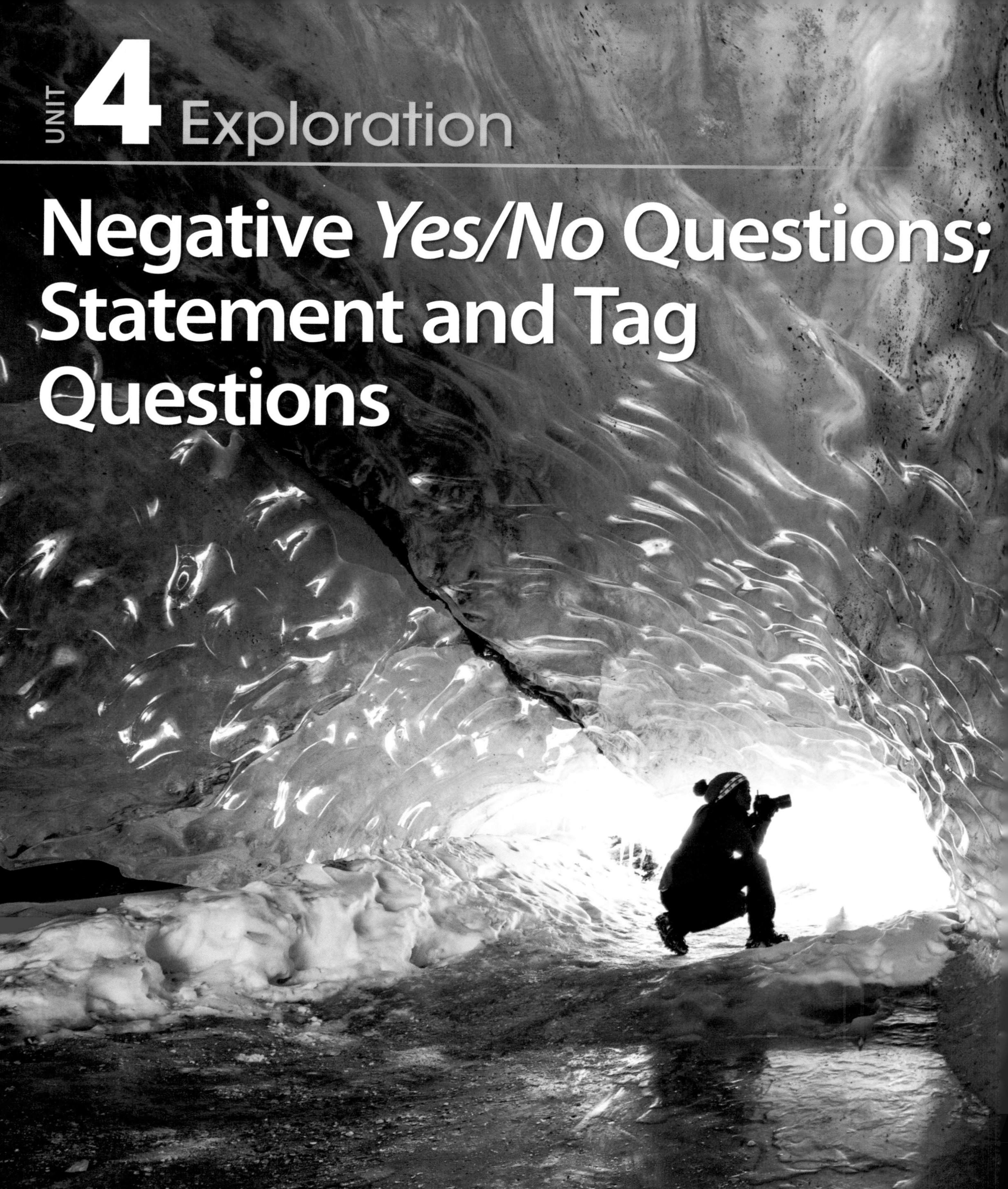

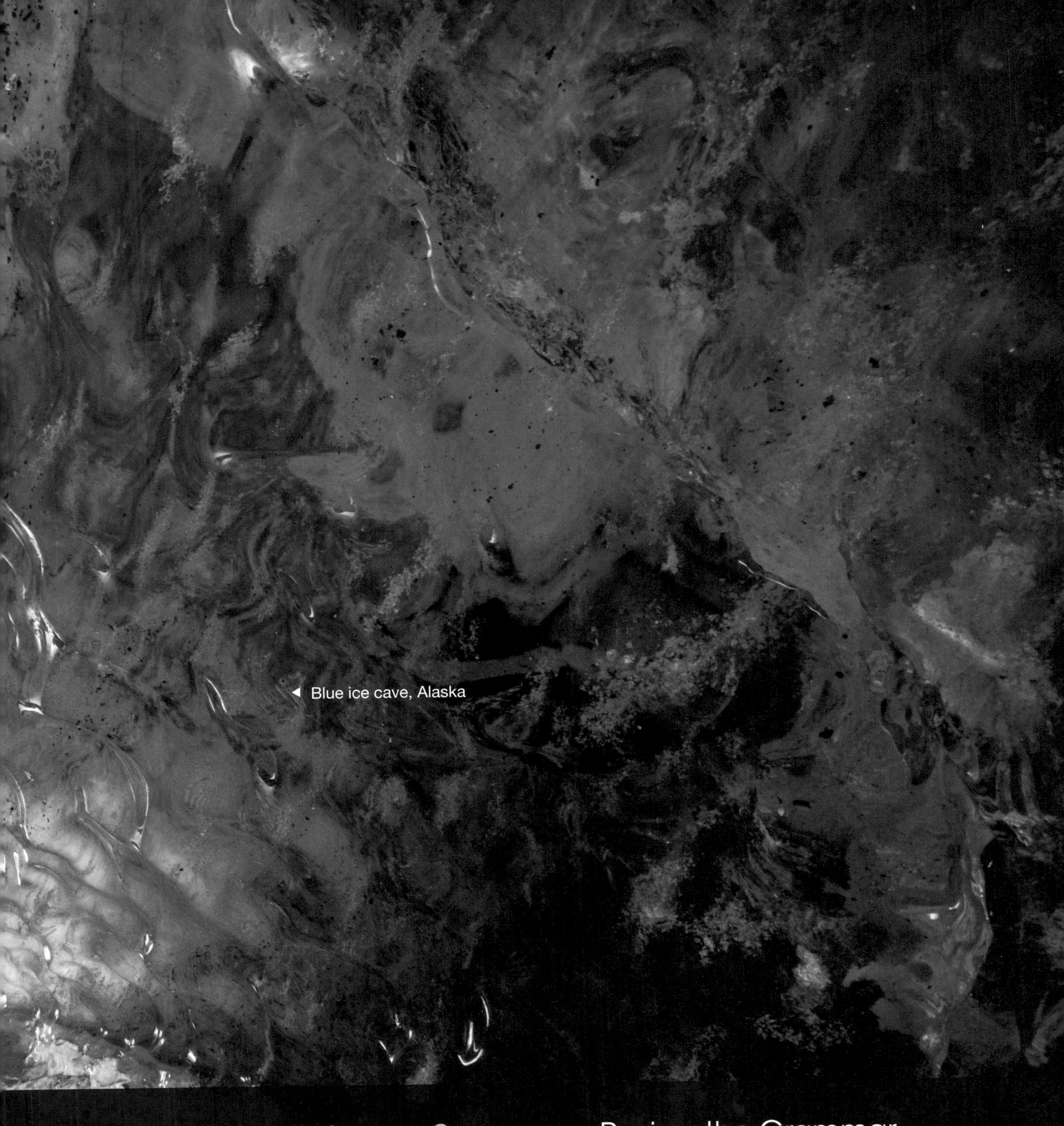

◀ Blue ice cave, Alaska

EXPLORE

1 READ the blog about how scientists are preparing for future travel to Mars. What are some of the challenges that the astronauts will face?

MARS ON EARTH

Marta Mirsky 8 hours ago

It will be many years before humans can safely go to Mars, but space scientists have already begun to prepare. They've been trying to figure out what astronauts will need for extended stays on the red planet. One research project—the Mars Desert Research Station—is right here on Earth. The station is located in a remote[1] desert area in Utah in the United States, and the crew[2] members experience challenges similar to those they would face on Mars. The crew works closely with a space psychologist.[3] In fact, psychology, more than aerospace engineering, may be the key to sending human crews to Mars.

spacecrazy115 6 hours ago

So life on Mars can drive you crazy?

Reply

Sure. Think of the tight living space, the lack of privacy, and the stress of working together every day. The crew has to be able to handle all that.

martianhead 4 hours ago

Isn't another challenge the special suits they have to wear?

Reply

Yes, those suits have many parts and they take hours to put on! But they're essential.[4] They protect the astronauts from radiation when they go out to explore.

redplanetlover 1 hour ago

Don't the astronauts start to feel claustrophobic in the research station? I wouldn't want to work in such a small, crowded space.

Reply

Yes, after a while, it becomes very uncomfortable. In addition, the work is hard, and the crew is under a lot of pressure to get everything done.

martianhead 20 minutes ago

I guess that's why they need a psychologist?

Reply

That's part of the reason. The research project presents many challenges, and the astronauts need someone to help them to deal with everything.

[1] **remote:** far away from where most people live

[2] **crew:** the people who work on and operate a ship or spacecraft

[3] **psychologist:** someone who studies how the mind works

[4] **essential:** extremely important or absolutely necessary

2 CHECK. Answer the questions. Write complete sentences.

1. Where is the Mars Desert Research Station? ______________________________

____

2. What kind of doctor helps the crew of astronauts? ______________________________

____

3. What do the astronauts have to do before they go out to explore? ______________________________

____

4. What are some of the challenges that astronauts have to deal with? ______________________________

____

3 DISCOVER. Complete the exercises to learn about the grammar in this lesson.

A Find these sentences from the blog in exercise **1**. Write the missing punctuation—a question mark (?) or a period (.).

1. So life on Mars can drive you crazy
2. Isn't another challenge the special suits they have to wear
3. Don't the astronauts start to feel claustrophobic in the research station
4. I guess that's why they need a psychologist

B Look at the sentences in exercise **A** and answer the questions. Write the number of each sentence next to the correct statement.

1. These questions have the same word order as statements. _____, _____
2. These questions begin with negative contractions (*-n't*) _____, _____

▲ Surface of the planet Mars

LEARN

4.1 Negative *Yes/No* Questions

Negative *Yes/No* Questions	Answers
Aren't you going to class?	Yes, I'll be there. / No, I'm busy today.
Didn't she know the answer?	Yes, of course she did. / No. She had no idea.
Haven't you seen the news?	Yes, I have. / No, I haven't. What happened?
Isn't she a teacher?	Yes, she is. / No, she isn't.

1. Contract *not* to *n't* and add it to the end of the auxiliary verb* or the main verb *be* in a negative *Yes/No* question.	Is**n't** he a student? Are**n't** you **going** to class? Did**n't** she **know** the answer?
2. A negative *Yes/No* question is often used instead of an affirmative one when the speaker: a. expects or wants the answer to be *yes* b. wants to check that information is correct c. is annoyed d. is surprised	 a. **Wasn't** that a terrible movie? b. **Isn't** Lima the capital of Peru? c. **Aren't** you going to say hello? d. **Haven't** you finished the book yet?
3. **Be careful!** The answers to negative and affirmative *Yes/No* questions are the same.	A: Isn't your house nearby? B: Yes, it is. / No, it isn't. A: Is your house nearby? B: Yes, it is. / No, it isn't.

* An auxiliary verb is used with a main verb. *Be, do, have, will,* and modals are auxiliary verbs. Auxiliary verbs are also called *helping verbs.*

4 Complete the exercises.

A Read the statements about space travel and underline the verbs. Then tell a partner which statements you believe are true and false.

Common Beliefs about Space Travel

1. The first person in space was American.
2. Space travel began in the 1960s.
3. The first astronaut stepped on the moon in 1969.
4. There have been trips to Mars already.
5. Space travel is expensive.
6. All objects are weightless in space.
7. Life in a space station seems exciting.
8. Everyone wants to travel to the moon.

▲ The NASA/ESA Hubble Space Telescope

B Write a negative question for each statement in exercise **A**.

1. Wasn't the first person in space American?
2. _____
3. _____
4. _____
5. _____
6. _____
7. _____
8. _____

CD1-31

C Choose the correct answer to the questions in exercise **B**. Then listen and check your answers.

1. a. Yes, it was not an American. (b.) No, it was a Russian named Yuri Gagarin.
2. a. Yes, it began in the 1950s. b. No, it actually began in the 1950s.
3. a. Yes, it was on July 21, 1969. b. No, it was on July 21, 1969.
4. a. Yes, people haven't gone there yet. b. No, nobody has gone there yet.
5. a. Yes, it's extremely expensive. b. No, it's extremely expensive.
6. a. Yes, they float around in the air. b. No, they float around in the air.
7. a. Yes, it seems amazing. b. No, it seems really interesting.
8. a. Yes, I don't think so. b. No, I don't think so.

4.2 Statement Questions

1. A statement question is a *yes/no* question with statement word order. Answers to statement questions are the same as to regular *yes/no* questions.	A: **That's the teacher?** B: Yeah. A: Is that the teacher? B: Yeah.
2. Statement questions are used: a. to check information b. to repeat and confirm information c. to show surprise or express annoyance	 a. **Your address is 22 Main Street?** b. **The lecture isn't on Friday?** c. **We're having fish again?**
3. Statement questions are more common in informal conversations. When using a statement question, the speaker expects the listener to agree with the statement.	A: **You went to the concert last night?** B: **Yes!** It was terrific! A: **You don't like the soup?** B: **No,** not really.
4. The speaker's voice usually rises at the end of a statement question.	**The meeting is going to take five hours?**

5 LISTEN & SPEAK.

CD1-32

A Listen to the sentences. Add a question mark (?) if the sentence is a statement question and a period (.) if the sentence is a statement. There are six statement questions.

1. There's a Mars research station on Earth?
2. The training at the station isn't for everyone
3. There are people who specialize in space psychology
4. Astronauts haven't gone to Mars yet
5. It will take years for humans to travel to Mars
6. It takes longer to travel to Mars than to the moon
7. We aren't going to read about other planets
8. We have to learn all this information about Mars

CD1-33

B Match the six statement questions in exercise **A** with the correct responses below. Write the numbers on the lines. Then listen and check your answers.

_____ a. Yes, the moon is much closer to Earth.

_____ b. Yes, but there aren't many.

__1__ c. Yes. It's located in a desert.

_____ d. Yes, but I'm sure you'll find it interesting.

_____ e. No, not this semester.

_____ f. No. No humans have gone there.

▼ Artist's concept of NASA Mars Science Laboratory Curiosity rover, a mobile robot for investigating Mars

PRACTICE

6 Complete the exercises.

A Complete the conversation about a Pacific Ocean expedition. Write statement questions or negative questions with the words in parentheses.

Reporter: You traveled all that distance in a canoe. (1) You weren't (you / not be) afraid? Statement Question

Explorer: Not really. I had done a lot of training before the journey.

Reporter: Yes, I think I read about that. (2) ______________ (you / train) for months to get ready? Negative Question

Explorer: Yes, I did. I had to be in excellent physical condition.

Reporter: Right. It would not be possible otherwise. But still . . .
(3) ______________ (it / be) hard? Negative Question

Explorer: Yes. It sure was. This kind of trip is not for everybody. Some people get lonely.

Reporter: What about for you? (4) ______________ (it / not get) lonely? Statement Question

Explorer: No, not for me. It was quiet, and I had a lot of time to think.

Reporter: How about the weather? Were there storms?

Explorer: Sometimes, but I was ready for them.

Reporter: (5) ______________ (you / be) ever afraid? Negative Question

Explorer: Not really. I had some good maps so I knew what I was doing. I can't wait to go out again.

Reporter: (6) ______________ (you / plan) another trip already? Statement Question

Explorer: Yes, I am. In fact, I'm training for it now.

Reporter: You're kidding. (7) ______________ (you / be) tired of the ocean by now? Negative Question

Explorer: No, I'm not. I love it.

CD1-34 **B** Listen and check your answers.

7 Complete the exercises.

A Read the statements about early Polynesian explorers. Add a question mark to make a statement question. Then write a negative question for each statement question.

1. The Polynesians were skilled explorers?
   Weren't the Polynesians skilled explorers?
2. It took only a short time to travel from Tahiti to Hawaii
   ____
   ____

3. The Polynesians discovered Hawaii and many other islands

____

____

4. The Polynesians traded with islanders thousands of miles away

____

____

5. Today's researchers are trying to find out how far the Polynesians traveled

____

____

B Work with a partner. Take turns reading each pair of questions.

C Look at the map and read the paragraph about Polynesian explorers. Which ocean did they sail on?

Polynesian Explorers

More than a thousand years ago, the Polynesians were skilled explorers of the Pacific Ocean. They sailed all over the South Pacific, including an extremely long journey from Tahiti to Hawaii. In addition to Hawaii, the Polynesians discovered many other islands, and they began trading goods[1] with the people on those islands, too. Why were the Polynesians so successful? Researchers today are trying to find out.

[1] **goods:** items that can be bought or sold

▼ Modern-day scientists follow an ancient route of Polynesian explorers.

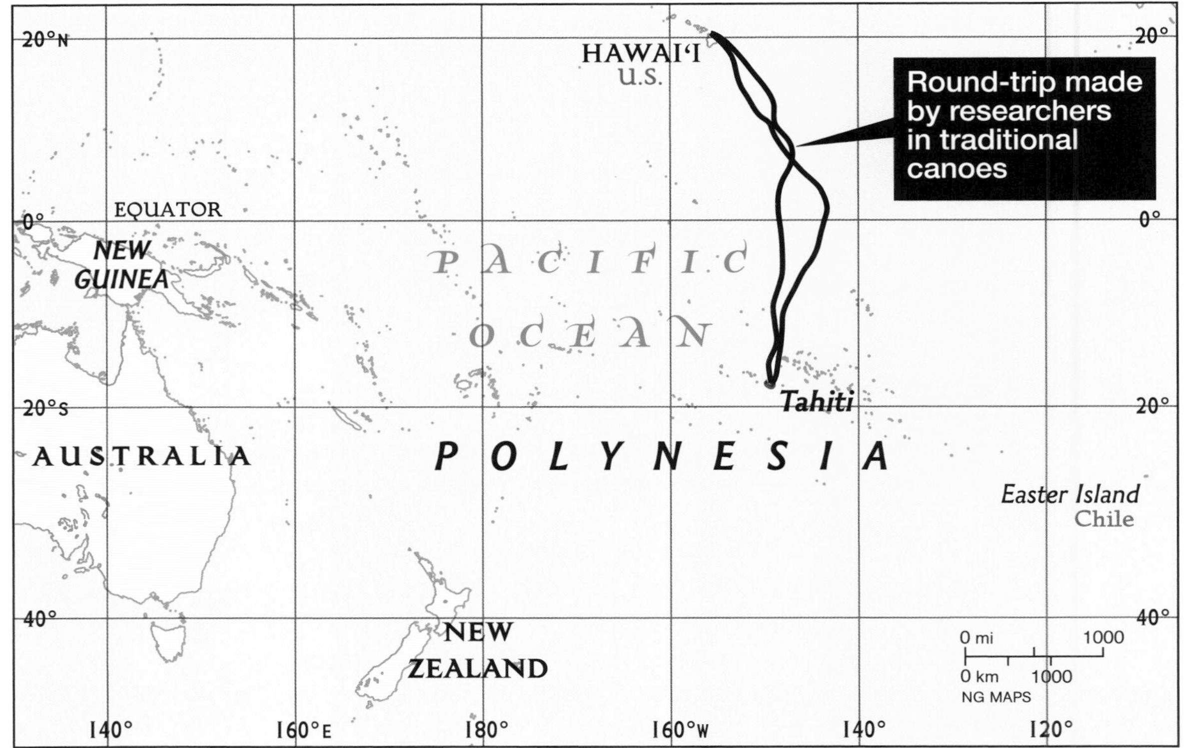

▲ A Polynesian canoe

D In your notebook, write the answer to each question in exercise **A** according to the information from the text in exercise **C**.

1. Yes, they were. They sailed all over the South Pacific.

8 LISTEN.

CD1-35

A Listen to the questions that a student asks his professor about the early Polynesians. Then read the responses. Which response do you think the professor will give? Choose the correct answer.

1. a. No, that's what the research shows.
   (b.) Yes, that's what the research shows.
2. a. No, they didn't. They had smaller boats called canoes.
   b. Yes, they did. They traveled in smaller boats called canoes.
3. a. No. They needed the wind.
   b. Yes. They waited for strong winds before they began their journeys.
4. a. Yes. They used the stars to find their way.
   b. No. They followed the direction of the stars.
5. a. No. They traveled in canoes.
   b. Yes. They didn't use sailboats.
6. a. No. They have proof.
   b. Yes. The proof is ancient Polynesian tools in Hawaii.
7. a. No. Hawaii is thousands of miles from Tahiti.
   b. Yes. Hawaii is thousands of miles from Tahiti.
8. a. No. They never had trouble.
   b. Yes. They never got lost.

CD1-36

B Listen to the full conversation and check your answers in exercise **A**.

▲ 1. Stonehenge

▲ 2. the Statue of Liberty

▲ 3. the Pyramid of the Sun

9 APPLY.

A Work with a partner. Look at the photos of famous places and match them with their locations. Ask and answer negative questions and statement questions about each place.

____ 1. Stonehenge	a. New York City
____ 2. The Statue of Liberty	b. Great Britain
____ 3. The Pyramid of the Sun	c. Mexico

A: *Isn't that Stonehenge?*

B: *Yeah, it's that place in Great Britain with the mysterious stones.*

B Match the famous places in exercise **A** with the descriptions below. Then ask and answer negative and statement questions about each place.

a. It has around 250 steps. 3

b. It's on an island. ____

c. It was built by the Aztecs. ____

d. It is over 500 years old. ____

e. It's over 5000 years old. ____

f. There are stones in a circle there. ____

A: *Isn't Stonehenge on an island?*

B: *Well, Stonehenge is in Great Britain, and that is an island. But what about the Statue of Liberty?*

C Work in a group. Tell your group the name of a famous place you have visited. The students in your group will then ask you negative and statement questions about the place. Can you answer all of the questions?

A: *I have been to St. Petersburg, Russia.*

B: *Interesting. Isn't there a famous museum there?*

A: *Yes. It's called the Hermitage.*

C: *You've been to St. Peterbsurg? I've always wanted to go there!*

EXPLORE

CD1-37

1 READ the information on the website about Børge Ousland. Then read the conversation between two friends below. Why do they enjoy videos about Ousland?

Børge Ousland, NORWEGIAN EXPLORER

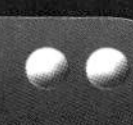

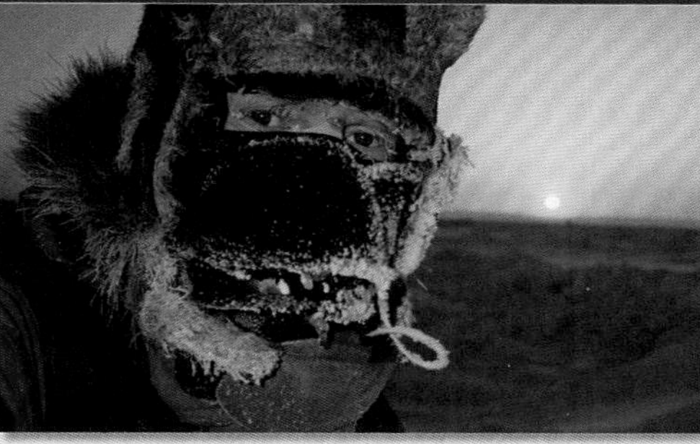

Børge Ousland's solo crossing of the North Pole was a great challenge. Pulling a heavy sledge of food and fuel, he covered 1240 miles (1996 kilometers) by walking, skiing, and even swimming. Alone in the icy Arctic for 82 days, Ousland faced many problems—a broken sledge, thin ice, bad snowstorms, polar bears—but he never gave up.

Birthplace: Oslo, Norway

First Occupation: Deep-sea diver

First Expedition: Ski trip across Greenland

Favorite Expedition: First solo trip to the North Pole

Other Passions: Fishing, sailing, and everything that relates to nature

Favorite Use of Free Time: Being with friends and family

Concerns: Global warming and the loss of Arctic ice

Jeff: Hey, what are you doing?

Flavio: Just watching this guy Børge Ousland. There are some great videos of him online. You've seen some of them, **haven't you?**

Jeff: Yeah. The guy is unbelievable! Did you see the one where he's swimming in the Arctic Ocean?

Flavio: No, I missed that one. It didn't show this sledge, **did it?**

Jeff: I think there was a quick shot of it. He was pulling 365 pounds of stuff everywhere . . . with all that snow blowing around. He's really incredible, **isn't he?**

Flavio: Uh-huh. And the sledge broke at one point, too.

Jeff: You're kidding! What did he do?

Flavio: Well, he tried to repair it, but he couldn't, so he called for a new one. And he kept going.

Jeff: He's not afraid of anything, **is he?**

Flavio: No, definitely not. Do you remember that scene with the polar bears?

Jeff: Yeah, that was great, **wasn't it?** That mother with her cubs looked so angry.

▶ Winter solstice during an Arctic expedition a few miles from the North Pole

2 CHECK. Read the statements. Circle **T** for *true* or **F** for *false*.

1. Børge Ousland is a Canadian explorer. **T** **F**
2. You can watch videos of Ousland's trip online. **T** **F**
3. Ousland fixed his sledge when it broke. **T** **F**
4. Ousland walked the whole way across the Arctic. **T** **F**
5. Ousland spends his free time with friends and family. **T** **F**

3 DISCOVER. Complete the exercises to learn about the grammar in this lesson.

A Underline the verbs in the sentences from the conversation in exercise **1** on page 101. Then complete each sentence with the missing words.

1. You've seen some of them, haven't you?
2. It didn't show this sledge, ________________?
3. He's really incredible, ________________?
4. Yeah, that was great, ________________?

B Look at the sentences in exercise **A**. Notice the patterns with the main verb and auxiliary verb forms. Then check (✓) the two correct rules.

_____ 1. The main verb and auxiliary forms are either both affirmative or both negative.

_____ 2. If the main verb form is affirmative, the auxiliary form is negative.

_____ 3. If the main verb form is negative, the auxiliary form is affirmative.

◂ A man pulls a sled through a blizzard (North Polar Ice Cap, Arctic Ocean)

LEARN

4.3 Tag Questions

Negative Tag Question

Affirmative Statement	Negative Tag
Vanessa **is** the teacher,	**isn't** she?
Class **starts** at 1:30,	**doesn't** it?
Carla and Luca **came** yesterday,	**didn't** they?
You**'ve** read that book,	**haven't** you?

Affirmative Tag Question

Negative Statement	Affirmative Tag
Philip **isn't** the writer,	**is** he?
The test **doesn't start** at 1:30,	**does** it?
Matt and Fran **didn't come,**	**did** they?
They **haven't arrived** yet,	**have** they?

1. Tag questions are used to ask someone to agree with or confirm information. A tag question is a statement with a two-word tag (auxiliary verb + pronoun) at the end. A comma is always used before a tag.	A: That was a hard test, **wasn't it?** B: Yeah, it was really hard. (agreement) A: Carlos is from Mexico, **isn't he?** B: Yes, he is. (confirmation)
2. If the statement is affirmative, the auxiliary in the tag is negative. If the statement is negative, the auxiliary in the tag is affirmative.	The Smiths **are going** home, **aren't** they? The Smiths **haven't come** home, **have** they?
3. Use *doesn't, don't,* and *didn't* in the tag with simple present and simple past affirmative statements that have verbs other than *be.*	Pedro **likes** the school, **doesn't he?** Gina and Tim **play** a lot of sports, **don't they?** Mariko already **saw** the movie, **didn't she?**
4. The pronoun in the tag matches the subject. If *there is/there are* is used in the statement, use *there* in the tag.	Carole **is** a hard worker, isn't she? Subject Pronoun **There aren't** any eggs, are **there?**

4 Complete the tag questions about the Arctic. Use the tags from the box.

aren't there	doesn't it	do we	haven't they	isn't it
didn't they	don't they	hasn't he	isn't he	~~wasn't it~~

1. Børge Ousland's experience in the Arctic was different from his normal life, wasn't it?
2. Ousland is worried about global warming, __________?
3. He has seen how warming temperatures are affecting Arctic ice, __________?
4. The Arctic is warming twice as fast as the rest of the planet, __________?
5. Scientists have collected a lot of information about sea ice, __________?
6. They used radar to show snow and ice thickness, __________?
7. There are many different types of ice, __________?
8. Arctic explorers have to wear many layers of warm clothing, __________?
9. The Arctic has one of the most extreme climates on Earth, __________?
10. We don't know exactly what will happen to Arctic ice in the future, __________?

4.4 Answering Tag Questions

1. When the statement in a tag question is affirmative, the speaker expects the answer to be affirmative. When the statement in a tag question is negative, the speaker expects the answer to be negative.	A: You **are coming** to the party, aren't you? B: **Yes, I am.** A: You **haven't eaten** lunch yet, have you? B: **No, I haven't.**
2. When the listener disagrees with the speaker or answers in an unexpected way, there is often an explanation.	A: Ahmed is from Egypt, isn't he? B: No, **he's from Canada.**
3. **Be careful!** The answers to tag questions and affirmative *Yes/No* questions are the same. It does not matter whether the tag is negative or affirmative.	A: Is Jim happy? B: Yes, he is. / No, he isn't. A: Jim is happy, isn't he? B: Yes, he is. / No, he isn't. A: Jim isn't happy, is he? B: Yes, he is. / No, he isn't.

5 Complete the interview with an explorer. Write *Yes* or *No*.

1. A: The life of an explorer is difficult, isn't it?
   B: Yes. It's hard, but it's very exciting.
2. A: Your journeys require a lot of planning, don't they?
   B: ______, I plan for months, and sometimes even years.
3. A: You take other people with you on these journeys, don't you?
   B: ______, most of the time I have two or three people with me.
4. A: There isn't a lot of free time, is there?
   B: ______, there's always something to do. We're busy all day long.
5. A: You're working on a new project now, aren't you?
   B: ______, I'm making plans for a trip next year.
6. A: You didn't get hurt on your last expedition, did you?
   B: ______. I didn't have any problems last time.
7. A: An expedition usually costs a lot of money, doesn't it?
   B: ______, supplies and equipment are very expensive.
8. A: You miss your family during these expeditions, don't you?
   B: ______, very much.
9. A: You don't go on more than one expedition a year, do you?
   B: ______, definitely not.
10. A: Your last journey was to the Gobi Desert, wasn't it?
    B: ______, I went to the Sahara Desert.

PRACTICE

6 Complete the exercises.

A Complete the conversation at a meeting of the Young Explorers Club. Write the missing tags.

Leon: You're new here, (1) <u>aren't you</u>?

Yuri: Yeah. I joined the club last month. It's a lot of fun, (2) ______________?

Leon: I love it. Have you done any of the activities yet?

Yuri: Uh-huh. I did the cave trip two weeks ago.

Leon: Really? I did that one, too. That was great, (3) ______________?

Yuri: Yeah. It was awesome. I didn't see you there. You weren't with the first group, (4) ______________?

Leon: No, I was with the second. Hey, you probably don't know many people here, (5) ______________?

Yuri: Not really.

Leon: OK. Let me tell you about some of them. That's Vera over there.

Yuri: Right. She collects spiders, (6) ______________?

Leon: Really? How did you know that?

Yuri: She was in my group on the trip. I heard her talking about her spiders. They're a strange thing to collect, but she seemed really nice.

▲ A Usofila cave spider

Leon: Look. She's coming over here. Let me introduce you. Hi, Vera. You haven't met Yuri, (7) ______________?

Vera: I haven't met you, but I remember you. You were on the cave trip two weeks ago, (8) ______________?

Yuri: Yeah. We were in the same group. So, how are your spiders?

Vera: They're great. I have one with me. You're not afraid of them, (9) ______________?

B Work with a partner. Compare your answers from exercise **A**.

7 **PRONUNCIATION.** Read the chart and listen to the examples. Then complete the exercises.

CD1-38

PRONUNCIATION **Intonation in Tag Questions**

The intonation in a tag question helps the listener understand the meaning of the question.

1. When the voice falls at the end of a tag question, the speaker is certain about the answer and expects the listener to agree.	A: This is a terrific party, **isn't it?** B: Yeah. It's great!
2. When the voice rises at the end of a tag question, the speaker is not certain about the answer and wants to confirm that something is true.	A: You invited Paul to the party, **didn't you?** B: No, I forgot. Sorry.

◂ a Maya cave painting

CD1-39

A Listen to each interview question for an explorer. Does the speaker expect agreement or confirmation? Check (✓) the correct box.

	Agreement	Confirmation
1. It's very hot in the Maya caves, isn't it?	☐	☑
2. The Maya lived thousands of years ago, didn't they?	☐	☐
3. There were many interesting things in the caves, weren't there?	☐	☐
4. The cave paintings are unusual, aren't they?	☐	☐
5. We can learn a lot about the Maya from the paintings, can't we?	☐	☐
6. You don't know the meaning of the symbols on the walls, do you?	☐	☐
7. You needed the help of the local people to find the caves, didn't you?	☐	☐
8. There isn't a lot of information about Maya cave traditions, is there?	☐	☐

CD1-40

B Match each response with the correct question in exercise **A**. Write the number of the question on the line. Then listen and check your answers.

__7__ a. Yes, of course. They know the area very well.

_____ b. Yes, they're very unusual.

_____ c. No, not yet. We hope to figure out the meaning soon.

_____ d. No, actually the temperature is very comfortable.

_____ e. In fact, there is quite a lot. There are many books on the subject.

_____ f. Yes, and there are Maya people today who live in southern Mexico and parts of Central America.

_____ g. Yes, the artwork is full of information about how the Maya lived.

_____ h. Yes, many amazing things.

C Work with a partner. Ask and answer the questions in exercises **A** and **B**. Be sure to use the correct intonation.

8 LISTEN & SPEAK.

A Read the conversations. Does the speaker ask the question to confirm facts? Or does the speaker expect the listener to agree? Write *C* (confirm) or *A* (agree).

__A__ 1. A: Rock climbing seems dangerous, doesn't it?
B: That's why I don't want to do it.

____ 2. A: The view is beautiful, isn't it?
B: It's gorgeous.

____ 3. A: We start the hike tomorrow at eight o'clock, don't we?
B: No, eight-thirty.

____ 4. A: The climb was hard, wasn't it?
B: Yeah, unbelievably hard.

____ 5. A: There's plenty of water, isn't there?
B: Let me check.

____ 6. A: We're going to stop at four o'clock, aren't we?
B: I'm not sure, but we stopped at four o'clock last time.

REAL ENGLISH

Tag questions are often used to start conversations or to keep conversations going. Some topics that people talk about include the weather and their current surroundings.

It's a beautiful day, isn't it?
The band sounds great, doesn't it?

CD1-41 **B** Listen to the conversations in exercise **A** and check your answers.

9 Work with a partner. Read the conversations. Find eight more places where the speaker expects the listener to agree. Change those sentences to tag questions.

1. **Sandy:** The weather's great today~~.~~, isn't it?
Jessica: It's beautiful. And there are a lot of people here.
Sandy: Yeah. I never knew so many people loved rock climbing.
Jessica: We're going to see some great views today.
Sandy: I hope so.

▶ People climbing the Eve Tooth rock formation in the Needles

2. **Ray:** Have we met before?

Hamid: Right. We were in the same map and compass training course last month.

Ray: Oh yeah. I remember now. That was hard.

Hamid: It really was. But I don't think I'll ever get lost again.

Ray: Me neither!

3. **Gisela:** This climb can't get any harder.

Luca: I hope not. We've walked through a lot of dangerous spots already.

Gisela: I know. I'll be glad when it's over.

Luca: The next mile is going to be the last hard part.

Gisela: I think so. After that, the trail gets easier.

10 APPLY.

A Think of eight different ways to start a conversation with people at a party or other event. Use topics such as names, hometowns, weather, sports, the news, entertainment, school, or work. Write a statement to complete each tag question.

1. ____________________, aren't you?
2. ____________________, don't you?
3. ____________________, aren't there?
4. ____________________, isn't it?
5. ____________________, doesn't it?
6. ____________________, do you?
7. ____________________, are you?
8. ____________________, is there?

B Imagine that you are at a party. Stand up and walk around the room. Ask your classmates questions from exercise **A**.

A: *Hi, you're Yuri, aren't you?*

B: *Yeah, that's right. And your name is Jenny, isn't it?*

A: That's right. You're from Russia, aren't you?

Charts 4.1,4.3–4.4

1 READ, WRITE & SPEAK.

A Read the fact sheet below and underline eight facts. Then write a negative question and a tag question for each fact.

Valley of the Khans Project Fact Sheet

- Dr. Albert Lin is the creator of the *Valley of the Khans* project. He wants to help the Mongolian people locate Genghis Khan's tomb.
- Genghis Khan was the founder of the Mongol Empire, the largest land empire in history. He lived in the thirteenth century.
- Mongolians do not know the exact location of Genghis Khan's burial site.
- Genghis Khan conquered many different parts of Asia after years of war. He brought all these parts under one government.
- People from Mongolia honor the memory of Genghis Khan. He was the first ruler of their country.

◄ Dr. Albert Lin

Isn't Dr. Albert Lin the creator of the Valley of the Khans project?

Dr. Albert Lin is the creator of the Valley of the Khans project, isn't he?

B Work with a partner. Ask and answer the questions you wrote in exercise **A**.

Charts 4.1–4.4

2 LISTEN, SPEAK & WRITE.

CD1-42

A Listen to a radio interview with two volunteers who work on Dr. Lin's project. What kind of work is Dr. Lin doing? Take notes in your notebook.

B Work with a partner. Share your notes from exercise **A**. Discuss any other information you remember from the interview.

CD1-43

C Read each *Yes/No* question. Does the radio host ask this question as a statement question (S), a negative question (N), or a tag question (T)? Listen again and write *S*, *N*, or *T* for each question. Then edit the sentence to match.

1. __T__ ~~Are you~~ You're working on Dr. Albert Lin's project, aren't you?
2. _____ Is the use of technology especially important in Mongolia?
3. _____ Does Lin's team of explorers ever disturb the ground?
4. _____ Do you do this right from your home computers?
5. _____ Is Mongolia enormous?

CD1-43

D Listen again. Write the answer to each question from exercise **C**.

1. ______________________________
2. ______________________________
3. ______________________________
4. ______________________________
5. ______________________________

◀ Some people believe that this rock shrine marks the burial place of Genghis Khan.

Charts 4.1–4.4

3 EDIT. Read the conversation. Find and correct seven more errors with questions and answers.

A: You're here for information about our University Explorers Club, ~~isn't it~~ aren't you?

B: Yes. By the way, I'm only 18. I'm not too young for the program, do I?

A: No, you're not too young. The program is for anyone between the ages of 18 and 25.

B: I don't need a college degree?

A: Yes. A college degree is not necessary, but previous exploration experience is. You have some experience, do you?

B: Yes. Here is a list of the projects I've worked on.

A: You can keep that. First, you need to complete the application online.

B: Do not you want to see my list of projects?

A: No, I don't need to see anything. You're going to list your projects in your application.

B: There isn't a deadline, is it?

A: Yes. You can apply all year long.

B: And the application is online?

A: Yes, it is.

B: It isn't difficult to find, was it?

A: No. It's at the very top of the website. You can't miss it.

Charts 4.1, 4.3–4.4

4 WRITE & SPEAK.

A Think of a nearby area to explore. In your notebook, write three negative questions and three tag questions about exploring the area.

You've been to Wildforest Park, haven't you?

B Work with a partner. Take turns asking and answering your questions from exercise **A**.

A: *You've been to Wildforest Park, haven't you?*

B: *Yes, I have. I went there once.*

A: *Doesn't it have some beautiful trails?*

B: *Yes, they're great. I'd like to go again sometime.*

Connect the Grammar to Writing

1 READ & NOTICE THE GRAMMAR.

A Read the short scene and visualize how it would look for a TV show or movie. Discuss your ideas with a partner.

The Great Maya Cave Quest

Characters: (1) Pierre L'Aventure, an archaeologist and adventurer

(2) Rosa Delacruz, Pierre's former coworker, an archaeologist

Situation: Pierre has not seen Rosa for ten years. He wants to find a hidden Maya cave. He thinks that there is a map in an old book that she owns. He goes to ask her if he can borrow it.

Scene: Rosa is at work putting books away. Suddenly, she hears a familiar voice behind her.

"Hello, Rosa," says Pierre. Rosa turns around in surprise.

"Pierre? You're here?" she cries out angrily.

"Yes, I am," he says. "What's wrong? Aren't you happy to see me again?"

Rosa does not answer. She only glares at him. Pierre continues, "I actually came to see you because I want to borrow something from you."

"You want to borrow something?" Rosa asks in disbelief.

"Yes—" Pierre starts to say, but then Rosa turns away and grumbles, "Don't you remember? You got that archaeology grant[1] instead of me. It wasn't fair!"

"You're not still upset about that, are you?" he asks.

"Yes, I am still upset about it. It was completely unfair," says Rosa, still angry.

"Look," says Pierre slowly, "I don't want to fight. I just want to borrow your old book about Maya caves. You know which book I'm talking about, don't you?"

Rosa looks surprised. She asks, "You want to borrow my Maya caves book? Why?"

"I can't explain," answers Pierre, "but it's important. You'll lend it to me, won't you?"

Rosa looks at him carefully for a minute. Then she continues putting books away as she says, "I'll think about it. Come back tomorrow."

[1]**grant:** money given for a specific purpose, such as research

GRAMMAR FOCUS

In this scene, the writer uses different questions to express emotions. For example:

Statement question: ***"You're here?"*** *she cries out.* (surprise)
Negative *yes/no* question: Rosa . . . grumbles, ***"Don't you remember?"*** (annoyance)
Tag question: *"You'll lend it to me,* ***won't you?"*** (expectancy)

B Read the scene in exercise **A** again. Underline one statement question, one negative *Yes/No* question, and a tag question. With a partner, decide which emotion the character is expressing with each question.

C Work with a partner. Look at the storyboard and tell your partner which part of the text in exercise **A** matches each picture. Draw a picture in the last square to match the scene. Then compare your drawings.

The Great Maya Cave Quest Storyboard

2 **BEFORE YOU WRITE.**

A Think of a scene in a movie or TV show in which two characters have an emotional conversation, or make up an imaginary scene. Draw four parts of the scene in your notebook. Use the storyboard in exercise **1C** as a model.

B Work with a partner. Share your storyboard from exercise **A** and describe the scene. Tell your partner what the characters are saying in each part.

WRITING FOCUS Using Quotation Marks

Notice how quotation marks ("...") and commas (,) are used in the story in exercise **1A**. Quotation marks are used around someone's exact words. Verbs such as *say* and *ask* often indicate quotes. Commas are used to separate the quote and the verb.

When the quote is first, put the comma inside the quotation marks and before the verb.
"Hello, Rosa," says Pierre.

When the quote is second, put the comma after the verb and outside of the quotation marks.
She asks, *"You want to borrow my old Mayan caves book? Why?"*

When the verb is in the middle of the quote, put the comma in both places.
"Look," says Pierre slowly, "I don't want to fight. . . ."

3 **WRITE** your scene as if it were part of a story. Make sure that the characters use the best question types to express their emotions. Use the scene from exercise **1A** and your storyboard from exercise **1C** to help you.

4 **SELF ASSESS.** Read your scene and underline the questions. Then use the checklist to assess your work.

- ☐ I used negative *Yes/No* questions and answers correctly. [4.1]
- ☐ I used statement questions correctly. [4.2]
- ☐ I used tag questions and answers correctly. [4.3, 4.4]
- ☐ I used commas and quotation marks correctly. [WRITING FOCUS]

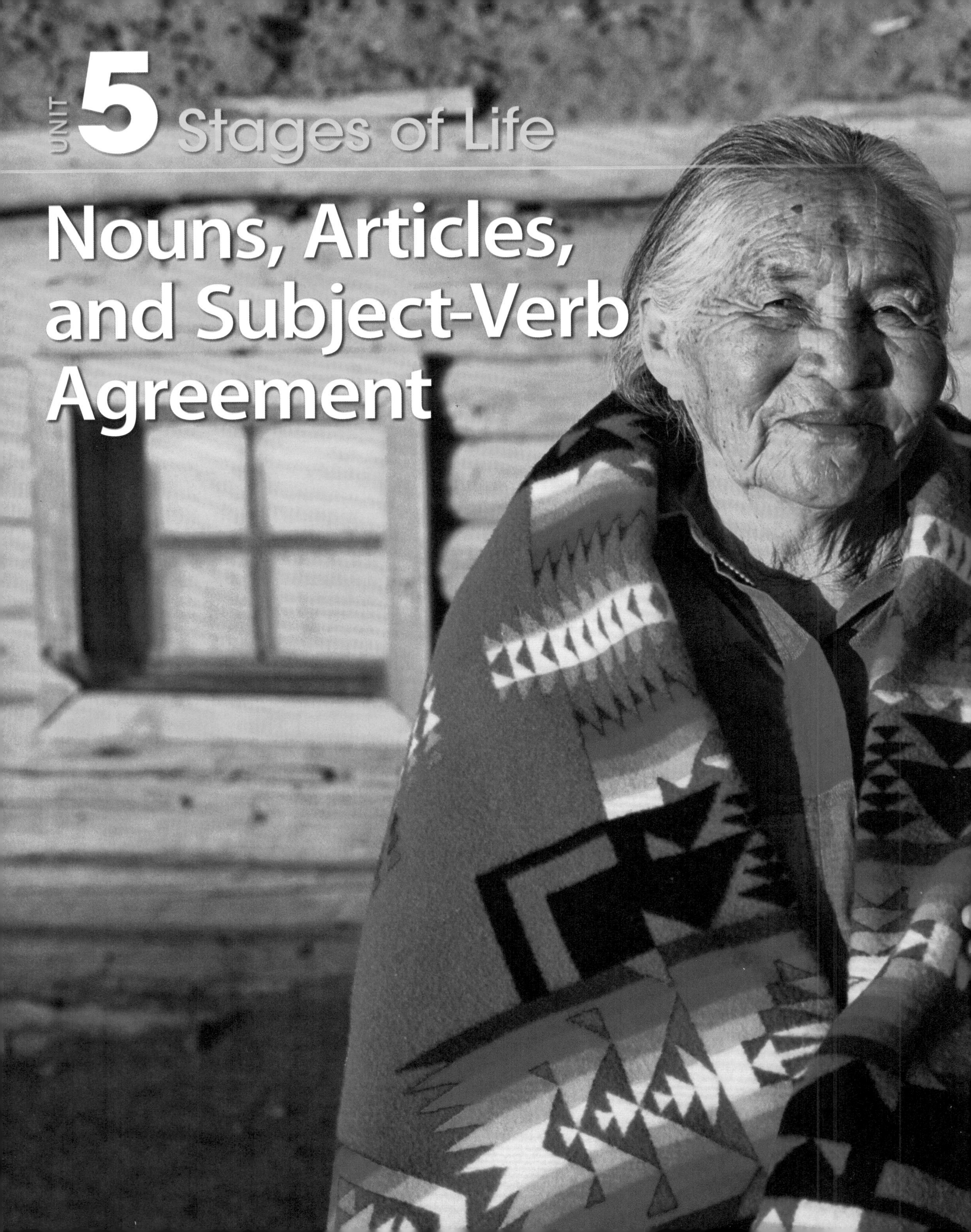

UNIT 5 Stages of Life

Nouns, Articles, and Subject-Verb Agreement

◂ Navajo woman and girl stand in front of their hoja home in Nazlini, Arizona, USA.

EXPLORE

1 READ the web page about baby-naming traditions in different parts of the world. Are any of the customs similar to traditions in your culture or family?

Naming Customs

Naming a baby is an important **event** throughout the world, and different cultures have their own **traditions**. Just **a few examples** can demonstrate a wide variety of **customs**.

In Indonesia, Balinese children are named according to their birth order. Normally, **every** first-born **child** is named *Wayan* or *Putu*; the second child, *Made* or *Kadek*; the third child, *Nyoman* or *Komang*; and the fourth child, *Ketut*. The names can be given to either **boys** or **girls**, but there is a **way** to distinguish **gender**. Male **names** start with *I* and female **names** start with *Ni*. For example, *I Made* is the name of a second-born boy, and *Ni Ketut* is the name of a fourth-born girl.

The Luo people of East Africa typically give their newborns two names. The first is usually a Western name, and the second often refers to the **time**, the **weather**, or other **information** related to the day of the child's birth. For example, a baby boy born at night could be named Michael Otieno. *O* indicates "male," and *-tieno* means "night." A baby girl born on a rainy **day** might receive a name such as Vivianne Akoth. *A* indicates "female" and *-koth* is the word for "**rain**."

The Wikmungkan people of northeastern Australia conduct a naming **ceremony** during the **birth** of a baby. At the birth, the names of all the infant's living **relatives** are called out, one by one. The name that is called at the final stage of birth is the one that the baby receives. From that time on, there is a close **relationship** between the baby and the relative whose **name** the **newborn** shares.

◄ A father holds up his child, Bali, Indonesia.

2 CHECK. Read the statements. Circle **T** for *true* or **F** for *false*.

1. Balinese children's names are based on the order in which they are born. **T** **F**
2. The Balinese use *I* for the first-born child and *Ni* for the second-born. **T** **F**
3. A Luo baby's name often relates to the day the child was born. **T** **F**
4. In the Luo culture, *O* indicates male. **T** **F**
5. A Wikmungkan naming ceremony takes place after the birth of a baby. **T** **F**

3 DISCOVER. Complete the exercises to learn about the grammar in this lesson.

A Look at the underlined words in the sentences. Write **S** above the three singular count nouns, **P** above the three plural count nouns, and **NC** above the three non-count nouns.

1. The names can be given to either boys or girls, but there is a way to distinguish gender.
2. . . . and the second often refers to the time, the weather, or other information related to the day of the child's of birth.
3. *A* indicates "female" and *-koth* is the word for "rain."

B Check (✓) the correct information about the nouns in exercise **A**.

	Singular Count Nouns (S)	Plural Count Nouns (P)	Non-Count Nouns (NC)
1. This type of noun cannot be plural.	☐	☐	☐
2. This type of noun follows *a/an*.	☐	☐	☐
3. This type of noun ends in *-s*.	☐	☐	☐

LEARN

5.1 Count and Non-Count Nouns

	Count Nouns	Non-Count Nouns
Singular	She wears that **necklace** every day. Is there a **copier** in the office? This English **assignment** looks hard.	She has beautiful **jewelry.** What **equipment** does the office need? The **homework** is pretty difficult.
Plural	She has two gold **necklaces.** Both **copiers** were broken. The **assignments** took a long time.	

1. Count nouns name things that can be counted. They have a singular and a plural form. To make most nouns plural, add *-s* or *-es.**	We have a **son** at home and two **sons** in college. This **box** is small. Those **boxes** are large.
2. Non-count nouns name things that cannot be counted. They do not have plural forms. Use singular verbs and pronouns with non-count nouns.	Sugar **isn't** good for your teeth. ✓The information **is** interesting, isn't **it?** ✗ The informations are interesting, aren't they?
3. Do not use *a/an* before a non-count noun.	✓Do you have **homework** tonight? ✗ Do you have a homework tonight?
4. An abstract noun refers to an idea or quality rather than a physical object. Abstract nouns are usually non-count.	Feelings: **anger, happiness, hate, love** Ideas: **beauty, friendship, intelligence** School subjects: **art, history, math, science** Weather: **fog, rain, snow, sunshine, wind**
5. **Be careful!** Some nouns have both count and non-count meanings. Use the context to determine if the noun is countable or not.	He had a long **life.** / **Life** is wonderful. Here's a **glass** of water. / It's made of **glass.** Your horse is a **beauty.** / There's **beauty** in nature.

*See page **A2** for spelling rules for regular plural nouns.

4 Complete the paragraphs about naming traditions. Add a plural *-s/-es/-ies* when possible.

In China, (1) **girl** _____ often receive (2) **name** _____ that suggest (3) **beauty** _____. (For example: *Mei Hua* means "beautiful flower.") (4) **Boy** _____ typically receive names that represent (5) **health** _____ and (6) **strength** _____. (For example: *Gang* means "strong.") It is customary to let some (7) **time** _____ pass before celebrating a (8) **birth** _____. Families have parties called "Hundred Days" to celebrate the (9) **survival** _____ of (10) **baby** _____ during the first three (11) **month** _____ of (12) **life** _____.

(13) **Buddhist** _____ in India name (14) **infant** _____ when they are certain that the baby can hear. A (15) **mother** _____ writes the baby's name on a banana leaf and covers the leaf with (16) **rice** _____. Then, she puts the baby on the leaf and whispers the name into the child's ear three (17) **time** _____.

5 **SPEAK.** How do people in your country or culture choose names? Do you know where your name comes from? Discuss your answers with a partner.

A: *In my country, children are usually named after their parents or grandparents. I am named after my grandmother.*

B: *This is true in my country, too. I am named after my father.*

6 Complete the exercises.

A Read the non-count and count definitions of each noun in bold. Then complete each pair of sentences with *a, an,* or Ø for *no article.*

1. **light** — **Non-Count:** energy from the sun that lets you see things
   Count: an electric lamp that produces light
   a. When I was a child, I always slept with __a__ light on.
   b. My house was filled with __Ø__ light every morning when the sun came up.

2. **appearance** — **Non-Count:** how someone looks and dresses
   Count: an arrival of someone in a place
   a. My parents told me that intelligence is more important than _____ appearance.
   b. Once a famous person made _____ appearance at my school and talked to the students.

3. **paper** — **Non-Count:** thin, smooth material that you can write on or wrap things with
   Count: a report or essay written by a student
   a. I always enjoyed making things out of _____ paper.
   b. I didn't know how to write _____ paper until high school.

4. **room** — **Non-Count:** enough empty space
   Count: a separate area that has its own walls inside a building
   a. When I was young, I used to share _____ room with two siblings.
   b. At home, we didn't have _____ room for a lot of furniture.

5. **experience** — **Non-Count:** knowledge or skill in a particular job or activity
   Count: something that happens to you
   a. I once had _____ very frightening experience.
   b. My babysitter had lots of _____ experience with children.

B **SPEAK.** Which sentences in exercise **A** are true for you? Tell a partner. Ask your partner follow-up questions for more information.

A: *Sentence 1a is true for me. When I was a child I always slept with a light on.*

B: *Really? Why?*

A: *I was afraid of the dark.*

5.2 Quantity Expressions with Count and Non-Count Nouns

Quantity Expressions	Singular Count Nouns	Plural Count Nouns	Non-Count Nouns
any, no	I'll read **any newspaper**. There is **no hotel** nearby.	Do you have **any ideas**? The store has **no eggs**.	I don't have **any advice**. He has **no patience**.
all, a lot of, lots of, more, most, some		I'll get **some candles**. Do **all babies** cry?	He has **more experience**. **Most fish** is good for you.
each, every, one	**Each photo** tells a story. **Every vote** counts.		
a couple of, a few, few, both, many		**Both parents** are here. Are there **many people**?	
a great deal of, a little, little, much			It's **a great deal of work**. There isn't **much time**.

1. A quantity expression is used before a noun to show the amount of the noun.	I got an e-mail from my friend. I get **a lot of e-mails** every day. The blog posts are interesting. **Each blog post** is informative.
2. *Any* and *no* are negative in meaning. Use *any* with a negative verb. Use *no* with an affirmative verb. *Any* can be used to mean *it doesn't matter which*.	They **haven't made any** progress. They **have made no** progress. Waiter: Would you like a table by the window? Customer: **Any table** is fine. Thank you.
3. *A few* + a count noun and *a little* + a non-count noun mean *some*. They indicate a positive amount.	**A few people** have arrived. Let's begin. We have **a little time.** Let's go for a walk.
4. *Few* + a count noun and *little* + a non-count noun mean *not many* or *not much*.	**Few people** went to the game. It was cold and windy. We have **little time.** Let's take a taxi. It's faster.
5. **Be careful!** *Much* is not usually used in affirmative statements.	✓ His boss gave him **a lot of** praise for his work. ✗ His boss gave him much praise for his work.

7 Circle the correct words to complete the article.

Babies Recognize Faces Better Than Adults, Research Shows

Researchers believe that (1) **all / each** babies start out with an ability to recognize (2) **many / much** different faces. However, by nine months they lose the skill if they don't have practice. When babies have (3) **a couple of / some** training during their first few months, they are better at recognizing faces when they get older.

Researchers tested a group of six-month-old babies by showing them (4) **a little / some** photographs of monkeys' faces. Then, the infants were divided into two groups. One group of babies was shown the monkeys' faces again and again over the next three months, so those infants spent (5) **a lot of / much** time with the photos. The other group didn't see (6) **any / no** photos of the monkeys during the same three-month period.

After nine months, the researchers showed (7) **both / each** groups (8) **more / a great deal of** photos: some monkey faces that the babies had seen before and some new ones. The babies without training showed (9) **few / little** interest in the new faces, and they saw (10) **any / no** differences between the old and the new faces. However, the trained babies recognized the differences.

What did the study show? Babies that had had (11) **a few / some** training didn't lose their ability to recognize faces, but those with (12) **any / no** training lost this ability by the time they were nine months old.

8 Complete each statement with *few, a few, little,* or *a little.*

1. Our children need ___little___ advice from us. They do everything right.
2. We have __________ problems with our children. They are very well behaved.
3. Our daughter is only sixteen months old, and she can already say __________ words.
4. Our daughter has __________ trouble learning anything new. She gets excellent grades.
5. Our son is seven and he already plays __________ musical instruments. He's gifted.
6. Our boys have __________ fights. They get along very well with each other.
7. Our girls have __________ free time. They are always busy studying.
8. Our children usually have __________ homework on the weekends, but not a lot.

PRACTICE

9 Complete the exercises.

A Circle the correct words to complete the paragraph.

Our daughter, Rosa, is already ten years old. Time (1) **has / have** gone so quickly! Before she was born, we had had (2) **few / little** experience with children. We didn't have (3) **any / some** knowledge about raising a child, but Rosa has taught us (4) **every / some** important things. She has (5) **a lot of / many** imagination, and so she always gives us (6) **a great deal of / many** pleasure. Fortunately, her health (7) **is / are** excellent, and that is the most important thing. We hope that Rosa meets (8) **many / much** kind people throughout her life and that she forms (9) **many / much** good relationships. We are happy that we're doing a good job as parents. There is (10) **little / a little** doubt in our minds that Rosa is going to be a successful adult with (11) **a lot of / much** self-confidence. (12) **Few / A few** of her teachers say that, too.

B **ANALYZE THE GRAMMAR.** Look at the chart. Then find at least four more examples of each kind of noun from the article in exercise **A** on page 121. Write them in the chart.

Singular Count Nouns	Plural Count Nouns	Non-Count Nouns
daughter	years	time

C Work with a partner. Compare your charts from exercise **B**.

10 **WRITE** eight sentences in your notebook. Use different quantity expressions, verbs, and nouns from the chart. Start each sentence with "When I was a child. . . ."

When I was a child, I didn't have many stuffed animals. I only had a few.

Verbs	Quantity Expressions	Nouns		
eat	a couple of	advice	fun	self-confidence
get	a great deal of	attention	game	stuffed animal
have	a lot of/lots of	candy	holiday	toy
like	a few/few	doll	junk food	truck
need	a little/little	fishing rod	money	video game
play	many/much	free time	praise	*Use your own ideas*
want	no	friend	problem	

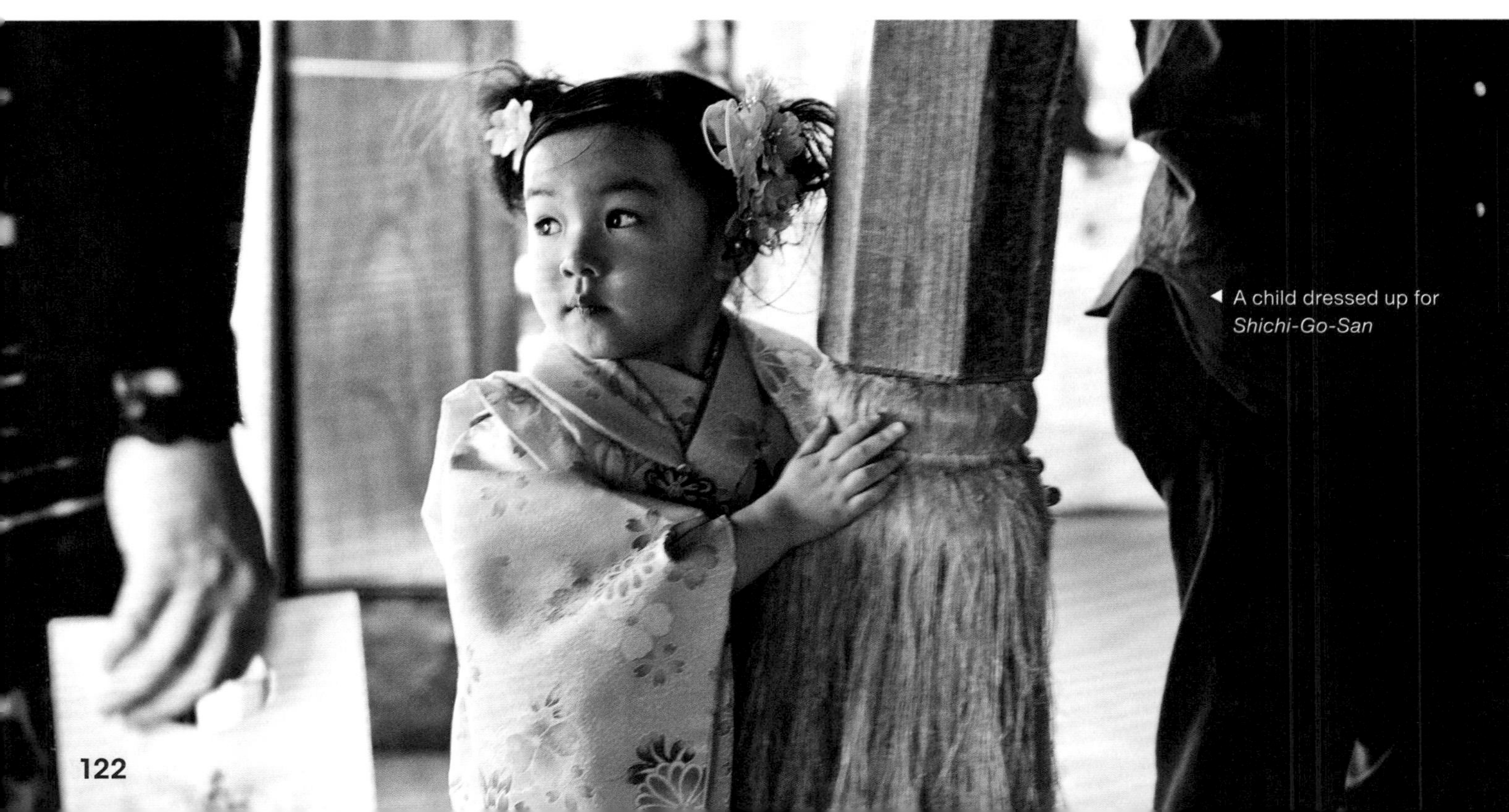

◀ A child dressed up for *Shichi-Go-San*

11 **EDIT.** Read the paragraph about *Shichi-Go-San*. Find and correct six more errors with count and non-count nouns or quantity expressions.

Shichi-Go-San

Shichi-Go-San ("Seven-Five-Three") is^a Japanese celebration. People have many fun at this time of year. *Shichi-Go-San* takes place on November 15 each year and celebrates different stages of childhood. Parents celebrate their children's growth and pray for their children's good healths. Every children receives a bag of candy. Boys receive bags of candy when they turn three and five years old. Girl receive them when they turn three and seven. In Japan, people think these are important ages in a child's life. The candy is shaped like a stick. All the candy bags have a picture of turtle and a crane on them. The candy, the crane, and the turtle are symbol of long life.

◄ A *Shichi-Go-San* candy bag

▲ *Shichi-Go-San* candy

12 **APPLY.**

A Write a paragraph in your notebook about a celebration from your childhood. It can be a national celebration or a personal one, such as a birthday. Answer the following questions.

What is the name of the celebration?
When does it take place?
What does the event celebrate?
Are there any symbols connected with the event?
Who celebrates this event?

Shichi-Go-San is a celebration in my country. It takes place on November 15th every year . . .

B Work with a partner. Read each other's paragraphs from exercise **A**. Then ask at least three questions about your partner's celebration.

A: *Do people wear any special clothing on that day?*

B: *Yes, the girls wear kimonos, and the boys wear traditional pants called hakama.*

EXPLORE

CD2-03

1 **READ** the article about why teenagers do the things they do. What are some typical teenage behaviors?

The Science of the Teenage Brain

Ask almost any parent of **a teenager** and you will hear **the** same **story**: adolescence[1] is a difficult time. Many parents will probably mention a few things that worry them such as high-speed driving, texting while driving, skateboarding, and other risky action sports.

Why do teens act the way they do? Nobody had **a** good **explanation** until **the** late **twentieth century** when **researchers** developed brain scanning. With this technology, scientists can see **the brain's** physical development and activity. **The brain scans** show that **the brain** develops slowly through childhood and adolescence. Therefore, **a** teenage **brain** is not yet fully developed. That's likely why most teens consider their desires more important than rules of behavior. For **the** same **reason**, they often don't consider **the consequences**, or results, of their actions.

In recent years, researchers have begun to view **the** teenage **brain** and teen behavior in **a** more positive **way**. Studies show that teens from all cultures have **some characteristics** in common such as **a desire** for thrills[2] and excitement. This desire may lead to **danger**, but it can also have **a** positive **effect**. Openness to new experiences can "get you out of **the house**," says brain researcher Jay Giedd. In other words, **the search** for excitement and risk prepares teens to leave **the safety** of their homes and move out into **the world**. According to this view, teens are very adaptable[3] human beings. When we look beyond their crazy behavior, we can see people who are getting ready to face **the challenges** of **the future**.

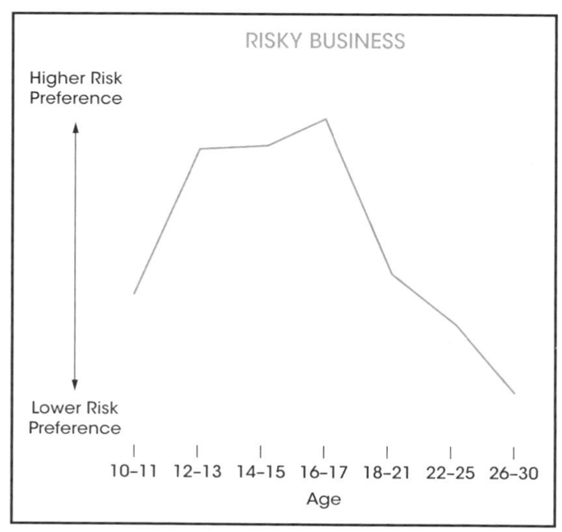

▼ For teens, pleasure is usually more important than its consequences.

[1] **adolescence:** the stage of life between childhood and adulthood
[2] **thrill:** a strong feeling of excitement, fear, or pleasure
[3] **adaptable:** able to handle changes; flexible

2 CHECK. Answer the questions about the article in exercise **1**. Write complete sentences.

1. What did late twentieth-century researchers find out about the teenage brain?

____

2. What are two characteristics that teens from all cultures share?

____

3. According to the graph, at what ages do teenagers take the most risks?

____

4. What is the positive side of teenage risk taking?

____

3 DISCOVER. Complete the exercises to learn about the grammar in this lesson.

A Read the sentences from the the article in exercise **1**. If there is an article (*a/an* or *the*) before the underlined noun, circle it.

1. Ask almost any parent of (a) teenager . . .
2. Nobody had a good explanation until the late twentieth century.
3. The brain scans show that the brain develops slowly through childhood and adolescence.
4. . . . researchers have begun to view the teenage brain and teen behavior in a more positive way.
5. . . . the search for excitement and risk prepares teens to leave the safety of their homes and move out into the world.

B Check (✓) the statements that are true based on your answers in exercise **A**.

_____ 1. *A* or *an* is used before a plural count noun.

_____ 2. *The* is used before a singular count noun.

_____ 3. *The* is used before a plural count noun.

_____ 4. *The* is used before a non-count noun.

_____ 5. No article is used before a singular count noun.

_____ 6. No article is used before a non-count noun.

LEARN

5.3 Articles: Specific and Nonspecific

Articles	Singular Count Nouns	Plural Count Nouns	Non-Count Nouns
the	**The child** has brown eyes.	**The children** are tall.	Where is **the sugar?**
a/an	Do you have **a** blue **pen?**		
some		Do we need **some apples?**	I gave him **some advice.**

1. Use *the* to refer to a specific person, place, thing, or idea. A noun is specific when:	
a. it is clear which noun you mean	a. Did you feed **the cat?** (our cat)
b. there is only one of the noun	b. Look at **the moon.** Isn't it beautiful?
c. a prepositional phrase or relative clause comes after the noun and defines the noun	c. Do you know **the name** *of this lake*? I don't know **the people** *that arrived late.*
2. Use *a/an* before a singular count noun when:	
a. you are not referring to a specific person, place, thing, or idea; you are referring to one of many	a. Do you have **a picture** of your family? (Any picture is fine.)
b. the listener or reader does not know which person, place, thing, or idea you mean	b. I just read **an interesting article** about teenagers.
3. Use *some* before a plural count noun or non-count noun that is not specific. *Some* refers to an indefinite amount. Often the meaning with and without *some* is similar.	**Some people** are here already. **People** have already arrived. There's **some milk** in the fridge. There's **milk** in the fridge.
4. **Be careful!** Singular count nouns almost always need an article or other determiner (such as *this, many, . . .*).	✓ **The girl** has **a** new **bike.** ✗ Girl has new bike.
5. An article is not used in some common expressions (*to bed, in bed, in class, at work, after school/college, at home*).	I often read **in bed.** I went **to bed** late. **After college,** I plan to travel for a year.

REAL ENGLISH

When a noun is mentioned for the first time, *a/an* is often used. When it is mentioned again, *the* is used.

A: *He wrote **a paper** for class.*

B: *How long was **the paper**?*

4 Circle the correct articles to complete each sentence. Circle Ø for *no article*.

1. **Some / The** teens play soccer in **Ø / the** afternoon and others swim.
2. Nick had **an / the** injury, but he didn't let **an / the** injury stop him from playing soccer.
3. **A / The** coach of his soccer team told Raul to stay **Ø / the** home, but he didn't want to.
4. After **Ø / the** school, Mia babysits two young children in **Ø / the** neighborhood.
5. We have **a / Ø** test next Monday, so **a / the** teacher is going to review everything on Friday.

6. We have several schools in our town but only one hospital. **Ø / The** school that my children attend is near **a / the** hospital.

7. Gina sent me **a / the** text message when I got home, but I didn't understand **a / the** message.

8. Emily left **an / the** empty water bottle in **a / the** fridge.

9. **Ø / The** weather sometimes affects **the / Ø** people and makes them sad.

10. I'm so glad that I don't have to go to **a / Ø** work tomorrow. I can stay in **the / Ø** bed later.

5.4 Articles: Making Generalizations

Articles	Singular Count Nouns	Plural Count Nouns	Non-Count Nouns
No Article		**Cats** sleep during the day.	**Experience** is important in a job.
a/an	**A car** is a motorized vehicle.		

1. To make a generalization about something, use a plural count noun or a non-count noun without an article.	**Cows** are mammals. **Milk** comes from cows.
2. *A/an* can be used before a singular count noun to make a generalization, but it is less common.	**Less Common: A computer** is **a useful tool.** **More Common: Computers** are useful **tools.**
3. *The* can be used before certain adjectives to refer to a specific group of people.	**The poor** need our help. Sam works with **the elderly.**

5 Put the words in the correct order to make sentences. Add *a*, *an*, or *the* where necessary.

1. person's life / can be / difficult time in / adolescence
   Adolescence can be a difficult time in a person's life.

2. want / many teens / excitement
   ____

3. worries about / her / mother / children
   ____

4. risky things / young / sometimes do
   ____

5. like / their friends / to spend time with / teenagers
   ____

6. teenage behavior / elderly / often don't understand
   ____

7. enjoy / many teens / activities / dangerous
   ____

8. to have / teenagers / job / it is good for

____

9. responsibility / job / teaches

____

10. doesn't make / young people / happy / money

____

PRACTICE

6 Complete the exercises.

A Circle the correct articles to complete the statements. Circle Ø for *no article.*

1. "I love to play with (Ø) **/ the** dolls."
2. "There's nothing that I like more than just looking up at **a / the** sky."
3. "I enjoy just hanging out with **Ø / the** friends."
4. "I can't wait until I'm big enough to go to **Ø / the** school."
5. "You never appreciate **a / Ø** time until you don't have a lot of it."
6. "It's fun to go to **Ø / the** parties and stay up all night."
7. "I don't see why students have to do **a / Ø** homework. We already do enough work at **Ø / the** school!"
8. "Swimming in **some / the** ocean is fun."
9. "I don't mind most household tasks, but I dislike cleaning **Ø / the** oven."
10. "I just learned to ride **a / the** bike."

B **SPEAK.** Work with a partner. Discuss who probably said each statement in exercise **A**: a young child, a teenager, or an adult.

A: *I think a young girl said, "I love to play with dolls."*

B: *I agree, but I'm not sure about number two.*

7 **PRONUNCIATION.** Read the chart and listen to the examples. Then complete the exercises.

CD2-04

PRONUNCIATION ***The:* /ðə/ or /ði/**

The is pronounced two ways: /ðə/ with /ə/ as in *of* or /ði/ with /i/ as in *he*.

1. Say /ðə/ before consonant sounds (b, c, d, . . .).

the book	**the** question	**the** difficult exercise

2. Say /ði/ before vowel sounds (a, e, i, o, u).

the exercise	**the** answer	**the** easy question

CD2-05

A Listen for the word *the* in each sentence. Then check (✓) the pronunciation you hear.

	/ðə/	/ði/
1.	✓	
2.		
3.		
4.		

	/ðə/	/ði/
5.		
6.		
7.		
8.		

CD2-05

B Listen again. Repeat each sentence. Then write the noun phrase with the word *the* from each sentence.

1. ____the flowers____
2. ________________
3. ________________
4. ________________
5. ________________
6. ________________
7. ________________
8. ________________

8 Complete the text. Write *a, an, the,* or Ø for *no article.*

Coming-of-Age Day in South Korea

What does it mean when (1) __a__ person comes of age? It means that (2) _____ person is moving from (3) _____ childhood to (4) _____ adulthood. This transition happens at different ages and is celebrated in a variety of ways in different cultures. It can be (5) _____ simple event or a celebration that involves special ceremonies.

In South Korea, the third Monday in May is Coming-of-Age Day. Everyone who is turning 20 years old that year celebrates (6) _____ day. When (7) _____ young reach this stage of (8) _____ life, they have more freedom than they did when they were (9) _____ children. For example, some start to drive, vote, or get married. In addition to (10) _____ independence, a 20-year-old needs to accept (11) _____ responsibility of becoming (12) _____ adult in his or her country.

It has become (13) _____ tradition for Korean "coming-of-agers" to receive three gifts: (14) _____ flowers, perfume, and (15) _____ kiss. In some places, there is (16) _____ ceremony, too, where the 20-year-olds wear traditional Korean clothing. The boys wear black hats made partially of (17) _____ horsehair, and the girls wear special (18) _____ dresses and hairstyles.

Young women and men wear traditional clothing at a "Coming-of-Age" Day ceremony in South Korea.

9 LISTEN.

CD2-06

A Listen to the news report about three young people—David Dicks, Zac Sunderland, and Laura Dekker. Check (✓) the sentence that best describes what they have in common.

_____ 1. They are all from the same part of the world.

_____ 2. Their parents encouraged them to do unusual things.

_____ 3. Each of them wanted to have an adventure.

CD2-06

B Listen again. Then complete the sentences based on what you heard in the news report. Use the words and phrases from the box and *a, an, some, the,* or Ø for *no article.*

after-school jobs	bad weather	difficult trip	government officials	
problems with his boat	~~sailboat~~	West Coast	world	young person

1. Each of the three teens had _____a sailboat_____.
2. They all wanted to sail around __________ alone.
3. The two challenges David Dicks had to face were __________ and __________.
4. David Dicks completed __________ in nine months.
5. Zac Sunderland set out from __________ of the United States.
6. Zac Sunderland got money for his boat from __________.
7. __________ were worried about Laura Dekker's plans.
8. They thought the trip was too dangerous for __________.

10 APPLY.

A Work in a group. Discuss how being a child is different from being a teenager in your culture. Use the topics from the box in your comparison of children and teens.

interests	types of skills	rules to follow
responsibilities	types of worries	ways they get into trouble

Children in my culture are mostly interested in toys. Teens are interested in music and sports.

B Write five sentences about the ideas you and your group discussed.

____

____

____

____

____

EXPLORE

CD2-07

1 READ the article about longevity, or how long people live. Why do some people live to be a hundred?

How long will you live?

Will you live to be a hundred? **There is** still no way to predict a person's life span, but **scientists are** getting closer. In a study of over 1000 centenarians (people who are 100 years old or older), researchers have discovered a set of "long-life" genes.[1] These genes allow scientists to guess, with 77 percent accuracy, whether a person can live into their late 90s or longer. **The authors** of the study **think** that long-life genes may prevent other genes from causing the usual illnesses of aging such as heart problems and dementia.[2] However, it is not true that **every person** with long-life genes **is going to live** to be a hundred. **A number of other important factors** greatly **influence** life span. For example, **lifestyle, the environment, and plain good luck** also **play** a big role. In fact, **23 percent of the people** in the study **were** not found to have long-life genes. Perhaps these people simply lived healthier lives.

The scientific community is excited by the study and its implications[3] for further research. For example, scientists are learning how to use genes to help predict and prevent certain illnesses. **Dan Buettner**, an expert in long-life studies, **believes** in the value of such studies. He says that scientists may even learn how to slow the aging process, although this won't happen for a long time. **Years** of research **have taught** him that, for now, we must accept the genes we have and live well. For Buettner that means eating a healthy diet, being physically active, and having a purpose in life.

[1] **gene:** the part of a cell that controls the physical characteristics, growth, and development of living things

[2] **dementia:** a serious illness of the mind

[3] **implication:** something that is likely to happen as a result of something else

▼ A 100-year-old man water-skis near his home in Washington State, USA.

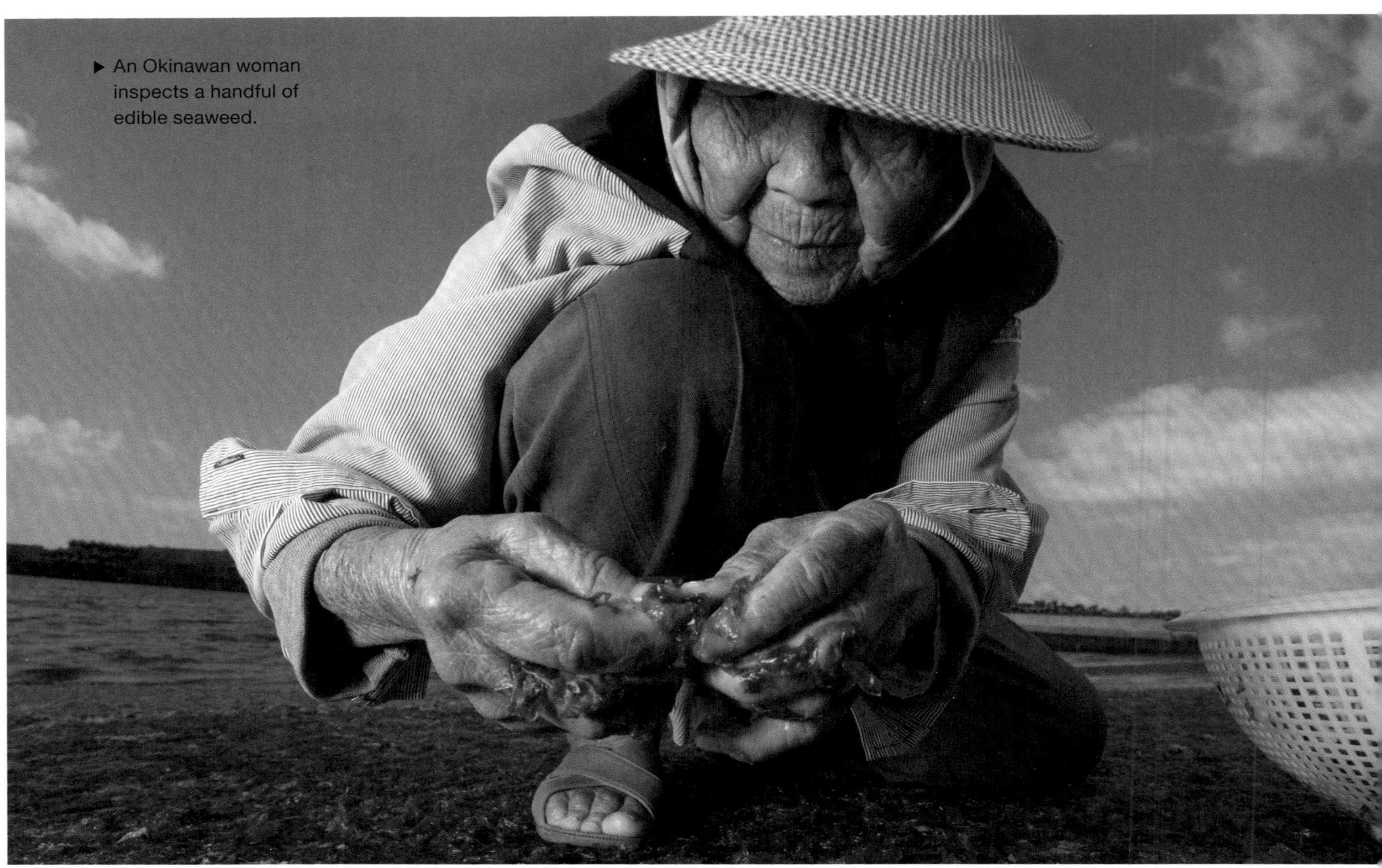

▶ An Okinawan woman inspects a handful of edible seaweed.

2 CHECK. Correct the error in each sentence to make it true according to the article from exercise **1** on page 131.

1. In a study of over 1000 ~~75-year-olds~~ centenarians, researchers have discovered a set of "long-life" genes.
2. Long-life genes may cause the typical diseases of the elderly.
3. Lifestyle, the environment, and plain good luck have little effect on life span.
4. Scientists are learning how to destroy genes to help predict certain illnesses.
5. Dan Buettner believes that scientists may even learn how to stop the aging process.

3 DISCOVER. Complete the exercises to learn about the grammar in this lesson.

A Look at the underlined subjects in the sentences. Circle the verb or verb phrase that agrees with each subject.

1. The authors of the study (think) that long-life genes may affect aging.
2. Every person with long-life genes is not going to live to be a hundred.
3. A number of other important factors greatly influence life span.
4. In fact, 23 percent of the people in the study were not individuals with long-life genes.
5. Years of research have taught him several things.

B Look the verb or verb phrase you circled in each sentence in exercise **A**. Then choose the noun or noun phrase that agrees with the verb or verb phrase.

1. (a.) the authors   b. the study
2. a. every person   b. genes
3. a. a number   b. factors
4. a. the people   b. study
5. a. years   b. research

LEARN

5.5 Subject-Verb Agreement

1. The main verb in a sentence must agree in number with the subject.	Singular: **The sofa looks** comfortable. Plural: **The chairs are** too hard.
2. When a subject includes a phrase or clause, the verb agrees with the head noun.	**The girl** with five brothers **is** very athletic. **A family** that has ten children **is** unusual.
3. Use a plural verb after subjects joined by *and*. Use a singular verb when *each* or *every* comes before subjects joined by *and*.	**Love and trust are** important to him. **Every day and night was** fun last summer.
4. Use a singular verb after an indefinite pronoun (*everybody, someone, anything, no one, etc.*).	**Everybody is going to come** to the party. **Someone has taken** the money. **Anything is** possible. **No one was sleeping** in the room.
5. **Remember:** Use a singular verb after *each* and *every*.	**Each class is** in a different room. **Every house costs** a different amount here.
6. In sentences beginning with *there is/there are* and *here is/here are*, the subject follows the verb. The verb still agrees with the subject.	There **is a dog** in the car. There **are two cats,** too. Here **is the lock,** and **here are the keys.**

4 Read the fact sheet about longevity, or long life. Circle the correct verb to complete each sentence.

Facts about Longevity

Here (1) **is / are** some information about longevity:

- There (2) **is / are** several factors other than genes that affect longevity.
- Lifestyle and the environment (3) **contributes / contribute** to the length of a person's life.
- Not every centenarian (4) **chooses / choose** the same lifestyle.
- Every man and woman (5) **needs / need** to exercise regularly.
- People who eat a balanced diet usually (6) **lives / live** longer.
- A good set of genes (7) **helps / help** some people stay active into their 90s.
- The people of Monaco (8) **has / have** the highest life expectancy in the world.

5.6 More Subject-Verb Agreement

1. Use a singular verb after a plural amount of money, time, or distance when it refers to one thing or idea (a price, a time period, a distance, . . .).	**Two hundred dollars is** a lot of money. **Three weeks seems** like a long time to wait. **Five miles isn't** too far to walk.
2. Some nouns look plural, but are used with singular verbs. For example: a. subjects ending in *-ics (physics, economics, . . .)* b. the noun *news*	 a. **Physics is** hard. b. **The news wasn't** good.
3. Use a singular verb with the names of: a. books, movies, and plays b. countries c. businesses ending in *-s*	 a. **"Romeo and Juliet" is** a famous play. b. **The United States is** a large country. c. **GREX Works is** a company near Boston.
4. When using *the* + adjective to refer to a group of people (*the young, the elderly, . . .*), use a plural verb.	**The wealthy live** in houses along the river. **The young are** comfortable with technology.
5. Use a singular verb with *the number of.* Use a plural verb with *a number of.*	**The number of** gardens in the city **is** small. **A number of** questions **are** impossible to answer.
6. The verb after a percentage (%), fraction (¼, ½), or quantity expression *(all, most)* agrees with the noun after *of.*	**Fifty percent of** the students **know** the answer. **Half of** the class **knows** the answer. **Most of** the survey **is** about aging.

5 Complete the sentences with *is* or *are.*

1. The average human life span __is__ 82 years in some countries.
2. Eighty-two years ______ not quite a century. There are 100 years in a century.
3. In Japan, more than one-fifth of the population ______ over the age of 65.
4. In India, more than 10 percent of the people ______ 60 or older.
5. Geriatrics ______ the name of medical care for older adults.
6. The number of centarians ______ increasing worldwide.
7. The elderly today ______ healthier than 50 years ago.
8. *Blue Zones* ______ the name of a book about longevity.
9. A number of interviews in the book ______ with centenarians.
10. The young ______ not likely to learn from the experience of the elderly.

PRACTICE

6 Complete the exercises.

A Circle the correct verb to complete each quotation.

Quotations about Aging

1. An old man (1) **continues / continue** to be young in two things – love of money and love of life. (Proverb)
2. There (2) **is / are** no medicine against old age. (Nigerian proverb)
3. To me, old age (3) **is / are** always 15 years older than I am. (Bernard Baruch, businessman)
4. Everyone (4) **is / are** the age of their heart. (Guatemalan proverb)
5. The elderly (5) **has / have** so much to offer. They're our link with history. (From the movie *Being John Malkovich*)
6. Anyone who stops learning (6) **is / are** old, whether at twenty or eighty. (Henry Ford, car manufacturer)
7. As we get older, things (7) **seems / seem** less important. (From the movie *Red*)
8. No man (8) **knows / know** he is young while he is young. (G. K. Chesterton, writer)

B **SPEAK.** Work with a partner. Choose one or two quotations in exercise **A** that you believe are true. Then tell your partner why you believe the quotations you chose are true.

7 **LISTEN.**

A You are going to hear an interview with Elvira Caceres Montero, a participant in a research study on the elderly. Before you listen, predict which three things she will say are the most important as she looks back at her life.

☐ communication ☐ health ☐ money
☐ education ☐ honesty ☐ volunteer work
☐ family ☐ marriage ☐ technology

CD2-08

B Listen to the interview. Were your predictions correct?

CD2-08

C Listen again. Circle the correct word(s) to complete each sentence about Ms. Montero.

1. **All / Some** of her family **was / were** together for her 80th birthday.
2. **Some / All** of her family **live / lives** in Puerto Rico.
3. **One experience / Her experiences** in life **has taught / have taught** her to be a better listener.
4. **One / All** of her grandchildren **has been / have been** successful.
5. She believes that **education / experience is / are** important for success.

8 EDIT. Read the company newsletter. Find and correct six more errors with subject-verb agreement.

Meet Gene Guerro, 92, Briteroom Electronics's 60-Year Employee

Gene Guerro has been working at Briteroom for 60 years and nothing ~~have~~ has ever prevented him from going to work. Briteroom Electronics are going to be honoring him next month for being the company's longest-working employee. When he first started college, Gene majored in economics. But economics just weren't very interesting to him, so he changed to physics. "There was many exciting things to learn in every physics class. In fact, physics still excites me today," says Gene. "Everybody tell me I should retire." And I say, "Why should I do that? Watching TV all day isn't for me. Half of my friends does that, but they aren't happy. Every day are exactly the same for them." As Lucy Guerro says about her father, "Work is my dad's hobby."

9 READ, SPEAK & WRITE.

A Work with a partner. Read the chart about the results of a survey. Then discuss these questions with your partner.

What is the survey about?

Who responded to the survey questions?

Are your answers to the questions similar?

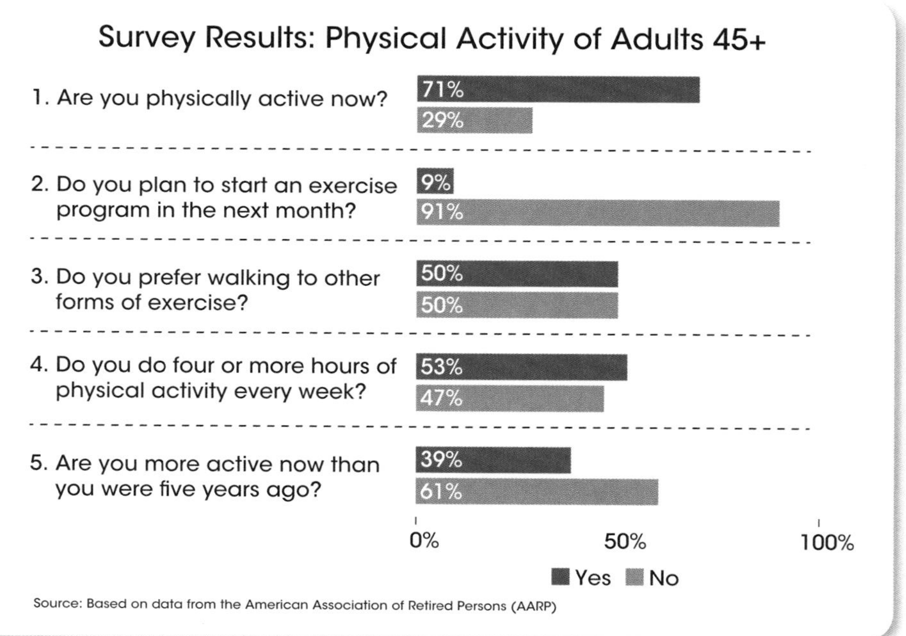

Survey Results: Physical Activity of Adults 45+
1. Are you physically active now?
71%
29%
2. Do you plan to start an exercise program in the next month?
9%
91%
3. Do you prefer walking to other forms of exercise?
50%
50%
4. Do you do four or more hours of physical activity every week?
53%
47%
5. Are you more active now than you were five years ago?
39%
61%
0%
50%
100%
Yes
No
Source: Based on data from the American Association of Retired Persons (AARP)

B Complete each statement about the survey results in exercise **A**. Use a phrase from the box and the correct form of the verb. Add *not* where necessary. More than one answer is sometimes correct.

~~be over 45 years old~~	plan to start an exercise program next month
be physically active now	do a few hours of physical activity per week
have the same level of activity as five years ago	prefer walking to other forms of exercise
be more active now than five years ago	

1. All of the respondents were over 45 years old.
2. A little less than 40 percent of the group ________.
3. Almost three-quarters of the respondents ________.
4. Nearly a third of the group ________.
5. Almost nobody ________.
6. Fifty percent of the people ________.
7. A little over half of the group ________.
8. Almost two-thirds ________.

10 APPLY.

A Work in a group. Brainstorm *Yes/No* questions to ask your classmates about their physical activity. Write as many questions as you can.

Do you exercise regularly?

Do you prefer going to the gym to exercising outdoors?

B Choose the four best questions from exercise **A** and write them in the chart. Then walk around the classroom and ask five students to take your survey. Ask each student all four of your questions. Record each student's answers in your chart. Write **Y** for *Yes* or **N** for *No*.

Class Survey on Physical Activity	Classmates (Y or N?)				
Questions	1	2	3	4	5
1.					
2.					
3.					
4.					

C Return to your group and discuss the results of your survey. Then write five sentences about the results.

Every person in the class exercises on a regular basis now.

Two-thirds of the students do not prefer exercising in the gym to exercising outdoors.

Charts 5.1, 5.3–5.5

1 Complete the exercises.

A Read about storytelling in Native American culture. Circle the correct answers.

Storytelling: A Native American Tradition

There (1) **is / are** a long tradition of (2) **the / Ø** storytelling among many Native American (3) **person / people**. Stories are often told by elders to teach younger generations important lessons about (4) **a / Ø** history and culture. Virginia Driving Hawk Sneve, (5) **a / the** Native American writer, remembers how it felt to sit with a group of other children and listen to the fascinating stories that her grandmother told. Sneve and her family (6) **is / are** Lakota Indians; however, (7) **a / the** tradition is not unique to them.

(8) **The / A** Lakota culture is just one example of a society in which grandmothers became the storytellers. Hunting for food was (9) **the / Ø** responsibility of the adult men, and household tasks such as food preparation (10) **was / were** the job of the strong, younger mothers. Therefore, it was up to the grandmothers to educate the children, and they told stories to do it.

A Lakota language class at Red Cloud Indian School in South Dakota

B **ANALYZE THE GRAMMAR.** Find four singular count nouns, four plural count nouns, and four non-count nouns from the text in exercise **A**. Write them in your notebook. Then work with a partner and compare your lists of nouns.

Charts 5.1–5.6

2 **EDIT.** Read the information about stories. Find and correct eight more errors with nouns, articles, and subject-verb agreement.

Every culture and country ~~have~~ has stories to pass down to the younger generation, and the young learns a lot of things from the stories. The stories also bring joy to a great deal of children.

There are many different kinds of stories, but a number of themes is common across cultures. For example, the importance of family relationships appear again and again. Hard work and honesty is also important theme in children's stories. What else do the children learn? Perhaps most importantly, they learn that all human beings are the same. There is a little difference between people. Everybody have the same dreams, hopes, and fears.

Charts 5.1–5.5

3 LISTEN, WRITE & SPEAK.

A You are going to listen to an excerpt from a traditional Native American story told by the Chippewa people of North America. The title of the story is "The Wonderful Turtle." Read the first part of the story. Write the articles and verbs that you think are missing.

Near a Chippewa village was (1) _____ large lake, and in (2) _____ lake there lived (3) _____ enormous turtle. This (4) _________ no ordinary turtle because he would often come out of his home in that lake and visit with his Indian neighbors. He made most of his visits to (5) _____ head chief of the tribe, and on these occasions he stayed for hours talking with him.

The chief, seeing that (6) _____ turtle was very smart and showed great wisdom, took a great fancy to him,[1] and whenever (7) _____ difficult question came up before the chief, he generally asked Mr. Turtle to help him decide.

One day there (8) _________ a great misunderstanding between two different groups in (9) _____ tribe. Each side became so angry that the argument threatened to become (10) _____ bloody fight. The chief was unable to decide which side was right, so he said, "I will call Mr. Turtle. He will judge for you."

[1] **took a great fancy to him:** liked him a lot

CD2-09

B Work with a partner. Compare your answers from exercise **A**. Then listen and check your answers.

CD2-10

C Listen to the next part of the story. Take notes to help you answer the questions that follow. Then ask and answer the questions with a partner.

1. Who did Mr. Turtle listen to carefully?
2. Who did the turtle say was right?
3. Why did he make this decision?
4. How did the people react to the turtle's decision? What did they do?

D Work in a group. Make up an ending to the story. Then tell your ending to the class. Decide as a class which group had the best ending.

Connect the Grammar to Writing

1 READ & NOTICE THE GRAMMAR.

A What are some kinds of risks have you taken in your life? Discuss them with a partner. Then read the narrative.

Teen Daredevil: A SURVIVOR'S STORY

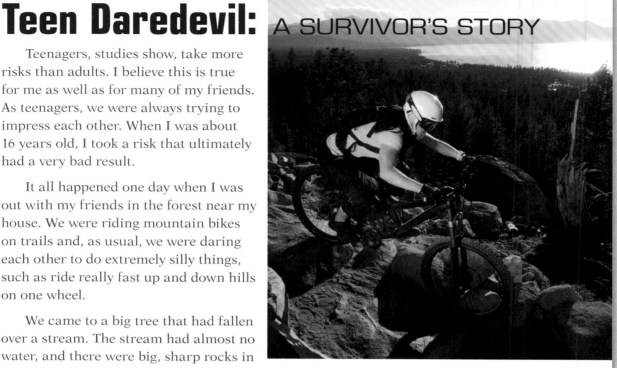

Teenagers, studies show, take more risks than adults. I believe this is true for me as well as for many of my friends. As teenagers, we were always trying to impress each other. When I was about 16 years old, I took a risk that ultimately had a very bad result.

It all happened one day when I was out with my friends in the forest near my house. We were riding mountain bikes on trails and, as usual, we were daring each other to do extremely silly things, such as ride really fast up and down hills on one wheel.

We came to a big tree that had fallen over a stream. The stream had almost no water, and there were big, sharp rocks in it. My friends dared me to ride my bike over the fallen tree. "No problem," I said coolly. There was no way I was going to chicken out[1] now. Everybody was cheering as I rode my bike at top speed. My fear was not as strong as my desire to impress my friends.

Suddenly, I lost control and slipped off the tree, crashing onto the rocks below. I landed on my right arm and felt a sharp pain unlike any I'd ever experienced before. Hours later at the hospital, where my parents had driven me after the accident, I learned that my arm was broken in several places.

After that experience, I became much more cautious. To this day, whenever someone dares me to do something, I think twice before doing it.

[1] **chicken out:** to agree to do something and then not do it because of fear

GRAMMAR FOCUS

In this story, the writer follows these rules of subject-verb agreement.

Subjects follow *be* in sentences with *there.*

*. . . and **there were big, sharp rocks** in it.*

Subjects with *every-, some-, any-,* or *no-* take a singular verb.

***Everybody was** cheering . . .*

Non-count nouns as subjects take singular verbs.

***My fear was** not as strong as . . .*

B Read the narrative in exercise **A** again. Underline more examples of *subject + verb* combinations such as those in the box. Then work with a partner and compare your answers.

2 **BEFORE YOU WRITE.** Work in a group of three or four students. Use the information about the writer of the narrative in exercise **1** as an example. Then tell your group about a risk that you have taken. What were the results of your actions? Complete the chart with notes about people in your group.

Name	Risky Action	Result
Lucy	rode her bike over a tree	broke her arm

WRITING FOCUS Past Perfect Review

Notice how the past perfect is used in the narrative in exercise **1A**.

Writers use the past perfect to describe the sequence of actions or events in the past. The past perfect shows that one action or event happened before another past action or event in the story.

We came to a big tree that ***had fallen*** *over a stream.*

tree fell — came to tree — now

*. . . , and felt a sharp pain unlike any I'****d*** *ever experienced.* (before in her life)

pain experienced before

felt sharp pain — now

3 **WRITE** about a risk that either you or a classmate once took. Write three or four paragraphs. Use your notes from exercise **2** and the narrative in exercise **1A** to help you.

4 **SELF ASSESS.** Read your narrative again. Underline the subjects and verbs in your sentences. Then use the checklist to assess your work.

- ☐ I used count and non-count nouns with the correct quantity expressions. [5.1, 5.2]
- ☐ I used articles correctly. [5.3, 5.4]
- ☐ I used proper subject-verb agreement with count and non-count subjects. [5.5, 5.6]
- ☐ I used the past perfect to describe actions or events that happened before other actions or events in the past. [WRITING FOCUS]

UNIT 6 Wellness

Gerunds and Infinitives

▲ Young Afghan girls play on swings in Kabul, Afghanistan.

EXPLORE

CD2-11

1 READ the article about sleeping. What are sleep researchers trying to find out?

The Mysteries of Sleep

Sleeping takes up about one-third of our lives, and most people need seven to nine hours of sleep a night. Why do we need so much sleep? After decades of research, scientists still don't have an answer, but they do have some theories.

Sleep seems to benefit both the mind and the body. According to some researchers, **sleeping** may improve our memory. It might be that the sleeping brain helps us remember important things **by letting** us forget unimportant things. Other research suggests that the body repairs damaged cells during sleep. Therefore, **not sleeping** may slow the healing process when we get injured. There is also a theory that sleep helps protect us from infection.

Although theories on sleep differ, researchers agree on its importance. Sleep is a necessary part **of living** a healthy life. Unfortunately, conditions such as insomnia are common. In the United States, for example, one-fifth of the population **has difficulty sleeping**. **Working** long hours and **managing** the stresses of modern life are common causes of sleeping problems.

Not getting enough sleep can have serious consequences, including traffic accidents and low productivity at work. Some people are trying to find solutions. In Spain, for example, businessman Ignacio Buqueras y Bach thinks that **watching** late-night television is a problem. In his opinion, TV networks should **consider changing** their schedules so that people can **spend** more **time sleeping**. Now, prime-time[1] programs don't end until midnight or later. Buqueras y Bach's words are relevant[2] for people throughout the world: "Every once in a while we have to close our eyes. We're not machines."

[1] **prime time:** the hours, usually in the evening, when the largest number of people are available to watch television or listen to the radio
[2] **relevant:** important or appropriate

▲ A hiker rests in the grass on the Mount Fox trail. Mount Fox, Westland National Park, Southern Alps, South Island, New Zealand.

2 CHECK. Write answers to the questions with information from the article.

1. What is one theory that researchers have for the reason we sleep?
   ____
2. What is one reason that some people don't get enough sleep?
   ____
3. What can happen if you don't get enough sleep?
   ____
4. What does Ignacio Buqueras y Bach think TV networks should do?
   ____

3 DISCOVER. Complete the exercises to learn about the grammar in this lesson.

A Write the missing words in the sentences from the article in exercise **1**.

1. ___Sleeping___ takes up about one-third of our lives.
2. It might be that the sleeping brain helps us remember important things by ______________ us forget unimportant things.
3. Sleep is a necessary part of ______________ a healthy life.
4. ______________ enough sleep can have serious consequences.
5. In his opinion, TV networks should consider ______________ their schedules so that people can spend more time ______________.

B The words you wrote in exercise **A** are gerunds. Look back at exercise **A**. Then read the statements below. Circle **T** for *true* or **F** for *false*.

1. A gerund can be the subject of a sentence. **T** **F**
2. A gerund can be the object of a preposition. **T** **F**
3. A gerund can be the main verb in a sentence. **T** **F**

LEARN

6.1 Gerunds as Subjects and Objects

	Gerund as Subject	Gerund as Object
Gerund	**Reading** is my favorite hobby.	I love **cooking**.
Negative Gerund	**Not eating** at restaurants saves money.	We considered **not going**.
Gerund Phrase	**Running in the park** is good exercise.	They enjoy **baking cookies**.

1. A gerund is an *-ing* form of a verb.* It functions as a noun (subject or object) in a sentence.	**Hiking** is fun for all ages. We enjoy **traveling**.
2. A gerund can be part of a gerund phrase. A gerund phrase can be the subject or object of a sentence.	**Seeing a movie** is a great idea. They enjoyed **hearing that song**.
3. Add *not* to make a gerund negative.	**Not sleeping** enough is a problem.
4. These common verbs can be followed by gerunds: *avoid, consider, dislike, enjoy, finish, keep, involve, mind, quit, practice, require, suggest.***	Have you **finished eating**? **Keep practicing**. Your skills will improve.
5. Use the third-person singular form of the verb when a gerund or gerund phrase is the subject.	Winning the race (Gerund Phrase) was (Verb) an accomplishment.
6. **Remember:** The *-ing* form of a verb can be a progressive verb or a gerund.	Progressive: She **was jogging** on the beach. Gerund: **Jogging** is her hobby.

*See page **A2** for spelling rules for the *-ing* form of verbs.
See page **A4 for a longer list of verbs followed by a gerund.

4 Complete the exercises.

A Check (✓) the sentences with gerunds or gerund phrases. Then underline each gerund or gerund phrase.

____ 1. The baby is taking a nap. Try to be quiet.

__✓__ 2. Taking a nap in the afternoon is good for you.

____ 3. Not getting eight hours of sleep a night is often a problem for adults.

____ 4. I haven't seen a sleep expert yet, but I'm considering the idea.

____ 5. Meditating helps some people sleep better.

____ 6. Most people dislike waking up early in the morning.

____ 7. Do you mind sleeping with a light on?

____ 8. Staying up late is a common habit of teenagers.

____ 9. I like exercising. It helps me sleep.

____ 10. Too many teens aren't getting enough sleep.

B **ANALYZE THE GRAMMAR.** Work with a partner. Label each gerund or gerund phrase in exercise **A** with **S** for *subject* or **O** for *object of a verb*.

S
Taking a nap in the afternoon is good for you.

6.2 Gerunds as Objects of Prepositions

1. A gerund is the only verb form that can follow a preposition (*about, at, by, for, in, of . . .*).	✓ You can achieve your goals **by working** hard. ✗ You can achieve your goals by work hard.
2. These common verb + preposition combinations can be followed by a gerund: *believe in, dream about, succeed in, think about.*	She has finally **succeeded in getting** a license. He is **thinking about getting** his own apartment.
3. These common noun + preposition combinations can be followed by a gerund: *advantage of, benefit of, purpose for/of, reason for.*	What's the **advantage of taking** vitamins? I don't know his **reason for writing** the letter.
4. These common adjective + preposition combinations can be followed by a gerund: *afraid of, interested in, tired of, worried about.*	I'm **interested in learning** more about baseball. I'm **tired of waiting** for the bus.

*See page **A4** for a list of verbs, nouns, and adjectives often followed by a preposition + gerund.

5 Complete the sentences with the correct preposition and the gerund form of the verb in parentheses.

1. Not everyone is interested in thinking (think) about their dreams.
2. What is the purpose ______________ (dream)?
3. What is a possible reason ______________ (have) bad dreams?
4. Have you ever succeeded ______________ (understand) your dreams?
5. Sometimes I dream ______________ (meet) a famous person.
6. In other dreams, I'm afraid ______________ (stay) home alone.
7. Some people don't believe ______________ (analyze) their dreams.
8. I never get tired ______________ (try) to figure out my dreams.

6.3 Gerunds with Nouns and Special Expressions

1. Some common nouns are often followed by gerunds. For example: *fun, difficulty, experience, problem, trouble.*	I had **fun playing** the video game. Did you have **difficulty finding** the house?
2. Some common expressions with *time* and *money* are often followed by gerunds. They occur with these verbs: *spend, waste,* and *have.*	She didn't **spend time exercising** yesterday. Don't **waste money buying** a new exercise bike. I've always **had a hard time losing** weight.

6 Complete the exercises.

A Complete the conversations with the correct form of the words in parentheses.

1. **A:** Lately, I've had ___trouble staying___ (trouble / stay) awake at my job.

   B: Why? Are you having ______________ (difficulty / fall) asleep?

2. **A:** Yes. I'm wasting ______________ (time / lie) in bed for hours.

   B: I'm sorry to hear that. Do you have ______________ (problems / deal) with stress?

3. **A:** Sometimes I worry about work. Then I have ______________ (trouble / calm down).

   B: You know, I have ______________ (experience / teach) people effective sleep techniques.

4. **A:** Really? It would be ______________ (fun / learn) from you.

   B: Come to my class tonight. We have a great ______________ (time / practice) relaxation techniques.

B **SPEAK.** Work with a partner. Discuss any techniques you know for falling asleep.

I like doing yoga or meditating.

PRACTICE

7 Complete the paragraph with the words in parentheses. Use a gerund and add a preposition when necessary.

(1) ___Dreaming about___ (dream) insects can be scary. However, not all insects are bad. In fact, many people in the world have positive feelings about insects. People in Eastern Europe, for example, believe that if a person sees a red butterfly, it means that he or she will have good health. In addition, some people (2) ______________ (believe / eat) insects as part of a healthy diet.

People (3) ______________ (enjoy / dine) on insects in many parts of the world. (4) ______________ (cook and eat) these creatures is common, for example, in Asia and Latin America.

▶ Grasshopper, cricket, and giant scorpion lollipops. France and the Netherlands are two countries making insect sweets.

▼ Peacock butterfly in the Netherlands. Butterflies have symbolism in many countries, including China, Russia, and Japan.

There are actually many (5) ______ (benefits / eat) bugs. If you (6) ______ (have difficulty / believe) this, I (7) ______ (suggest / look) at the facts. Insects have a high amount of protein. Just take grasshoppers. They have 60 percent protein and they are rich in calcium.

Do people ever have any (8) ______ (problems / eat) insects? Yes. Some contain toxins. It's best to (9) ______ (avoid / eat) yellow, red, or orange bugs and any bugs that smell strong. Black, brown, or green bugs are generally fine.

Are you interested (10) ______ (try) something new and healthy? Then (11) ______ (think / include) more bugs in your diet.

8 LISTEN, WRITE & SPEAK.

CD2-12

A Work with a partner. Read the choices to complete each tip for losing weight. Which do you think are good? Tell your partner. Then listen and choose the answers you hear.

TIP 1: Eat ______.

a. food with bread   b. food cut in pieces   c. one piece of food

TIP 2: Schedule your biggest meal ______.

a. in the morning   b. in the afternoon   c. at night

TIP 3: Eat ______ and stop when you are full.

a. slowly   b. quickly   c. slowly or quickly

CD2-12

B Listen again. Then complete the sentences with the words you hear. You can use a verb more than once.

1. a. ___Cutting your food___ into small pieces may help you eat less.
   b. ______________________ of food may satisfy people more than having one large piece.
2. a. Some researchers believe that ______________ the largest meal of the day in the early afternoon helps people control their weight better than ______________ late in the day.
   b. One theory is that when we eat late in the day, it causes our body to have problems ______________.
3. a. ______________________ gives your body a chance to process food properly.
   b. ______________ the total amount of food you eat helps you avoid ______________ and other health problems.

C Work in groups. Discuss your ideas for eating well. Use gerunds

A: *Eating several small meals a day is better than eating one large one.*

B: *I have problems finding time to eat during the day. That's why I eat at the end of the day.*

9 WRITE & SPEAK.

A Read the sentences about healthy habits that help you live longer. Then rewrite the sentences with gerunds. Use *by* where necessary.

1. If you floss your teeth every day, it could add three to five years to your life.
   ___Flossing your teeth every day could add three to five years to your life.___
2. You may add six years to your life if you don't smoke.
   ____
3. You should lift weights. It could add five to six years to your life.
   ____
4. You could add five years to your life if you eat fruits and vegetables.
   ____
5. You should get enough sleep. It may add three years to your life.
   ____
6. You could add two years to your life if you walk every day.
   ____

B Work with a partner. Suggest five more pieces of advice to help people live longer. Use gerund form of the verbs *avoid, consider, think about, spend time,* and *practice.*

People should spend more time relaxing.

10 EDIT. Read the paragraph about fitness and technology. Find and correct seven more errors with gerunds.

Tech Tools for Healthy Living

~~Use~~ Using technology is a big part of daily life. Today there are many products that can help us succeed in reach our dietary and fitness goals. Is planning meals a problem for you? Are you tired of spend time search for healthy recipes? Downloading diet-related apps to your cell phone may be the answer. Apps can put the fun back into eat well.

Apps are also great for helping you get a good workout. If you are a runner, perhaps improve your speed is your goal. If so, a GPS watch is perfect for you. Do you need to be especially careful during your run? Take advantage of the heart monitor. It will prevent you from overdo your workout. If you swim, you may find that doing laps can get boring, especially when you are swimming long distances. But swimming is much more fun with a pair of waterproof headphones that play your favorite music.

Try these different products—you will have no excuse for being not able to stay fit!

11 APPLY.

A Complete the sentences about your habits. Use gerunds.

1. I don't have fun ______________________________.
2. I have thought about ______________________________ in order to stay fit.
3. When I exercise, I avoid ______________________________.
4. ______________________________ doesn't bother me.
5. I am always worried about ______________________________.
6. A while ago I quit ______________________________ because ______________________________.
7. ______________________________ gives me a headache.
8. When I was younger, I had a hard time ______________________________.

B Work in groups. Tell each other four of your sentences from exercise **A**. Ask questions to get more information. Use gerunds when possible.

A: *I don't have fun exercising.*

B: *Why not?*

A: *I think being in the gym is boring.*

EXPLORE

CD2-13

1 READ the article about a place where ancient healing is helping to advance modern medicine. Why are scientists in a hurry to learn as much as they can?

Medical Riches in the Rainforests

The world's rainforests are of great interest to medical scientists. In those forests, scientists have found treatments for a wide range of conditions, from headaches to malaria. Researchers also **hope to find** cures for cancer there. According to the National Cancer Institute, 70 percent of plants that may be useful in cancer treatment grow only in rainforests. Only some of them have been studied so far.

Scientists often depend on the knowledge of traditional healers. The scientists **want the healers to show** them where plants are growing in the rainforest. Gervasio Noceda, for example, is a well-known healer in Paraguay. He is a shaman[1], and his knowledge of medicinal plants equals that of a medical library. When Noceda **prepares to lead** a group of researchers on a search for plants, he chants and prays. Perhaps he **is hoping to establish** a spiritual connection with the forest. When he is ready, the search begins. The researchers often **ask him to find** a plant root[2] called *suruvi*. When *suruvi* is made into a tea, it is used to treat a variety of illnesses. With Noceda's help, some researchers have published a book on medicinal plants. It is a rich source of information that **helps people to identify** and **study** plants more easily.

Scientists feel **fortunate to have** the benefit of the healers' knowledge. They **need to work** quickly, though. Deforestation[3] is a serious problem, so it is urgent[4] **to identify**, **record**, and **analyze** the plants of the rainforests before it is too late.

[1] **shaman:** a wise person who is thought to have magic or spiritual powers
[2] **root:** the part of a plant that grows underground
[3] **deforestation:** the cutting down or destruction of trees for farming, wood, or fuel
[4] **urgent:** needing attention as soon as possible

▲ A shaman in the Cofan region, Ecuador

▶ The cinchona tree grows in the rainforests of South America. Its bark is used in a medicine for malaria.

2 CHECK. Check (✓) the statements that are true according to the article.

_____ 1. There is a large number of medicinal plants that you can find only in rainforests.

_____ 2. Researchers have studied most of the medicinal plants of the rainforest.

_____ 3. Scientists and healers work together to find and identify useful plants.

_____ 4. Gervasio Noceda learned about plants in a medical library.

_____ 5. The loss of rainforests in the future is a possibility.

3 DISCOVER. Complete the exercises to learn about the grammar in this lesson.

A Write the missing words in the sentences from the article in exercise **1**.

1. Researchers also hope ___to find___ cures for cancer there.
2. The scientists want the healers ____________ them where plants are growing in the rainforest.
3. The researchers often ask him ____________ a plant root called *suruvi*.
4. Scientists feel fortunate ____________ the benefit of the healers' knowledge.
5. They need ____________ quickly, though.

B The verbs you wrote in exercise **A** are infinitives. Look back at the word that comes before each infinitive. Write it in the chart. Then check (✓) the correct column.

	Adjective	Noun	Pronoun	Verb
1. hope				✓
2.				
3.				
4.				
5.				

LEARN

6.4 Infinitives: Verbs (+ Object) + Infinitive

Verb + Infinitive	Verb + Object + Infinitive	Verb (+ Object) + Infinitive
We **have decided to go** to Chile. She **promised to be** on time.	He **reminded his son to study**. He **convinced me to study** medicine.	I **want to see** the doctor. I **want you to see** the doctor.

1. Certain verbs can be followed by an infinitive (*to* + the base form of a verb) or an infinitive phrase.	I like to eat. (Infinitive) I like to eat chocolate cake. (Infinitive Phrase)
2. These verbs can be followed by an infinitive: *afford, decide, hope, know how, plan, promise, seem.*	I **hope to get** better at diving. Do you **know how to swim**?
3. These verbs can be followed by an object + an infinitive: *advise, allow, convince, encourage, remind, teach, tell, urge, warn.**	The teacher **encourages us to ask** questions in class. I **urge you to consider** your plans carefully.
4. Some verbs can be followed by either an infinitive or an object + an infinitive, but the meaning is different: *ask, expect, need, pay, want, would like.**	He **expected to pay** for dinner. He **expected me to pay** for dinner.
5. Add *not* before the infinitive to make the infinitive negative.	They promised **not to be** late.
6. **Be careful!** Use an infinitive after *want* and *would like*, not *that*.	✓ I want you to exercise more. ✗ I want that you exercise more.

*See page **A5** for a list of verbs followed by an infinitive and verbs followed by an object + an infinitive.

4 Circle the correct answers.

Dear Professor Bartoli,

I'm writing to tell you that I've decided (1) **not to continue / to not continue** my medical research here. My family in Paraguay (2) **needs / needs me** to come home. While I still plan (3) **to finish / me to finish** my degree, I will do so in Paraguay. Thank you so much for everything you have taught me. I now know how (4) **to present / me to present** my research findings in a professional way. You have also taught (5) **to use / me to use** lots of new techniques to study plants. I promise (6) **not to forget / to not forget** anything I have learned. Please tell me if you would like (7) **to return / me to return** any of your papers before I leave. Finally, I want to encourage (8) **to come / you to come** to Paraguay in the future. It will give me great pleasure to show you some of our wonderful rainforest plants.

Sincerely,

Mariana Vera

5 Complete a health care worker's statements. Use the words given. Put the words in the correct order. Use the infinitive form once in each sentence.

1. ask / people / we / be patient

   We ask people to be patient in the waiting room.

2. follow / my patients / would like / I

   ______________________ their doctors' orders.

3. everyone / I / stop smoking / advise

   ____

4. our patients / we / exercise / encourage

   ______________________ every day.

5. avoid / advise / we / them

   ______________________ certain foods.

6. be careful / older people / need

   ______________________ about their diet.

7. not worry / I / urge / our patients

   ____

8. people / I / not lose / remind

   ______________________ their sense of humor.

6.5 Verbs Followed by a Gerund or Infinitive without a Change in Meaning

1. Some verbs can be followed by a gerund or an infinitive with no or almost no difference in meaning. These verbs include: *begin, (not) bother, can't stand, continue, hate, like, love, prefer, start.*	I **began exercising** regularly last year. I **began to exercise** regularly last year. Don't **bother making dinner**. We'll go out tonight. Don't **bother to make dinner**. We'll go out tonight.
2. You can use *prefer* to compare two activities in the following ways: a. *prefer* + gerund + *to* + gerund/noun b. *prefer* + infinitive + *rather than* + verb	 a. I **prefer swimming to running**. b. I **prefer to swim** rather than **run**.

6 Complete the exercises.

A Rewrite the sentences. Change the gerunds to infinitives (sentences 1–4) and the infinitives to gerunds (sentences 5–8).

1. I can't stand staying in bed all day long when I'm sick.

   I can't stand to stay in bed all day long when I'm sick.

2. I prefer using medicinal plants to taking medicine.

____

3. I like getting phone calls from my friends when I'm sick.

____

4. When I feel ill, I start looking up my symptoms on the Internet.

____

5. I begin to worry right away when I have symptoms.

____

6. I prefer to wait rather than go to the doctor immediately.

____

7. I don't bother to tell anyone when I don't feel well.

____

8. I hate to sit in the waiting room at the doctor's office.

____

B SPEAK. Work with a partner. Say which sentences in exercise **A** are true for you.

A: *When I don't feel well, I can't stand to stay in bed all day long.*

B: *Me neither. I get bored and my back starts to bother me.*

6.6 Verbs Followed by a Gerund or Infinitive with a Change in Meaning

1. Some verbs can be followed by a gerund or infinitive, but with a change in meaning. These verbs are *stop*, *remember*, and *forget*.	I'll never **forget meeting** you for the very first time. Sorry, I **forgot to meet** you at the gym yesterday.
2. Use *stop* + a gerund to say that a person or thing ended an activity. Use *stop* + an infinitive to tell the reason why a person or animal stopped. The infinitive gives the reason.	He **stopped drinking** coffee a year ago. My car **stopped working**. It was a long drive. We only **stopped to eat** lunch. The cat **stopped to watch** the bird.
3. Use *remember* + a gerund to talk about a memory or something in the past. *Remember* + an infinitive means you remember to do a necessary task or action.	I **remember calling** last week, but I don't remember what day it was. He never **remembers to call** when he arrives safely.
4. Use *forget* + a gerund to talk about a memory. It is often used with a negative. *Forget* + an infinitive means someone did not remember to do a necessary task or action.	I'll never **forget hiking** to the top of the mountain. I **didn't forget meeting** him. I just forgot his name. He often **forgets to do** his homework. Did you **forget to pay** the rent?

7 Complete the stories with the gerund or infinitive form of each verb in parentheses.

Nina Garfield, Avalanche Survivor

Nina Garfield almost didn't survive her recent ski trip. She remembers (1) ___enjoying___ (enjoy) a beautiful day on the mountain with her friends, all expert skiers. All of a sudden, the snow started moving underneath her. Nina remembers (2) ________ (fall) and rolling around in the snow. Luckily, the snow didn't bury her. What saved Nina's life? When she was packing, she remembered (3) ________ (put) airbags into her backpack. When the avalanche began, the airbags opened and helped Nina keep her head above the snow. She says that she'll never forget (4) ________ (bring) airbags with her on ski trips in the future.

Juan Ramos, K2 Climb Survivor

When Juan Ramos was close to the top of K2, the second highest mountain in the world, it was evening and already getting dark. He stopped (5) ________ (admire) the view. Then, he began his return trip down to the camp. However, it began to snow hard, so he had to stop (6) ________ (move) because he couldn't see. He stayed on the mountain for two freezing, stormy nights before the weather cleared. Fortunately, he had not forgotten (7) ________ (bring) a lot of water with him. Not drinking enough can be life-threatening in high altitudes. Ramos says he'll never forget (8) ________ (feel) such fear.

PRACTICE

8 Complete the exercises.

A Read each statement. Complete the sentence so that it is similar in meaning to the statement. Use infinitives in your answers.

1. "Last time I had a cold, I forgot about taking vitamin C. This time, I took it." (Aaron)

   Aaron remembered ___to take vitamin C___.

2. "My grandfather thinks I should take a walk by the sea." (James)

   James's grandfather wants James ________.

3. "I don't like to take medicine. I think drinking hot milk is much better." (Suzana)

   Suzana prefers ________.

4. "Make sure you rub plant oil on your back." (Li's mom)

   Li's mom reminded him ________.

5. "My parents say that I can't drink coffee or soda." (Lisa)

   Lisa's parents don't allow Lisa ________.

6. "My mother can make noodle soup that cures colds." (Sang)

   Sang's mother knows how ____.

7. "I still have a cold, so I need to keep resting as much as possible." (Felipe)

   Felipe should continue ____.

8. "My mother said adding garlic to my soup will cure anything." (Oscar)

   Oscar's mother reminded him ____.

B **SPEAK.** Work in groups. Discuss ways you deal with a cold. Use gerunds and infinitives.

My mother always told me to drink a lot of orange juice.

9 Complete the exercises.

A Complete the article. Use the correct form of the verbs in parentheses. Add an object pronoun where necessary. Sometimes either the gerund or the infinitive form of the verb is correct.

Can venom be good for you?

While Michael was on vacation in Mexico, he (1) ___decided to go___ (decide / go) for a swim. It was very hot, and he (2) ____________________ (want / get) some cool relief. He jumped into the pool, but instead of relief, all of a sudden he (3) ____________________ (start / feel) a burning pain in his leg. He looked down and saw his attacker—a poisonous scorpion. Michael got to a local hospital quickly, and about 30 hours later, the pain (4) ____________________ (seem / disappear). He was very relieved.

But that isn't the end of the story. Before the scorpion bite, Michael had been suffering from back pain. Doctors had often (5) ____________________ (encourage / him / do) regular exercise such as swimming. Surprisingly, days after the scorpion bite, his back pain went away, and it never came back. The scorpion's venom had cured him. Whenever he (6) ____________________ (remember / suffer) from his horrible back pain, he is grateful for that scorpion.

Experts (7) ____________________ (advise / people / not go) anywhere near scorpions or snakes. But if scorpion researchers (8) ____________________ (stop / work) with these creatures, we might not find out more about the medical benefits their venom can provide.

A venomous bark scorpion, Arizona, United States ▶

CD2-14

B Listen and check your answers.

10 **EDIT.** Read the poster. Find and correct seven more errors with gerunds and infinitives.

First-Aid Tips for Treating Cuts

Do you remember ~~to cut~~ cutting yourself when you were a child? Did you know how take care of the cut, or did you ask to someone to help you? Of course, it's not only children who cut themselves. That is why we urge everyone having a first-aid kit at home. We also want you follow this advice.

- For minor cuts: After the cut stops to bleed, start rinsing the wound with clear water. Clean the area around the wound with soap and a washcloth. Avoid getting soap directly in the wound.
- For deep cuts: Put pressure on the cut to stop the bleeding. Continue to putting pressure on the wound for 20 or 30 minutes.
- If the wound can get dirty, put a bandage on it and remember changing it every day.
- Remember! Teach your children about first aid, and remind them to not play with sharp objects.

11 Read the situations about sports injuries. Then complete the sentences. Use infinitives and gerunds where necessary.

Lucy used to run every weekend, but she doesn't now because her feet have been hurting her a lot. She hates to miss her runs, and she's tired of being in pain, so she goes to see a foot specialist. The specialist's advice: "Wear proper shoes. Ice your feet often. Your feet will always give you trouble unless you follow my advice."

1. Lucy has stopped running every weekend.
2. Lucy can't stand ______________________.
3. Lucy decides ______________________ because of the problem with her feet.
4. The foot specialist warns Lucy ______________________ or she will continue to have pain.
5. The specialist also tells Lucy ______________________ often.
6. The specialist tells her she needs to follow his advice or her feet will continue ______________________.

Jake's favorite sport is mountain biking, but recently he's been biking less because of pain in his knees. It costs him a lot of money, but Jake goes to see a sports injury specialist. Some advice from the specialist: "Raise the seat of the bike. Do leg muscle exercises in the gym." Jake will remember to do the exercises every day because he wants to go mountain biking again soon.

7. Jake loves ______________________________.
8. Jake pays ____________________________________.
9. The specialist has advised Jake ______________________________.
10. The specialist wants Jake ______________________________ in the gym.
11. Jake won't forget __________________________________.
12. Jake hopes _______________________________________.

12 APPLY.

A Check (✓) the medical problems you have had. Then make notes about how you have dealt with the problems.

Medical Problems	(✓)	Ways That I Have Dealt with the Problem
Burn		
Earache		
Headache		
Muscle pain		
Sprained ankle		
Toothache		
Other:		

B Write six sentences about the problems you checked in exercise **A**. Use some of the verbs in the box. Remember to use gerunds and infinitives appropriately.

advise	begin	encourage	forget	remember	start	want
ask	continue	expect	prefer	remind	stop	warn

The last time I had a burn, my friend advised me to put ice on the burn. I felt better right away, and I think my burn healed faster.

C Work in groups. Share your sentences. Ask questions to get more information.

EXPLORE

CD2-15

1 **READ** the article about the work of one man, Feliciano dos Santos, in his home country. What are some serious problems in the part of Mozambique where he is from?

The Guitar Man

For Feliciano dos Santos, a guitar is an excellent weapon in the fight against disease. Along with his band, Massukos, Santos plays music to educate people about how personal hygiene[1] helps to prevent illness. In fact, one of the band's greatest hits is *Tissambe Manja*, which means "Wash Our Hands."

Santos performs in some of the poorest, most remote[2] villages of his home country, Mozambique. His songs provide information and motivation for villagers. He uses traditional music, rhythms, and local languages to get his message across.

Santos has focused his efforts on Niassa, the part of Mozambique where he is from. He has not forgotten the challenges of growing up there. In Niassa, there is **not enough clean water to meet** people's needs. Unclean water is the cause of many diseases, including polio. As a child, Santos had polio, and he knows how it feels to be ill. He also knows that many of the people are **too poor to travel** for medical care.

In addition to performing, Santos works on projects to improve sanitation.[3] Thanks to Santos, there are now water pumps and low-cost, environmentally friendly toilets in many villages. **It wasn't easy to make** these changes, but the project was **effective enough to provide** Niassa with a basic sanitation system. Santos's projects have been so successful that they now serve as models for other development programs around the world.

"Music has the power to change people."
—Feliciano dos Santos

▼ Feliciano dos Santos

[1] **hygiene:** the practice of keeping yourself and your surroundings clean
[2] **remote:** far away from places where most people live
[3] **sanitation:** the process of keeping a place clean and healthy

2 CHECK. Correct the error in each sentence so that it is true according to the article.

1. Feliciano dos Santos uses a ~~piano~~ guitar to teach people about keeping clean.
2. Santos's band plays songs in English to communicate their message.
3. Santos does most of his work in small cities in Mozambique.
4. Santos thinks that Niassa needs more traditional music.
5. Other countries have little to learn from Santos's sanitation projects.

3 DISCOVER. Complete the exercises to learn about the grammar in this lesson.

A Underline the infinitives in the sentences from the article on page 161.

1. In Niassa, there is not enough clean water to meet people's needs.
2. He also knows that many of the people are too poor to travel for medical care.
3. It wasn't easy to make these changes.
4. The project was effective enough to provide Niassa with a basic sanitation system.

B Look back at the sentences in exercise **A**. Pay attention to the words before the infinitive and after the main verb. Write the number of the sentence that has each pattern.

_____ a. adjective + *enough* + infinitive

_____ b. adjective + infinitive

_____ c. *enough* + (adjective) + noun + infinitive

_____ d. *too* + adjective + infinitive

▲ Feliciano dos Santos

LEARN

6.7 Infinitives after the Subject *It*; Infinitives after Adjectives

1. An infinitive phrase is often used in a sentence that has *it* as the subject. *It* has the same meaning as the infinitive phrase at the end of the sentence.	**It** is fun **to go to the beach**. Subject Infinitive Phrase
2. The following verbs are common between *it* and the infinitive phrase: *appear, be, cost, seem, take.*	**It costs** a lot **to take** the course. **It takes** time **to lose** weight.
3. The following adjectives are common between *it* and the infinitive phrase: *challenging, difficult, easy, exciting, important, necessary, rewarding.*	**It** is **easy to learn** English. **It** is **important to pay** attention in class.
4. The following adjectives do not follow *it*, but they are also common before an infinitive: *afraid, determined, disappointed, easy, glad, lucky, relieved, reluctant, willing.**	I'm **determined to get** a good score on the exam. I'm **reluctant to pay** for private lessons. We're **not willing to share** one book.
5. When an infinitive follows an adjective, use *for* + an object (*for someone*) before the infinitive to indicate who or what the adjective refers to.	The exercises are hard **for young children** to do.

*See page **A5** for a list of adjectives followed by infinitives.

4 Rewrite the first part of each sentence with *it* as the subject. Use infinitives.

1. Helping people from Niassa is rewarding for Feliciano dos Santos.

   It is rewarding for Feliciano dos Santos to help ________ people from Niassa.

2. Communication is possible through music.

   ________________________ through music.

3. Learning about sanitation is important for children.

   ________________________ about sanitation.

4. Educating people about good hygiene takes a lot of thought.

   ________________________ about good hygiene.

5. Washing your hands frequently is necessary to prevent disease.

   ________________________ to prevent disease.

6. Getting clean water to a remote village takes time.

   ________________________ to a remote village.

5 Complete the sentences. Use the verb *be*, the adjectives in parentheses, and infinitives.

1. Some people are uncomfortable with trying new health practices.

   Some people are reluctant to try new health practices (reluctant).

2. Governments must be open to solving problems.

   Governments ________________ (willing).

3. Some countries are afraid of making changes.

   Some countries ________________ (unwilling).

4. Many people feel strongly about getting good health care.

   Many people ________________ (determined).

5. Some people do not like talking about illness.

   Some people ________________ (hesitant).

6. We really want to make the world a healthier place.

   We ________________ (ready).

6.8 *Too* and *Enough* with Infinitives

Too + Infinitive	*Enough* + Infinitive
The hospital is **too small to treat** everyone. We have **too much homework to do**. The doctor has **too many patients to see**.	The hospital is **big enough to treat** everyone. Is there **enough food to feed** everybody? Are there **enough eggs to make** an omelet?

1. *Too* + an adjective means "more than what is wanted or possible." You can use the infinitive after *too* + an adjective to explain why something is not possible.	He is **too weak to walk**. The medicine is **too strong to take daily**.
2. You can also use the infinitive after *too* + a noun to explain why something is not possible. Use these patterns: a. *too much* + non-count noun + infinitive b. *too many* + plural count noun + infinitive	 a. I have **too much work to do**. b. There are **too many children to take** care of.
3. *Enough* means "an amount that is wanted or possible." *Not enough* means "less than is wanted or possible." Use the infinitive after an adjective + *enough* or after *enough* + a noun.	They are **(not) tall enough to reach** the shelf. We have **enough data to write** the report.
4. A noun object or pronoun may come before the infinitive in sentences with *too* and *enough*. Use *for* before the noun or pronoun.	The music isn't loud enough **for me to hear**. The chair is too small **for my father to sit** in. There is not enough time **for her to visit**.

6 Circle the correct words to complete the paragraph about an African health clinic that is mobile (on wheels).

Sometimes people don't have (1) **enough information / information enough** to make the right health choices. At our mobile clinic, it's hard for the staff to explain (2) **too many / too much** things at one time. That's why we hold educational workshops several times a week. Our meeting room is (3) **enough big / big enough** to hold 30 people. The doctors and nurses have learned to speak the local language, so their language skills are good enough (4) **for them / for they** to communicate with the villagers. At the meetings, we explain all the medical services we offer. At the end of the meetings, we always have (5) **enough / too many** time to answer questions.

If people find that it costs (6) **too many / too much** money to use our services, we treat them for free. When they live (7) **far enough / too far** away to travel to a hospital, we can help them instead. There aren't (8) **enough health clinics / health clinics enough** in many areas of Mozambique, so it's really important to have mobile health clinics that can come to the areas that need them.

6.9 Infinitives of Purpose

	Purpose
She went to the store	**in order to** get bread. **to get** bread.

1. Use an infinitive of purpose to say why someone does something or what something is for.	He teaches **in order to help** others. We use this scale **to weigh** ourselves.
2. Use *in order not to* for negative purposes.	I drink a lot of water **in order not to get** dehydrated.
3. **Be careful!** Do not use *for* to say why someone does something.	✓ I'm taking this class **to learn** English. ✗ I'm taking this class for learning English.

7 Complete the sentences. Use *to* or *in order not to* and the verbs in parentheses.

1. Paulo practices medicine to help (help) people around the world.
2. He follows several steps ______________ (make) mistakes or waste supplies at work.
3. He volunteers ______________ (bring) health care to poor places.
4. Paulo is working in a lab ______________ (develop) a new medicine for diabetes.
5. He writes papers ______________ (inform) other doctors about his research.

6. He also pays attention to other doctors' work ______________________ (learn) as much as he can.
7. He avoids complex language ______________________ (confuse) patients.
8. He listens to people ______________________ (try) to understand their health concerns.
9. Paulo's organization always needs money ______________________ (pay) for projects.
10. It organizes concerts with famous performers ______________________ (raise) money.

PRACTICE

8 Read the paragraph about Dr. Hayat Sindi and her research to improve health care. Insert *to* where it is missing in each sentence in **bold**.

Dr. Hayat Sindi is a medical researcher from Saudi Arabia. (1) **She has co-invented and developed a way** ^to **detect disease with a tiny piece of paper.** (2) **It appears be an ordinary piece of paper, but it is not.** (3) **It took a lot of time for her develop the device**; (4) **however, she was determined find a simple, inexpensive way monitor health**. Sindi's organization, Diagnostics for All (DFA), brings affordable health diagnoses to the world's poorest people.

(5) **There has never been a problem too great for Sindi solve**. (6) **When she moved to England continue her studies,** (7) **her English was not good enough attend university**. But that did not stop her. She improved her English by watching news broadcasts, and (8) **she studied up to 20 hours a day prepare for college entrance exams.** (9) **She was the first Saudi woman study at Cambridge University in the field of biotechnology.** Sindi's accomplishments have made her a role model for women and girls around the world. (10) **She feels it is important for women know that they can transform society.**

▶ Hayat Sindi, emerging explorer and science entrepreneur

9 Read the information in the chart about medical innovations. Then use the words to write sentences with infinitives. Use the simple present. Add *not* and *for* when necessary.

Medical Innovations		
Device	How It Works	Purpose
Diagnostics for All (DFA) patterned paper	The paper "reads" a sample from a patient. If there is an illness, the paper changes color.	Detects illness cheaply and without a lot of equipment
CellScope Oto™ cell phone attachment by CellScope, Inc.	People use their smartphone as a microscope.	Lets parents diagnose their children's ear infections easily, without going to a doctor
Headache-curing implant by Autonomic Technologies, Inc.	The device sends a message to the brain before a headache starts.	Improves the lives of headache sufferers

Patterned Paper by Diagnostics for All

1. the paper / cost / too much / produce

   The paper doesn't cost too much to produce.

2. DFA / produce / the paper / provide inexpensive medical care

   ____

3. it / be / difficult / detect / an illness / with DFA

   ____

The CellScope Oto™ by CellScope, Inc.

4. parents / use / a cell phone / diagnose their children's ear infections

   ____

5. the CellScope Oto / is / hard / parents / use

   ____

6. parents / have / enough time / go to the doctor for every earache

   ____

Headache-Curing Implant by Autonomic Technologies, Inc.

7. people / are / glad / have / relief from headaches

   ____

8. the device / act / early enough / prevent a headache

   ____

10 WRITE & SPEAK. Work with a partner. Answer the questions about health using infinitives and your own ideas. Then share your answers with your partner.

1. Why shouldn't people eat too many sweets?
   To avoid problems with their teeth.
2. Why do researchers invent new things?
   ____
3. Why should we support health research?
   ____
4. Why should every home have a first-aid kit?
   ____
5. Why do people choose to be medical workers?
   ____

REAL ENGLISH

Infinitives of purpose are often used to answer questions with *Why*.

A: ***Why*** *are you going to the store?*
B: ***To buy*** *some fruit.*

11 LISTEN & WRITE.

CD2-16

A Listen to an interview with a public health researcher in Thailand. Check (✓) the statements that are true according to what you hear.

Thailand: A Health Care Success Story

_____ 1. The government of Thailand has universal health care for Thai people.

_____ 2. Thailand was a wealthy country 20 years ago but is not as wealthy today.

_____ 3. Other countries are studying the health model in Thailand to improve their own health care.

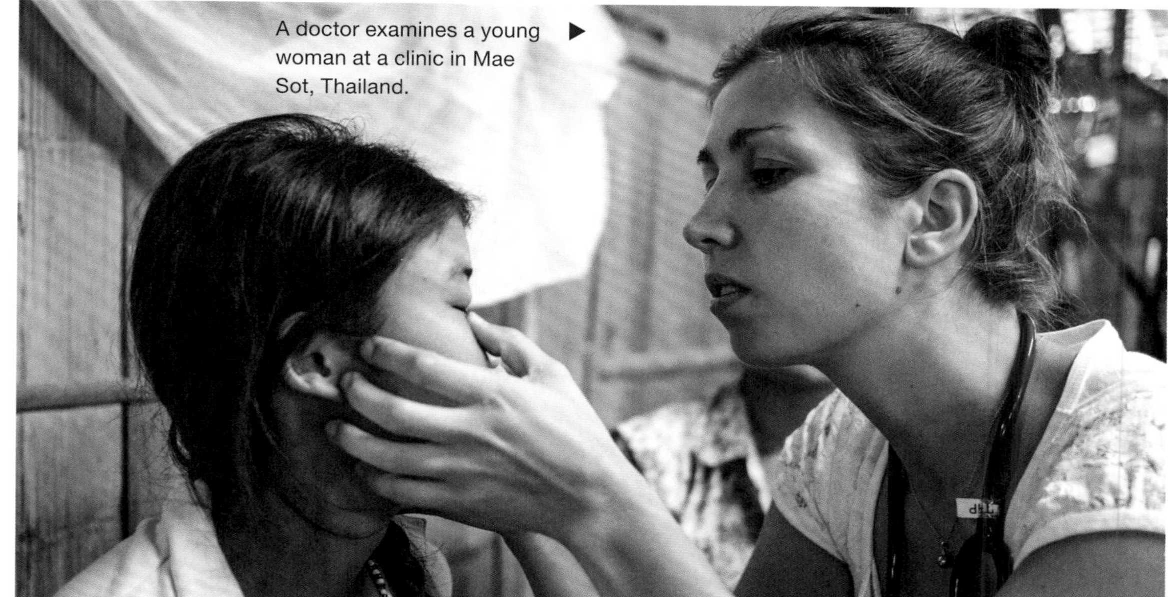

A doctor examines a young woman at a clinic in Mae Sot, Thailand. ▶

CD2-16

B Listen again. Then complete the chart about public health in Thailand with information from the interview. Use infinitives of purpose, *too*, and *enough*.

1. **Problem**: People in rural areas ___lived too far away___ to get medical treatment in hospitals.

   Solution: The government of Thailand ___decided to spend money on the countryside___ in order to bring health care to the rural areas.

2. **Problem**: There wasn't ______________________ to meet people's needs.

   Solution: The government gave more people safe ______________________ drink.

3. **Problem**: People lived ______________________ to access health services.

   Solution: The government built highways ______________________ remote areas to the cities.

4. **Problem**: There ______________________ medical workers to give people medical care in remote areas.

   Solution: New medical graduates must serve in rural areas, so there will always be ______________________ people who live outside cities.

12 APPLY.

A Work in groups. Discuss areas in the world where changes could help solve people's health problems. Then complete the chart with two more problems and possible solutions.

Country	Problem	Possible Solutions
	not enough food to feed all people	give farmers seeds to plant more vegetables

B Write five sentences for the problems and solutions you listed in the chart. Use infinitives.

In ____, there isn't enough food to feed all the people. The government should give farmers seeds to plant more vegetables.

Charts 6.1–6.4, 6.6, 6.7, 6.9

1 Circle the correct words to complete the sentences.

1. When Sam doesn't remember **taking / to take** his allergy medicine in the morning, he sometimes has difficulty **breathing / to breathe** later in the day.
2. Marina stopped at the pharmacy **buying / to buy** some tissues because she couldn't stop **sneezing / to sneeze**.
3. Jamal would like **tasting / to taste** the bread, but he had to stop **eating / to eat** bread of any kind because he's allergic to it.
4. Henry has to be careful **not eating / not to eat** eggs or anything made with eggs. That's why he often has a hard time **ordering / to order** food in a restaurant.
5. Ana's allergy to cats prevents her from **visiting / to visit** any of her friends with cats. It's hard for her **being / to be** around cats for more than an hour or so.
6. Ali tried allergy pills for his hay fever. They didn't work, so he stopped **taking / to take** them.
7. Gina was surprised **learning / to learn** that she had a peanut allergy. She remembers **eating / to eat** bowls of peanuts when she was younger.
8. Ed is pretty good at **cleaning / to clean** his apartment every week. If he doesn't clean it, he is likely **to having / to have** an allergic reaction to the dust.

2 LISTEN.

Charts 6.1–6.4, 6.8

CD2-17

A Listen to the radio broadcast. Then complete the answers to the questions with the word in parentheses. Use gerunds, infinitives, prepositions, *too*, and *not enough* where necessary.

1. How do many people spend a lot of their time?

   They spend a lot of time sitting at a computer (sit).
2. Why are many people unable to enjoy nature?

   They are ______________ (busy) outside.
3. What does Richard Louv write about?

   He writes about the ______________ (benefits) outside.
4. What did Louv's first book do?

   It encouraged ______________ (start) nature programs.
5. When the high school principal gave him a choice, what did Martinez do?

   Martinez decided ______________ (join).

6. According to Louv, what changed Juan Martinez's life?

_______________ (connect) changed his life.

7. What does Martinez think many children don't have enough of?

They _______________ (connect) with nature.

8. What does Martinez emphasize in his lectures?

He emphasizes the importance _______________ (get) outdoors.

CD2-17 **B** Listen again and check your answers.

Charts 6.1–6.7 **3** **EDIT.** Read the article about student stress. Find and correct eight more errors with gerunds and infinitives.

A Furry Solution to Student Stress

~~Deal~~ Dealing with stress is becoming more and more of a problem for young people. Many students say that they are having trouble falling asleep at night because of the pressures of school. They also say that they are constantly worried about get good grades.

Some schools are trying to do something about the problem. In one high school, five-year-old Maddy greets the students as they enter the building every morning. Maddy seems happy being there, and the students like to see her. They have fun greeting her, and they walk away with smiles on their faces. It doesn't cost much for the school have Maddy there every day because Maddy is a dog.

The school considered to set up a special room where students could go to relax, but it was too expensive do. In addition, some parents didn't want their children to take time out from classes in order relax. They thought that it was important for their children to be in class as much as possible.

Experts disagree and warn parents not putting too much pressure on their children. Encouraging children to relax are the best way for parents to help them.

Charts 6.1–6.7 **4** **SPEAK.** Work in groups. Have a discussion about stress in people your age. Then draw a chart like the one below. Write five things in every column.

Causes of Stress	Physical and/or Emotional Effects	Things You Can Do to Relieve Stress

1 READ & NOTICE THE GRAMMAR.

A Have you ever bought a product after you read a review of it? What kind of product was it? Tell a partner. Then read the product review.

Keeping Fit with the Zip by Fitbit

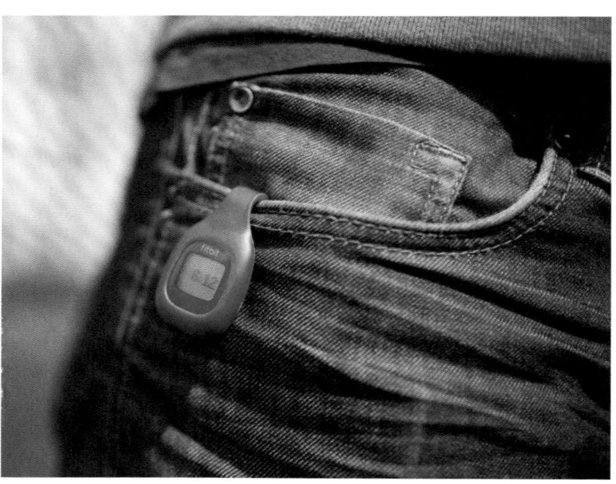

Starting a new exercise routine is not a problem for me, but I always have difficulty sticking to one. However, things have changed ever since I got my Zip by Fitbit. The Zip is a small device that measures the number of steps you take every day. It also measures your distance and the number of calories that you burn. It really encourages you to be active. Exercising becomes more fun!

One great thing about the Zip is its small size. Also, it's very easy to clip on. Knowing that it is measuring your steps encourages you to get out of your chair more often. With your Zip on, you will probably decide to walk or take the stairs instead of driving or taking the elevator.

Another great aspect of Zip is that it is easy to connect to your smartphone or computer, so you can share your goals and progress with others. It challenges you to try to take the most steps and burn the most calories. I convinced my brother to get a Zip a few months ago, and now we are competing with each other. I am determined to beat him; sometimes, I go for long walks at night in order to get a higher score. The competition is fun, but more important is my achievement: I've started to exercise regularly, and I feel great.

GRAMMAR FOCUS

In this product review, the writer uses gerunds and infinitives with the following patterns:

Gerunds
- as the subject of the clause (***Starting*** *a new exercise routine is not a problem . . .*)
- after certain nouns (*. . . I always have* ***difficulty sticking*** *to one.*)
- after prepositions (*. . . instead* ***of driving*** *or* ***taking*** *the elevator.*)

Infinitives
- after a verb + an object (*It really* ***encourages you to be*** *active.*)
- after a verb + an adjective (*I* ***am determined to beat*** *him . . .*)
- after *it* + a verb + an adjective (***It's*** *very* ***easy to clip on*** *. . .*)

B Read the product review in exercise **A** again. Find one more gerund and one more infinitive. Write the pattern for each. Use the box above and the grammar charts in the unit to help you.

Gerund/Infinitive	Pattern

C Look at the graphic organizer that the writer used to generate ideas for the product review in exercise **A**. Cross out the features that the writer did NOT choose to write about.

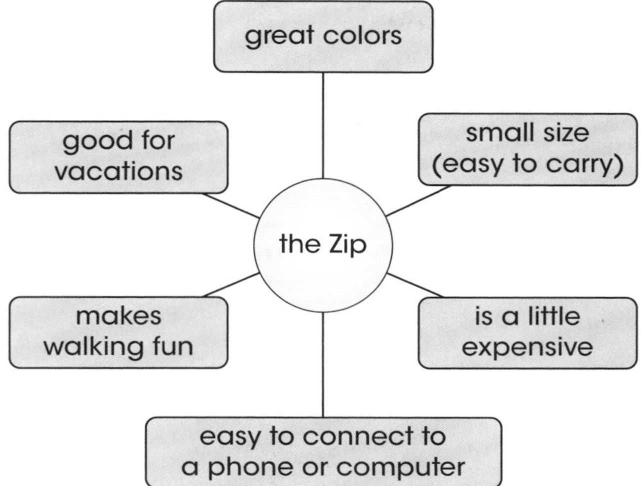

2 BEFORE YOU WRITE.

A Work with a partner. Discuss a product that you like or dislike. Brainstorm its positive or negative features. Then write your ideas in a graphic organizer like the one in exercise **1C**.

B Look at your graphic organizer and choose two or three features to include in your product review. Cross out the features that you do not want to write about.

3 WRITE two or three paragraphs about the product. Your review can be either positive or negative. Use your ideas from exercise **2B** to organize your writing.

WRITING FOCUS Avoiding Comma Splices

A comma splice is an error that occurs when two independent clauses are separated by a comma. A comma splice can be fixed by:

- adding a conjunction (*and, but, so*) after the comma
- changing the comma to a period and beginning a new sentence with the second clause
- changing the comma to a semicolon (;) between the two clauses

Comma splice:

✗ I went for a walk in the forest, at 9 o'clock I came home.

Corrected:

✓ I went for a walk in the forest**, and** at 9 o'clock I came home.
✓ I went for a walk in the forest**. At** 9 o'clock I came home.
✓ I went for a walk in the forest**; at** 9 o'clock I came home.

4 SELF ASSESS. Read your product review. Underline the infinitives and circle the gerunds. Use the checklist to assess your work.

☐ I used gerunds as subjects and objects. [6.1]
☐ I used gerunds and infinitives after the correct verbs. [6.3, 6.4, 6.5]
☐ I used infinitives with *it* as the subject or with *too* and *enough*. [6.6, 6.7]
☐ I avoided comma splices. [WRITING FOCUS]

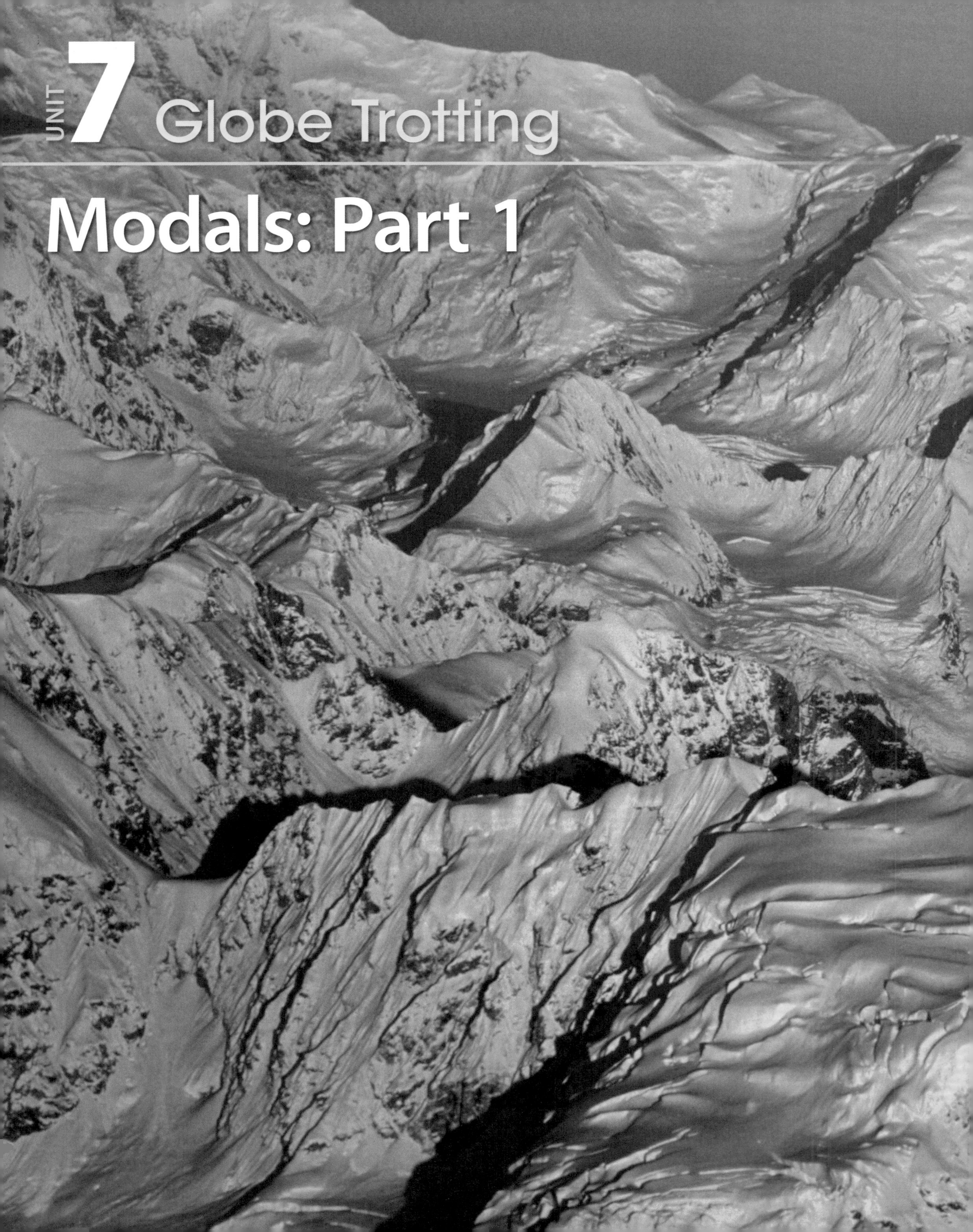

UNIT 7 Globe Trotting

Modals: Part 1

▼ Plane flying over mountains, Wrangell St. Elias National Park, Alaska

EXPLORE

CD2-18

1 **READ** the web page. What should people think about when they scuba dive?

What is scuba diving? SCUBA refers to the equipment that divers **must wear** so that they can stay underwater for long periods of time. When you scuba dive, you can explore exotic places, take terrific pictures, and exercise your body and mind. It's also a great way to make friends because you **have to** dive with other people. In the past, divers could not stay underwater very long. They often **had to hold** their breath.[1] Now, divers have air tanks that give them fresh oxygen so they can stay down for a long time.

Here are answers to some common questions.

Q: Do I **have to be** a great athlete to scuba dive?

A: No, but you **have to be** healthy. Before taking a diving class, you **must fill out** a medical questionnaire. You **will have to take** a water-skills assessment[2] test, too.

Q: Is scuba diving dangerous?

A: It can be. At the end of the dive, for example, you **must not come** to the surface too quickly. If you do, you can get sick.

Q: Where is a good place to scuba dive? I've heard that Bali **is supposed to be** great. Is that true?

A: Yes, Bali is a popular destination for diving. Go in June, and you **won't have to worry** about heavy rain at that time of year.

[1] **hold your breath:** take air in and not let the air out
[2] **assessment:** evaluation

2 CHECK. Write the missing words to make true sentences according to the web page.

1. Scuba equipment allows divers to stay underwater for ____________ periods of time.
2. Not all scuba divers are great ____________.
3. It's very important for a scuba diver to be ____________.
4. A diver should avoid coming to the surface of the water very ____________.
5. Springtime in Bali is good for scuba diving because there won't be a lot of ____________.

3 DISCOVER. Complete the exercises to learn about the grammar in this lesson.

A Use information from the web page in exercise **1** to complete these sentences about SCUBA.

1. SCUBA refers to the equipment that divers ____________ wear.
2. They often ____________ hold their breath.
3. You ____________ be healthy.
4. You ____________ come to the surface too quickly.
5. Bali ____________ great.

B The words you wrote in exercise **A** change the meaning of the main verbs. Match the words with their meanings.

____ 1. *have to*	a. prohibition
____ 2. *be supposed to*	b. expectation
____ 3. *must not*	c. necessity

LEARN

7.1 Expressing Necessity and Prohibition

Must	*Have To*
You **must check** your luggage. She **must fill in** another form.	We **have to get up** early for the tour. He **has to be** careful when he flies.

Must Not	*Not Have To*
You **must not text** while driving. She **must not miss** any more classes.	We **don't have to get up** early tomorrow. **Doesn't** he **have to go** to class tonight?

1. *Must* and *have to* are used before a verb to show that something is necessary.	Sue **must pass** the course in order to graduate. Sue **has to pass** the course in order to graduate.
2. *Have to* is a modal-like expression. It has different forms for the present, past, future, and present perfect.	He always **has to arrive** at work by 9:00. She **had to work** late yesterday. I **will have to read** the notes tomorrow. I **have had to work** on this problem all night.
3. *Must* is often used with rules, laws, and commands. It is not usually used in questions. *Have to* is used to express necessity in most other situations. *Have to* is more common in conversation than *must*.	Drivers **must obey** the rules of the road. To get a license, you **must take** a test and **complete** a written exam. I **have to finish** the report today. You **have to think about** your future. **Do** we **have to hand in** our homework?
4. *Must not* means that something is prohibited or not allowed. *Not have to* means that it is not necessary to do something.	Workers **must not enter** the building until the doors open at 9:00. I **don't have to go** to school tomorrow. It's a holiday.
5. *Have got to* is also used to talk about necessity, but it is less formal than *have to* or *must*. It is usually used only in affirmative statements, not in questions or negative statements.	✓ I **have got to study** more next time. ✓ I'**ve got to study** more next time. ✗ Have you got to study more next time? ✗ I haven't got to go.

*Modals are words such as *can, could, should,* and *will*. They add meaning to the main verb that follows them. Modals do not have different forms and are always followed by the base form of a verb.

4 Circle the correct words to complete the conversation. In some sentences, more than one answer is possible.

A: How was the scuba diving trip?

B: It was terrific. But I (1) **must / had to** get my diving certification first.

A: Really? (2) **Did you have to / Must you** get it, or did you want to get it?

B: Well, I (3) **didn't have to / must not** have the certification to do basic diving, but that got boring after a while. I (4) **must / had to** do the certification training in order to dive more freely.

A: So what (5) **do people have to / have people got to** do for the certification? Are there a lot of tests?

B: Well, everyone (6) **has got to / must** float or tread water for 10 minutes, and you (7) **have got to / must** be able to swim 200 yards.

A: Oh, about 180 meters. That's not very much. I guess you (8) **don't have to / haven't got to** be an excellent swimmer to get the certification.

B: No, you don't. There are also written tests, pool work, and diving practice; but you can do it all over a period of several weeks. It (9) **doesn't have to / must not** be an intensive course. I actually think it's better to do the training over a period of time.

A: I (10) **have got to / have to** try it soon. I've always wanted to go scuba diving.

5 Complete the paragraph with *must, must not,* or a form of *have to/not have to.* More than one answer is sometimes possible.

Diving Safely

You can have a great time scuba diving, but you (1) __________ remember that it can be dangerous. In order to dive safely, you (2) __________ forget the possible dangers underwater. For example, watch out for sea creatures. Divers don't get attacked very often, but you (3) __________ know which animals to stay away from. You also (4) __________ consider the effect of the force of the water on the body. A diver (5) __________ go down slowly to avoid ear pain or injury. Coming up slowly is important, too. You (6) __________ rise to the surface too quickly, or you could get very sick. Most importantly, a diver (7) __________ stay alert. If you follow these rules, you (8) __________ worry, and you will enjoy your dive.

▼ A green turtle swims near a scuba diver.

7.2 Expressing Obligation and Expectation: *Be Supposed To*

Be Supposed To
I'**m supposed to buy** textbooks before the first class. You're late. You **were supposed to be** here an hour ago.

1. *Be supposed to* is a modal-like expression. It expresses an obligation because of expectations, rules, laws, or other people's requests.	You **are supposed to call** the hotel to cancel the reservation. Aren't you going to do that?
2. *Be supposed to* can also express an expectation based on a schedule, plan, or a person's opinion.	We **are supposed to be** at the boarding gate a half hour before departure.
3. *Was/were supposed to* means that the action or event was expected, but it did not happen.	I **was supposed to drive** my friend to the station, but my car broke down.

6 Complete the paragraphs. Use the correct form of *be supposed to.*

According to some travel websites, volunteering on a boat (1) <u>is supposed to</u> be a great way to see the world without spending a lot of money. You help out on a boat and you get a place to sleep in exchange. Everyone on the trip (2) <u>is supposed to</u> share the cost of food.

This kind of volunteering seemed like a great idea, so I read the blogs of a couple of people who had done it. One person, Manny, went on a trip to the South Pacific with an older couple. Their daughter (3) <u>supposed to</u> travel with them, but she changed her mind at the last minute. The couple heard about the volunteer program and asked Manny to come with them instead for six months. While he was on the trip, he (4) <u>suppose to</u> help with the cooking, cleaning, and boat chores.

Unfortunately, the trip turned out to be much shorter than expected. Manny and the couple (5) <u>was supposed</u> go around the world, but they had to end the trip in the South Pacific because of a problem with the boat. Manny enjoyed himself anyway and said he can't wait to do it again. He (6) <u>is supposing to</u> meet some new boat owners soon to arrange a couple months at sea.

PRACTICE

7 Complete the statements about the Galápagos Islands. Use the words in the box. You can use some words more than once.

didn't have to	had to	was supposed to	have got to
don't have to	are supposed to	were supposed to	will have to

1. There are a lot of optional day trips. You ___don't have to___ go on any of them, but some are really great. You ___had to___ sign up for the trips the night before, but I think you can also just show up in the morning and go.
2. Our plane ___was supposed to___ arrive at 4:30 in Quito, but it didn't land until 11:00 at night. Our tour guide ___were supposed to___ wait at the airport for over six hours. Then, when our luggage was not on the plane, the guide located it for us. We ___will have to___ do anything.
3. We ___are supposed to___ bring our own wetsuits. We didn't know that, so we ___didn't have to___ rent some.
4. You ___have got to___ check out my photos of the iguanas! I took this shot from just a few feet away. Next time, I ______________ try to get a shot of the sea lions, too.

8 **PRONUNCIATION.** Read the chart and listen to the examples. Then complete the exercises.

CD2-19

PRONUNCIATION **Reduced Forms of *Have To* and *Have Got To***

Have to, has to, have got to, and *has got to* are often reduced.

Examples:	**Full Pronunciation**	**Reduced Pronunciation**
	We have to help Mom.	We /hæftə/ help Mom.
	Nobody has to know.	Nobody /hæstə/ know.
	You don't have to pay right away.	You don't /hæftə/ pay right away.
	I have got to go now.	I've /gatə/ go now.
	Jack has got to get up.	Jack's /gatə/ get up.

CD2-20

A Listen to the statements. Write the full form of the words you hear.

1. We ___have to___ be there in 20 minutes, or we'll miss the plane.
2. Everybody ______________ be back on time. We leave at 6 o'clock sharp.
3. You ______________ call us every day.
4. Max ______________ learn some basic Chinese before he goes.
5. I'm sorry that I'm late. I ______________ take an earlier train next time.
6. We ______________ buy gifts before we go back home.

CD2-20

B Listen again and repeat the sentences from exercise **A**.

9 READ, WRITE & SPEAK.

A Look at the airport arrival and departure information. Complete the sentences with the correct form of *have to, have got to,* or *be supposed to.* Add *not* where necessary. More than one answer is sometimes possible.

DEPARTURES

Destination	Scheduled Departure Time	Status	Gate
Beijing	8:00	Now boarding	E4
London	7:30	I hour delay	B3
Seoul	9:45	On time	C1
Istanbul	11:30	Canceled	
Addis Ababa	3:10	Departed 3:40	

ARRIVALS

Departure City	Scheduled Arrival Time	Actual Arrival Time	Status
Tokyo	6:30		Expected 8:30
Jakarta	2:40	2:15	Arrived
Cairo	4:30		5-hour delay
Quito	5:45	5:45	Arrived
Mexico City	6:30		2-hour delay

1. It's 7:35 A.M. Lynn is flying to Beijing. She's just finished going through security. She ______ *has to OR has got to* ______ get to the gate quickly.

2. It's 8:00 A.M. The passengers for the flight to London are still at the gate, and they're not happy. The plane ______ depart at 7:30.

3. It's 9:40 A.M. The flight to Seoul ______ take off in five minutes, but the doors of the plane are still open.

4. Hank ______ fly to Istanbul at 11:30 A.M. Now he ______ find another way to get there.

5. It's 2:20 P.M. Mr. Halim is on the flight from Jakarta. He was worried about getting to his meeting at 4:00 P.M. Now, he ______ worry about being late.

6. It's 7:00 P.M. Celia is returning from Mexico City. Her brother thought he ______ leave for the airport at 5:45 P.M., but now he ______ rush to get there.

B Imagine that it's 12:00 P.M. Write two sentences about the arrival and departure information in exercise **A**. Leave a blank for the names of the cities. Use the correct forms of *have got to, have to,* or *be supposed to.* Add *not* where necessary.

Passengers from ______ are supposed to arrive at the airport very early in the morning.

C Read your sentences to the class. Ask your classmates to say the correct city for each of your sentences.

10 EDIT. Read the e-mail. Find and correct eight more errors with modal verbs and modal-like expressions.

Addis Ababa, Ethiopia

Hi Tom,

I'm writing to tell you some exciting news. I'm suppose to go to Ethiopia in May. I know you had a great time there last year, so I want to ask you a few questions. First of all, when you were there, must you stay in Addis Ababa, or were you able to find good accommodations outside the capital? I also want to go to Bale Mountain National Park. Have I got to camp there, or is there a hotel? Either way, I got to make a reservation very soon, so let me know. How about food? According to my travel guide, visitors are suppose to try *injera*, an interesting kind of bread. I also read that in Ethiopia you have to use a fork. It's not the custom. You're supposed to use *injera* as both the fork and the plate. Is that true?

I don't have a visa yet, but I know that I got to have one. What am I supposed to doing to get one? Do I have to go to the Ethiopian embassy, or can I do the application online? I'm sorry about all these questions. I promise that you must not answer anymore . . . until my next e-mail!

Best,

Linda

11 LISTEN to the podcast about coffee ceremonies in Ethiopia. Then complete the sentences with an appropriate modal or modal-like expression. More than one answer is sometimes possible.

CD2-21

1. You __________________ plan to spend a lot of time at a coffee ceremony.
2. You __________________ leave the ceremony early.
3. You __________________ say that the coffee and its preparation are excellent.
4. According to tradition, the oldest person __________________ get the first cup of coffee.
5. You __________________ say "no" to any of the cups of coffee.
6. You __________________ speak the language of your host in order to enjoy yourself.

12 APPLY.

A Write six sentences about a ceremony or ritual in your country or in a country you know. Use *have to, have got to, must,* and *be supposed to*. Add *not* where necessary.

The host of a Japanese tea ceremony must serve Matcha tea, a kind of green tea.

B Read your sentences to the class. Answer any questions your classmates may have.

EXPLORE

CD2-22

1 READ the web page from a travel website. Which of the hotels would you like to stay in?

Traveling Feet

When you travel, your accommodations should be as interesting as the rest of your trip. Today's post is about some of the world's most unusual places to stay.

Nine Hours capsule hotel, Kyoto, Japan

Capsule hotels became popular years ago in Japan, especially among businessmen who worked late and **couldn't catch** the last train home. Nine Hours is a modern capsule hotel with a simple, clean design. Each tiny boxlike room for sleeping has a special alarm clock that wakes guests up with light, not noise. The hotel is right in the center of Kyoto, so it's a quick walk to shops, buses, and subways. Capsule hotels are also good for people who **can't afford** expensive hotel rates.

▲ Khao Sok Rainforest Resort

Jules' Undersea Lodge, Florida, USA

This hotel is completely underwater. In fact, you **have to be able to scuba dive** down 21 feet (6 meters) to reach it. The lodge **is able to accommodate** four people and has showers, a microwave, and a refrigerator. For entertainment, see if you **can identify** the different fish that swim past your window.

Khao Sok Rainforest Resort, Phanom, Thailand

Here you **will be able to observe** the plants and animals of the rainforest from your room in the treetops. Visitors like taking boat trips on the river or elephant rides through the jungle.[1] One guest reports that she **was** even **able to enjoy** visits from monkeys.

[1] **jungle:** a hot, humid area with many trees and plants growing close together

2 CHECK. Match the accommodations with the features.

_____ 1. Nine Hours — a. a view of fish

_____ 2. Jules' Undersea Lodge — b. special alarm clocks

_____ 3. Khao Sok Rainforest Resort — c. monkeys

3 DISCOVER. Complete the exercises to learn about the grammar in this lesson.

A Read the sentences from the web page in exercise **1**. Underline the words that show ability or lack of ability.

1. Capsule hotels became popular years ago in Japan, especially among businessmen who worked late and couldn't catch the last train home.
2. Capsule hotels are also good for people who can't afford expensive hotel rates.
3. In fact, you have to be able to scuba dive down 21 feet (6 meters) in order to reach it.
4. For entertainment, see if you can identify the different fish that swim past your window.
5. Here you will be able to observe the plants and animals of the rainforest from your room in the treetops.
6. One guest reports that she was even able to enjoy visits from monkeys.

▲ A monkey, Thailand

B Look at the words you underlined in exercise **A**. Circle **T** for *true* or **F** for *false*.

1.	There is more than one way in English to express ability.	**T**	**F**
2.	We use *can* with infinitives	**T**	**F**
3.	We use *can* after *will*.	**T**	**F**
4.	There are two ways to talk about ability in the past.	**T**	**F**

LEARN

7.3 Expressing Ability: Present and Future

Can	*Be Able To*
I **can speak** Chinese, but I **can't speak** Japanese.	Ana and Ella **are able to swim**, but they **aren't able to dive**.

1. *Can* and *be able to* both express ability. *Can't* and *be not able to* express a lack of ability.	We **can speak** English fairly well now. We **are able to speak** English fairly well now. She **can't speak** English very well. She **isn't able to speak** English well.
2. *Can* is used more frequently than *be able to*. *Be able to* is used in more formal situations than *can*.	Sam, I **can come** over now. Mr. Lugo, I'**m able to come** to your office now.
3. *Be able to* has different verb forms.	We **are able to buy** tickets online. He **hasn't been able to go** on vacation all summer.
4. Use *will be able to* (or *be going to*), not *can*, for a future ability that will be learned or new.	I **will be able to read** French after my course. I **am going to be able to write**, too.
Use *will be able to* or *can* when the future ability is possible or true now.	I'**ll be able to finish** the paper tonight. I **can finish** the paper tonight.
Remember: Do not use *can* with *will*.	✗ I can will speak English well a year from now.

4 Circle the correct words to complete the travelers' comments. Sometimes both answers are correct.

Flora and Federico

If you visit Nanuku Island in the South Pacific, you won't regret it. We (1) **can / have been able to** do a lot of wonderful things since we got here. With coconut trees all around, you (2) **can / are able to** eat coconuts all day long. The food is delicious, too. We have been lucky on this trip because we (3) **can / have been able to** go fishing almost every day so far. It's too bad that we have to leave tomorrow. We (4) **can't / won't be able to** forget this paradise in the South Pacific.

Lucia

Here we are on beautiful Nanuku Island. We wake up every morning to the sound of the ocean. The accommodations aren't great, though. We (5) **can't / haven't been able to** take a shower since yesterday because of a problem with the hot water. The air-conditioning isn't perfect either. Hopefully, they (6) **are going to be able to / can** fix both problems soon. On the bright side, we (7) **can / have been able to** kayak around the island three times since we got here. Yesterday, I learned how to surf and stood up on the surfboard for over five seconds. Maybe next time I (8) **can / will be able to** stand up longer.

7.4 Expressing Ability: Past

Could	*Was Able To*
I **could ski** when I was 12, but I **couldn't ski** when I was 8.	I **was able to go** on the tour last week, but my friends **weren't able to join** me.

1. *Could* and *was able to* refer to general ability in the past.	My dad **could** always **fix** broken toys. My dad **was** always **able to fix** broken toys.
2. *Could* is used more frequently than *was/were able to*. *Was/Were able to* is more formal.	Informal: The kids **could ski** when they were four. Formal: The child **was able to read** by age four.
3. Use *was/were able to* (not *could*) to talk about ability at one time in the past. In the negative, use either *couldn't* or *wasn't/weren't able to*.	✓ I **was able to fix** the clock when it stopped. ✗ I could fix the clock when it stopped. ✓ I **couldn't fix** the clock when it stopped. ✓ I **wasn't able to fix** the clock when it stopped.
4. With verbs of perception (*see, hear, understand, remember*), you can use *could* or *was/were able to* to talk about ability at a time in the past.	We were at the back of the theater, but we **could hear** everything. He **was able to see** clearly from the front row.

5 Complete the paragraphs. Write the affirmative or negative forms of *could*, *was able to*, or *were able to* as appropriate. If two forms are correct, write both.

We drove up and down the narrow streets of Cerbère, but we (1) couldn't/weren't able to find a parking space. After driving around for 20 minutes, I finally (2) ________ find a space, but it was tiny. I'm not good at parking, so I (3) ________ get into the space. My friend had to get out of the car to direct me. Then, I (4) ________ park the car.

We had to walk a long way to the hotel and carry our bags. On my last hiking trip, I (5) ________ carry my backpack without difficulty. But this time, I had packed too much stuff, and the bags were heavy. It was very hot, too. When we saw that we were lost, we stopped and asked a woman for directions. My friend (6) ________ speak a little French, so he (7) ________ understand her directions. I (8) ________ understand anything. Believe me, we were very glad when we finally got to the hotel.

▼ Cerbère, France

7.5 *Be Able To:* Gerunds, Infinitives, and with Modals

Be Able To	
Gerund	**Being able to speak** Russian was helpful during her visit to Moscow.
Infinitive	I want **to be able to travel** by myself.
Modal	People near the emergency exit **must be able to open** the door.

1. *Be able to* describes the ability to do something. Use *being able to* when you need a gerund.*	We were upset about not **being able to** sit together on the plane.
2. Use *to be able to* when you need an infinitive.	She hopes **to be able to** work in Rome after she learns Italian.
3. Use *be able to* after another modal or modal-like expression.	You **should be able to** open the door quickly.

*To review gerunds and infinitives, see Unit 6, starting on page 142.

6 Complete the sentences about alternative travel ideas. Use the correct form of *be able to.*

1. On this yoga retreat, the instructors want you ___to be able to___ relax. You will enjoy ______________ spend a whole month focusing on your mind and spirit.

2. Do you want ______________ speak Italian or maybe Chinese? Studying a language abroad is a great way to travel. ______________ communicate with people in a foreign country can be very satisfying.

3. Why not take a cooking class in another country? You don't have to ______________ speak the local language, because many of the classes are in English. However, ______________ speak the local language is helpful when you visit the local markets to buy ingredients. It's fun ______________ eat at popular restaurants and meet their chefs. And when you return home, you are going ______________ cook some delicious food.

4. Archaeological digs make great vacations for people who love history and museums. When I went on a dig in Tanzania, I was worried about not ______________ do such hard work in the hot sun. But after a few days, I was happy about ______________ work for hours without any difficulty.

PRACTICE

7 Complete the conversation. Use the correct form of *be able to.* Add *not* when necessary.

Irene: Welcome back, Terry. How was your trip to Turkey? You stayed in a cave, right?

Terry: It wasn't really a cave. It was a cave house in Cappadocia, and it was wonderful. We (1) ___were able to___ experience how our ancestors lived, but we had all the modern conveniences. Our host was great. He (2) ______________ answer all of our questions.

▲ Cave houses in Cappadocia, Turkey

Irene: Was there a lot to do?

Terry: Tons. And we (3) ______________ walk everywhere. I really enjoyed (4) ______________ do that. We didn't need to take buses at all! The only thing we (5) ______________ do was go up in a hot-air balloon because the weather wasn't good enough. That was a disappointment.

Irene: I was wondering . . . Do you have to (6) ______________ speak Turkish in order to get around?

Terry: No, you don't have to, but it's great if you do. Hopefully, I (7) ______________ speak some Turkish next time. I'm taking a class now. I really want (8) ______________ communicate with the local people.

8 ANALYZE THE GRAMMAR. Read the sentences. Underline the form of ability in each sentence. If possible, write *can, can't, could,* or *couldn't* above the underlined words. Write **NC** if no change is possible.

1. NC
 Being able to ride in a hot-air balloon was the best part of my trip to Turkey.
2. can
 You are able to see so many things when you go up in a hot-air balloon.
3. I was able to see dozens of caves from the air, and they were beautiful.
4. We were able to take a lot of great pictures from the balloon.
5. My sister wasn't able to come with us on the balloon ride because she was sick.
6. If my sister visits Turkey again, she will be able to go up in a balloon.

9 Complete the sentences. Use an affirmative or negative form of *can*, *could*, or *be able to*. If two forms are correct, write both.

1. In Catalonia, Spain, people ___have been able to___ keep the tradition of human tower building alive since the eighteenth century.
2. Participants in the competition ___are able to / can___ build enormous towers using only their bodies.
3. It requires a lot of practice ___to be able to___ build a tower.
4. Men are usually on the lowest level of the tower because they ___can / are able to___ support the weight of the others.
5. Children need courage. They have to ___be able to___ stand on the top of the tower.
6. When children get older and heavier, they ___Can___ be on the top.
7. One year, a team ___can___ build ten levels.
8. Perhaps sometime in the future, people ___are able to___ form even taller towers.
9. ______________ trust the other people in the tower is important.
10. There is a competition every two years, so if you ______________ see it last year, you will have to wait another year to attend.

10 APPLY.

A Complete the sentences so that they are true about you.

1. When I travel, I can ______________, but I can't ______________.
2. The first time I went on a trip, I couldn't ______________.
3. I have never been able to ______________ on a trip.
4. One day, I would like to be able to ______________.
5. When people travel, they have to be able to ______________.
6. Being able to ______________ is important in a foreign country.

B Work in groups. Take turns reading your sentences from exercise **A**. Then ask each other follow-up questions. Use the affirmative or negative of *can, could,* or a form of *be able to*.

A: *When I travel, I can communicate with people in French or Greek, but I can't speak Chinese or Arabic.*

B: *Can you answer when people ask you questions in Greek and French?*

EXPLORE

CD2-23

1 READ the web page. Who would find this information useful?

WWOOFing It!

HOME FEATURE ARTICLES PHOTOS CONTACT US

Farm work isn't for everybody, but if you want an adventure that will give you hands-on experience on an organic farm, you ***should check out*** *World Wide Opportunities on Organic Farms (WWOOF). This organization connects volunteers with farmers who offer accommodations, food, and learning opportunities in exchange for work. Read some comments from WWOOFers on their experiences:*

WWOOFer in Greece

"Last summer, I helped a Greek family start an olive orchard. We spent hours every day digging stones out of a field to prepare it for planting. It was extremely hard work, and my muscles were sore by the end of the day. I really **should have gotten into** better shape before my trip. But I learned a lot about farming, and I picked up a little Greek, too."—*Angie, Scotland*

WWOOFer in Argentina

"I'm a city kid from Tokyo, so I didn't know what to do on a small Argentinian farm. On my first day I pulled up a whole row of carrot seedlings[1] because I thought they were weeds.[2] My hosts were nice about it, but I know they weren't happy. I **should have asked** more questions before I got started."—*Michio, Japan*

WWOOFer in Ireland

"I **should have found out** more about the accommodations before arriving. I had a tiny room and no electricity. I got used to it after a while, but it wasn't easy. WWOOF hosts will rarely be able to offer you the comforts of home; if you're not willing to rough it,[3] then you **ought to look into** other travel options."—*Marie, Canada*

[1] **seedling:** a young plant that has been grown from a seed
[2] **weed:** a wild plant that is not wanted in a yard or garden
[3] **rough it:** live without modern comforts

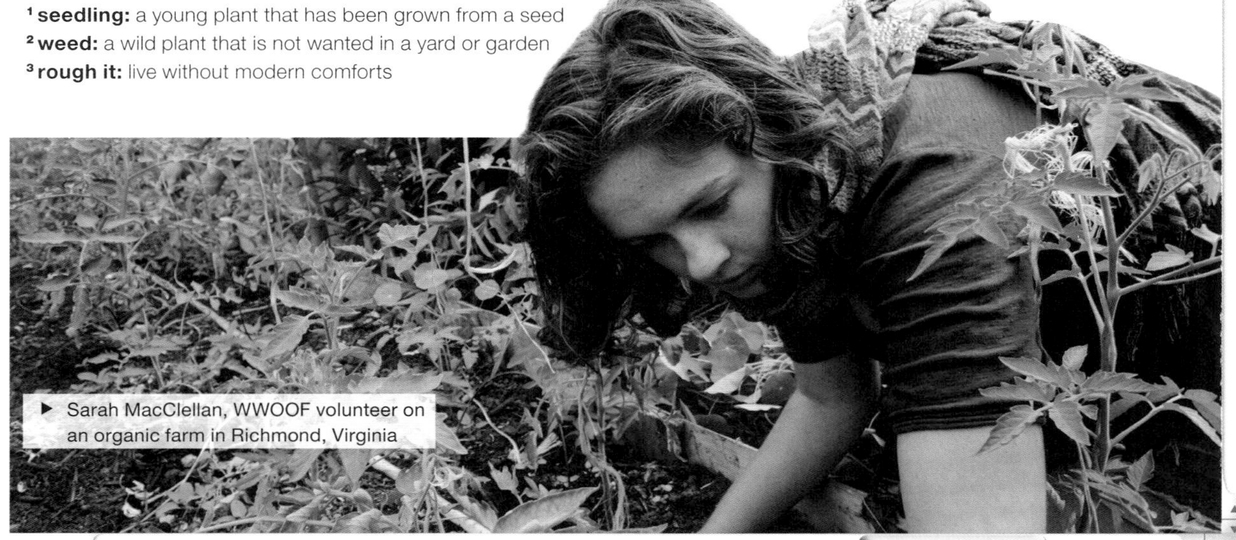

▶ Sarah MacClellan, WWOOF volunteer on an organic farm in Richmond, Virginia

▼ WWOOF volunteers have many possibilities, including working with herbs and flower gardens.

2 CHECK. Correct the mistake in each sentence to make it correct according to the information from the web page in exercise **1** on page 191.

1. Through WWOOF, you can ~~work for money~~ volunteer at an organic farm.
2. Angie was in great shape when she went to Greece.
3. Michio came from a village in Japan to work on a farm in Argentina.
4. Marie didn't get used to her accommodations in Ireland.

3 DISCOVER. Complete the exercises to learn about the grammar in this lesson.

A Look back at the web page in exercise **1** to find these sentences. Then circle the correct meanings.

1. You **should check out** World Wide Opportunities on Organic Farms (WWOOF).
   a. It is a bad idea for you to check out WWOOF.
   b. It is a good idea for you to check out WWOOF.
2. I really **should have gotten** into better shape before my trip.
   a. I didn't get into better shape before the trip, and I'm sorry I didn't.
   b. I got into better shape before the trip, and I'm glad I did.
3. I guess I **should have asked** more questions before I got started.
   a. I didn't ask enough questions before I got started.
   b. I asked enough questions before I got started.
4. You **ought to look** into other travel options.
   a. It is a bad idea for you to look into other travel options.
   b. It is a good idea for you to look into other travel options.

B Match the meanings with the grammar from exercise **A**.

1. advice about the present or future _____, _____
2. a regret about something in the past _____

a. *should* + verb
b. *should have* + past participle
c. *ought to* + verb

LEARN

7.6 Asking for or Giving Advice

	Should, Ought To, and *Had Better*
	Subject + Modal/Modal-like Expression + Base Form
Should	You **should get** your passport soon. You **shouldn't forget** to buckle your seat belt.
Ought To	You **ought to buy** your tickets online.
Had Better	We **had better take** a taxi, or we will be late. We **had better not be** late, or we will miss the plane.

1. *Should* or *ought to* + the base form of a verb can be used to give advice. *Should* is more common than *ought to.*	You **should pack** some warm clothes. Everyone **ought to watch** the video about the plane's safety procedures.
2. *Had better* + the base form of a verb is used to express strong advice or a warning. *Had better* suggests that there will be serious consequences if the advice is not followed.	You **had better stop shouting,** or the other passengers will get angry. We**'d better take** a taxi, or we'll miss the bus.
3. In negative statements, use *should not* or *had better not.* To ask for advice or an opinion, use *should.*	You **shouldn't put** your laptop in your bag. You**'d better not be** late. **Should** we **take** umbrellas, too?
4. To give advice in the progressive, use *should (not) be, ought to be,* or *had better (not) be* + verb + *-ing.*	You **shouldn't be texting** your friends. You **ought to be sleeping**. You**'d better be taking** notes.
5. **Be careful!** *Had* in *had better* does not refer to the past. It refers to the present or future.	You **had better** hurry, or we'll be late. We**'d better check out** ticket prices today.

4 Complete the exercises.

A Complete the sentences. Use *should* or *ought to* and the words in parentheses. Add *not* when necessary. If both *should* and *ought to* are correct, write both.

1. Marc is good at planting seeds. He <u>should do / ought to do</u> (do) that job all the time.
2. Lucy is a good worker. ______________ (we / offer) her a full-time job?
3. Tarek is scared of dogs. I ______________ (keep) them away from him.
4. Sarah has a fever. She ______________ (work) tomorrow.
5. Ru is always late, and it's causing problems. She ______________ (get) to work on time.
6. All the volunteers did a really good job today. We ______________ (tell) them.
7. We ______________ (pick) the apples yet. They aren't ready.
8. ______________ (we / ask) WWOOF to send us more volunteers?

B **ANALYZE THE GRAMMAR.** Which four sentences in exercise **A** can also use *had better* or *had better not*? Write the number of the sentences.

3, ____, ____, ____

5 Complete the conversation between people on a trip to Peru. Use modals and the progressive form of the verbs in parentheses. Add *not* when necessary.

Joe: It's hot today. We (1) shouldn't be wearing (should / wear) jeans.

Ani: I know. We (2) ____________ (should / wear) shorts.

Joe: You know, maybe it was a mistake to go to the market today. I feel like we (3) ____________ (ought / work) at the farm today. And I'm worried about the animals. Dan (4) ____________ (had better / feed) them right now, or I'll be very upset.

Ani: Don't worry. I talked to Señor Ortega, and he said that we've been working too hard lately. He thinks we (5) ____________ (should / have) some fun during our stay, too. And I'm sure Dan is taking good care of the animals.

Joe: I guess you're right . . . So where is this market anyway? We (6) ____________ (should / get) close to it by now. I think we (7) ____________ (ought / walk) the other way.

Ani: I'm pretty sure it's this way . . . Wow! Look at the cool hat that woman is wearing! Let me take her picture.

Joe: Ani, you (8) ____________ (should / take) pictures of people without asking them first!

Ani: Oops! I forgot. I'll put my camera away.

▼ A view of mountains in Chinchero, Peru

7.7 Expressing Regret or Criticism: *Should Have* + Past Participle

Statements
Subject + *Should (Not) Have* + Past Participle
I **should have bought** my ticket online. The online tickets were cheaper. I **shouldn't have bought** my ticket from a travel agent. It was more expensive.

Questions	Answers
(*Wh*- Word) + Subject + *Should Have* + Past Participle	
Should I **have arrived** here earlier?	Yes, you **should have**. / No, you **shouldn't have**.
What **should** we **have done** to prepare for the test?	You **should have started** studying earlier.

1. *Should (not) have* + past participle is often used to express regret about something that happened or did not happen in the past.	We **should have researched** hotels before we left. I **shouldn't have stayed up** so late last night. Now I'm tired.
2. *Should (not) have* + past participle is also used to talk about mistakes or to criticize someone for something they did or did not do in the past.	You **should have told** me about the cost. I can't afford to go. He **shouldn't have made** a reservation without asking me.

6 Complete the exercises.

A Read the situations. Then complete the sentences about the travelers' mistakes. Use *should have* and *shouldn't have* and the verbs in parentheses.

1. Carlos got thirsty during his train trip. He left his bag on his seat and went to get something to drink. When he came back, the bag was gone. He ___should have taken___ (take) his bag with him. He ___shouldn't have left___ (leave) it on the seat.
2. Anna made a photocopy of her passport, but she kept the copy with her passport. Then, she lost her passport. She ________________ (keep) the copy with the passport. She ________________ (put) the copy in a different bag.
3. Sylvia drank tap water and got sick. She ________________ (drink) water from the sink. She ________________ (buy) bottled water.
4. Jake went on a backpacking trip, and he packed too many things in his backpack. He couldn't carry it, and he had to throw away some of his belongings. He ________________ (pack) so much in his backpack. He ________________ (take) only a few important things with him on the trip.
5. Ira and Gina saw a crowd of people marching and carrying signs. They also saw police, but they went closer anyway. When they started to take photos, the police began to question them. They ________________ (take) photos. They ________________ (go) back to their hotel.

B Write questions about the people in exercise **A**. Use *should have.*

1. Carlos / leave / his bag on the seat
   Should Carlos have left his bag on the seat?
2. what / Carlos / do / with his bag
   ____
3. Anna / keep / the copy and the passport together
   ____
4. who / Anna / notify / about the lost passport
   ____
5. Jake / throw away / some of his belongings
   ____
6. what / Jake / bring / with him on his trip
   ____
7. Ira and Gina / take / photos of the crowd
   ____
8. where / they / go / when they saw the crowd
   ____

C **SPEAK.** Work with a partner. Ask and answer the questions in exercise **B**.

A: *Should Carlos have left his bag on the seat?*

B: *No, he shouldn't have.*

PRACTICE

7 Read the conversation about a homestay in India. Use the modals and the correct form of the verbs in parentheses. Add *not* where necessary.

Lee: So how was your homestay in that village? Was it everything you expected?

Ben: It was even better. You (1) ____ought to try____ (ought to / try) it some time.

Lee: Did you stay with a family in their home?

Ben: No, we had meals with the family, but my brother and I stayed in a mud hut. It had two beds, a fan, lighting, and a bathroom. It wasn't like home, but when you travel, you (2) ______________ (should / expect) everything to be just like home.

Lee: So you had no complaints?

Ben: None. You (3) ______________ (should / miss) the chance to do a homestay some day. I'm sure you'll love it. For us, the whole experience was great. In fact, we think we (4) ______________ (should / stay) longer. We were in the village for only two days. We (5) ______________ (should / spend) at least four days there, maybe even six or seven.

Lee: Did you do a lot of sightseeing, too?

Ben: Yes, but we were in big cities most of the time. We (6) ______________________ (should / spend) so much time there. I wish we had spent more time in the villages. Being with a family and learning about local customs was much more interesting than visiting temples and palaces.

Lee: It sounds interesting. Maybe I'll do it this summer.

Ben: Homestays in Rajasthan are becoming pretty popular. You (7) ______________________ (had better / make) arrangements soon, or the homestays will all be booked.

Lee: That's good to know.

Ben: Before you go, you (8) ______________________ (ought to / practice) eating with your hand, because you often eat meals that way. I (9) ______________________ (should / practice) before my visit because I wasn't very good at it. I held the bread the wrong way to eat my vegetables. I (10) ______________________ (should/fold) the bread the way I did. Finally, my host got me a fork and knife. He called them "gardening tools"!

8 PRONUNCIATION. Read the chart and listen to the examples. Then complete the exercises.

CD2-24

PRONUNCIATION **Reduced *Should Have, Shouldn't Have***

Should have and *shouldn't have* are often reduced. *Have* sounds like the word *of*.

Examples:	Full Pronunciation	Reduced Pronunciation
	We should have helped them.	We *should of* helped them.
	Chris should have asked for a ride.	Chris *should of* asked for a ride.
	I shouldn't have left so early.	I *shouldn't of* left so early.
	The children shouldn't have gone.	The children *shouldn't of* gone.

In informal conversation, *should have* is often pronounced *shoulda*.

	We should have helped them.	We *shoulda* helped them.

CD2-25

A Listen to the sentences. Do you hear *should have* or *shouldn't have*? Write the correct words.

1. I <u>shouldn't have</u> bought a ticket for her.
2. I ______________________ taken the bus.
3. We ______________________ come early.
4. She ______________________ invited her friend.
5. We ______________________ worn jeans today.
6. He ______________________ made a reservation online.
7. They ______________________ stayed at a hotel on the beach.
8. You ______________________ eaten the soup.

B Tell a partner two things you should have done and two things you shouldn't have done in the past. Use reduced pronunciation.

I should've studied harder for the last test. I shouldn't have made so many mistakes.

9 WRITE & SPEAK.

A Read a family's comments about their trip to Marrakesh, Morocco. Complete the next sentence in each comment. Use *should have* or *shouldn't have.*

1. We left the *suq* (marketplace) after two hours. The kids loved it and didn't want to leave.
   We shouldn't have left the suq so soon.
2. When the snake charmer gave our son some snakes to hold, my wife and I got scared.
   ______________________________ our son the snakes to hold.
3. We got into trouble when we took pictures of some people in the *suq*.
   ______________________________ of people in the *suq*.
4. I told a vendor that I really liked one of his lamps. He didn't lower the price.
   ______________________________ that I liked the lamp.
5. We were never able to find the Bahia Palace because we didn't know how to get there.
   ______________________________ for directions.
6. We took a day trip to the Atlas Mountains, but without a guide we missed a lot.
   ______________________________ a guide.
7. We walked around the walls of the old city in the heat of the day. That wasn't a good idea.
   ______________________________ in the heat of the day.
8. We hurried past the storytellers and didn't stop to listen. We were sorry later.
   ______________________________ to the storytellers.

B Work with a partner. Compare the sentences you wrote in exercise **A**.

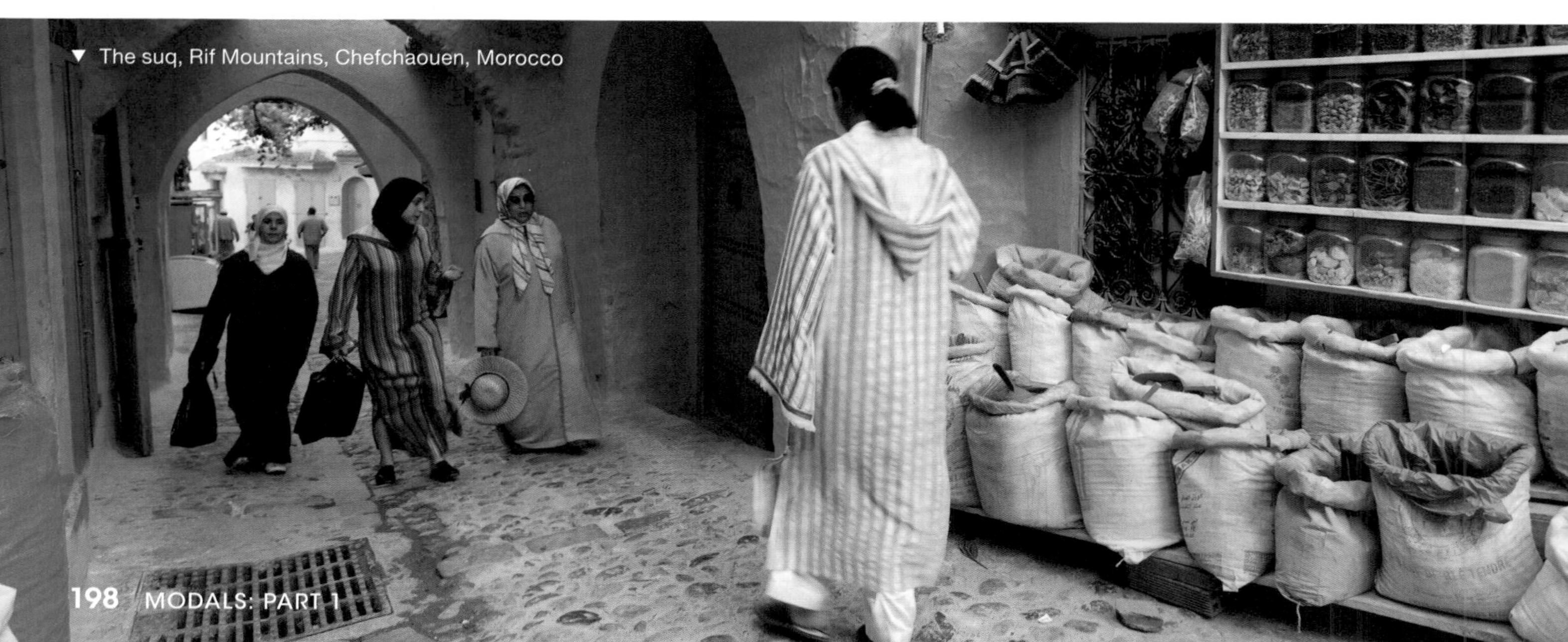

▼ The suq, Rif Mountains, Chefchaouen, Morocco

CD2-26

10 LISTEN to the conversation between a business consultant and the owner of a hotel with organized tours. Then check (✓) the things that the owner is doing already. Write **X** next to the things that the owner should have done.

_____ 1. Provide comfortable accommodations

_____ 2. Employ local people

_____ 3. Serve food from the local area

_____ 4. Start a recycling program at the hotel

_____ 5. Use local tour guides

_____ 6. Offer walking tours and camel tours

11 EDIT. Read the comment on the blog. Find and correct seven more errors with *should, ought to,* and *had better.*

Tina Grant:

The message of your recent blogs has been that we ~~have~~ had better limit our traveling because it is bad for the planet. Yes, travel has some negative effects on the environment, but people should be know the positive effects as well. You should have spend some time discussing the benefits of travel. People should to realize that the income from tourism helps local economies.

We had not better forget that without foreign money it is hard for some countries to build airports, roads, bridges, schools, and hospitals. All these things are very important, so tourists had better to keep visiting these countries and bringing their money with them! I believe we should thinking about the cultural benefits of tourism, too. When tourists are interested in another culture, it can encourage a sense of pride and identity in that culture. That's very important, so I think you ought to mentioned that as well.

12 APPLY.

A Work with a partner. List four ways that travel can have a negative effect on the environment.

B Write four sentences, two affirmative and two negative, with *should(n't) have* + past participle about a recent travel experience. Explain the effect your trip had on the environment.

My friends and I shouldn't have driven to Jakarta in separate cars. We should have gone in one car in order to save energy.

C Work in groups. Read your sentences to each other. Ask questions to find out more about your classmates' trips.

Charts 7.1, 7.2, 7.4, 7.6, 7.7

1 Circle the correct words to complete the story about David's first day in Moscow.

1. The train **had to / was supposed to** arrive at 10:00 P.M., but it didn't arrive until 2:00 A.M.
2. It was so late that I **can't / wasn't able to** call my friends to tell them about the delay.
3. I hadn't booked a hotel room because my friends **could / were supposed to** meet me and take me to a hotel near their apartment.
4. That was a big mistake. I **had to book / should have booked** a room before I arrived.
5. I **had to walk / should have walked** around for hours before I found accommodations.
6. I **could / was able to** find a hotel that had rooms, but it was expensive.
7. It was a good thing I **didn't have to pay / shouldn't have paid** cash because I didn't have any.
8. I **could / was supposed to** be at a language school at 10:30 A.M. for a job interview the next morning, but unfortunately, I didn't fall asleep until 6:00 A.M.
9. I **didn't have to go / shouldn't have gone** to sleep because I didn't wake up until 1:00 P.M.
10. I went to the school and apologized. I **had to / was supposed to** set up another interview time. I knew that I **don't have to / shouldn't** be late again.

Charts 7.1–7.3, 7.5–7.7

2 **LISTEN & SPEAK.**

A Complete the conversation with the modals or modal-like phrases in the box. Use the correct forms of the the verbs in parentheses. Add *not* where necessary. More than one answer is sometimes possible.

be able to	be supposed to	can	have to	should

The night before

Mara: OK. So we're going to start at the Lincoln Memorial, right? Everyone says we (1) ___shouldn't miss___ (miss) that.

Paul: Yeah. It's good to start at the Lincoln Memorial because we (2) __________ (visit) it early in the morning. It's open 24 hours a day.

Mara: Do we (3) __________ (buy) tickets?

Paul: No, it's free.

At the Lincoln Memorial

Mara: Look how clearly you (4) __________ (see) the Washington Monument from here. Isn't it a spectacular view?

Paul: It is. Are you ready to walk over there?

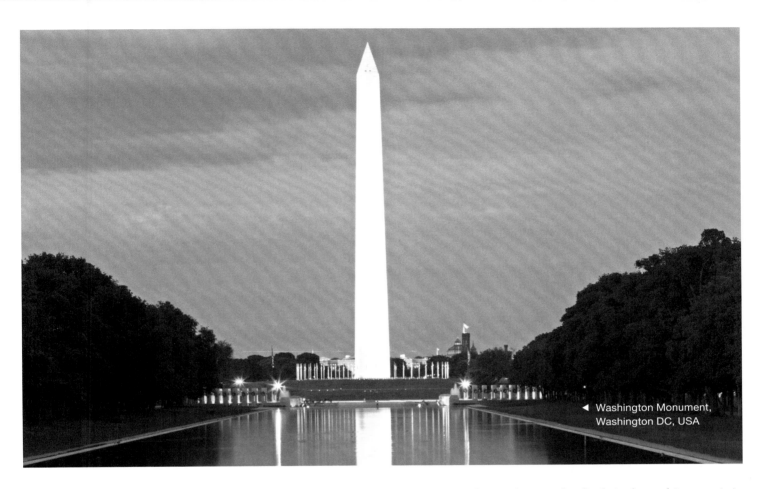

Washington Monument, Washington DC, USA

Mara: Almost. Let's take pictures of the monument first. Oh, no. The flash isn't working again! I (5) ______________________ (get) the flash to work at all on this trip.

Approaching the Washington Monument

Mara: Look at that line of people. Isn't it only a quarter to nine? The Monument (6) ______________________ (open) until 9 o'clock. Why are they standing there?

Paul: For tickets. You (7) ______________________ (have) a ticket to take the elevator. And you (8) ______________________ (go) to the top to see the view. It's great. You (9) ______________________ (see) the whole city from up there. And the Washington Monument is free. We (10) ______________________ (spend) any money on tickets. It's the same at the Jefferson Memorial.

A few hours later, leaving the Jefferson Memorial

Mara: That was great. I'm so glad we (11) ______________________ (wait) in a long line here. One long line a day is enough for me.

CD2-27

B Listen to the conversation. Compare your answers from exercise **A** to what the people actually say. Then work with a partner. Discuss the sentences in exercise **A** that have more than one correct answer.

C Use the map to complete Paul and Mara's conversation below with modals, modal-like expressions, and the verbs in parentheses. Then share your answers with the class.

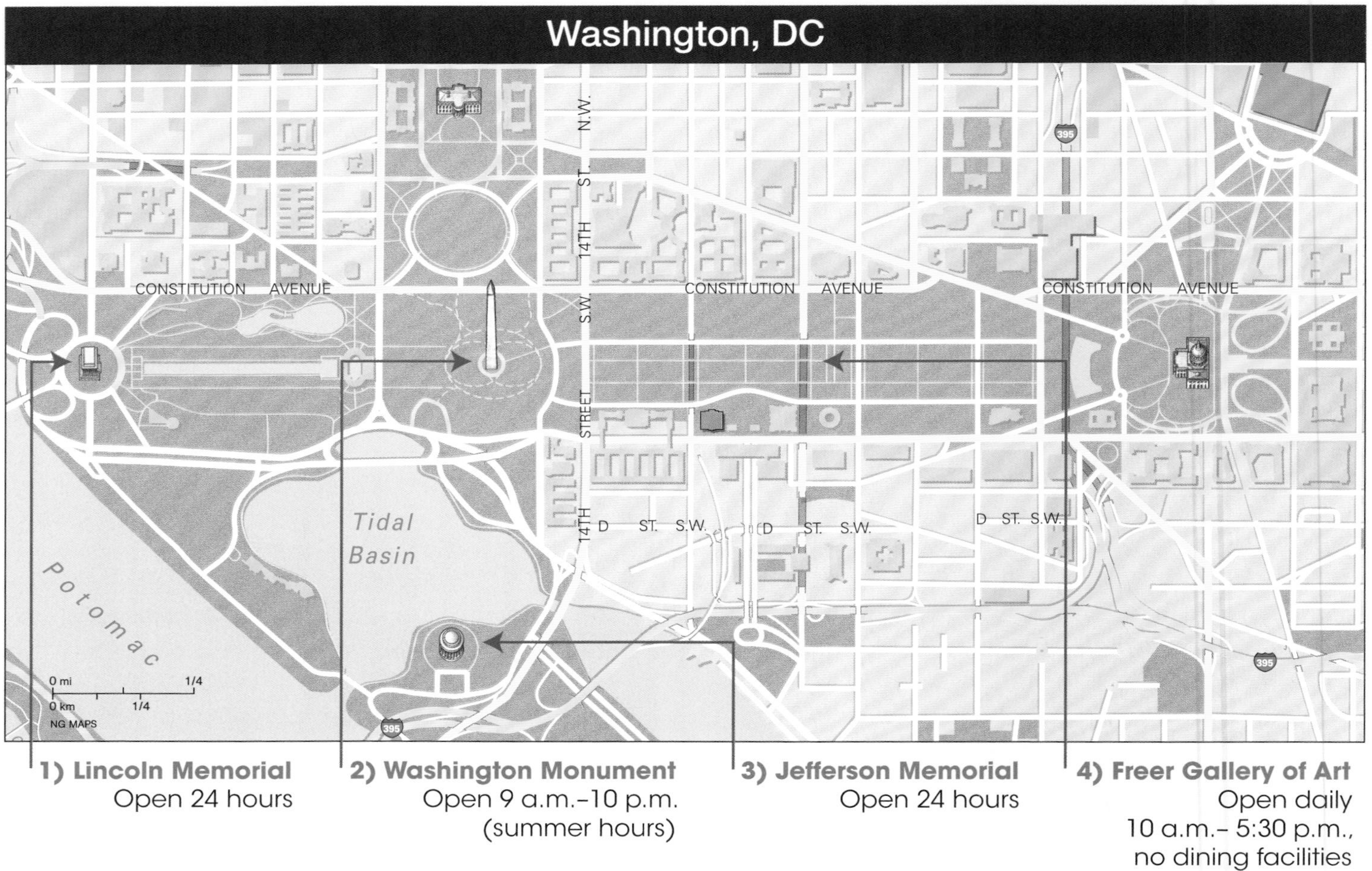

Looking for the Freer Gallery

Paul: OK. So how do we get to the Freer Gallery from here?

Mara: First, we go up 14th Street. Then, we (1) ______________ (make) a right.

A half hour later

Mara: I think we turned too soon. The map says we (2) ______________ (turn) on Constitution Avenue. This is D Street.

Paul: I think we (3) ______________ (ask) that police officer for directions. I don't want to walk all the way back to 14th Street.

At the Freer Gallery

Paul: I'm starving. (4) We ________________ (bring) sandwiches with us.

Mara: It's a good thing we didn't. Do you see that sign? People (5) ________________ (eat) here.

Paul: OK, then we (6) ________________ (find) a café nearby.

CD2-28

D Listen to the rest of Paul and Mara's conversation. Check your answers from exercise **C**.

Charts 7.1–7.7

3 EDIT. Read the paragraph about staying home for vacation. Find and correct nine more errors with modals and modal-like expressions.

Save Money: Take a Staycation!

Friends are always telling me that I should ~~taking~~ take a trip abroad. "You can learn so much. You will able to have new experiences," they say. "You had better to travel before you get married and have a family. When you have a family, you can't afford to travel so easily." I'm sure it's wonderful to go abroad, but I think people are able to learn a lot and have new experiences right at home. When I'm on vacation, I enjoy be able to see all the exciting things right in my hometown. I should not go abroad to visit a great museum. There's a great museum ten miles from my home. I went there yesterday. I could go for free. I had a wonderful time. I also don't have to go far to hear good music. I can enjoy the performances at our great concert hall. In fact, I ought go there more often. No, traveling isn't for me. At the end of the day I want to be able sleep in my own bed. I think all of my friends should had stayed in town for their last vacation like I did. I had a terrific time, and I must not to spend as much money as my friends did.

Charts 7.1–7.3, 7.6

4 SPEAK. Work in groups. Describe a good place for visitors to see in your town or country. Take turns answering the questions.

What place do you think visitors should see?

What are visitors able to see and do there?

How much do they have to pay to visit?

What do they have to bring with them?

Are they supposed to wear anything special?

What must people avoid doing to stay out of trouble there?

I think visitors should see the Forbidden City. Tourists are able to walk around the palace and its gardens . . .

Connect the Grammar to Writing

1 READ & NOTICE THE GRAMMAR.

A Do people tip in your country? Have you ever made a mistake when tipping someone in your country or abroad? Tell a partner about it. Then read the text.

When should I tip?

A tip is a small amount of money that you pay to certain service workers. In most countries, you don't have to tip much, if anything. However, in the United States, you are supposed to tip in a number of different situations.

- **Restaurants:** When you eat in a restaurant, you are supposed to leave your server a 15–20 percent tip. You don't have to tip when you order food and pick it up yourself, but you are supposed to offer a delivery person about 10 percent if he brings it to your home. Of course, if it's terrible weather, you probably ought to include a few extra dollars.
- **Hotels:** Hotels can be complicated. A lot depends on how much help you need. You are supposed to tip the concierge about \$10–\$20 when you check out. You should also leave some money for the cleaning staff, especially if you left your room a mess! Also, you really ought to hand anyone who carries your suitcases a small tip of about one or two dollars.
- **Taxis:** People generally tip taxi drivers about 15–20 percent. If the driver helps you with your bags, then you should probably offer him or her a few dollars more.

If you follow these basic rules, you won't have any problems traveling in the United States. If you get confused, don't be afraid to ask what to do.

GRAMMAR FOCUS

In this text, the writer uses the following modals and modal-like expressions.

be supposed to • is used to express an obligation *(When you eat in a restaurant, you **are supposed to leave** your server . . .)*

not have to • is used to show that something is not necessary *(In most countries, you **don't have to tip** much . . .)*

ought to/should • are used to offer advice *(. . . you probably **ought to include** . . .) (You **should** also **leave** some money for the cleaning staff . . .)*

B Read the text in exercise **A** again. Underline one more example of each of the following:

1. something that the writer considers a rule (with *supposed to*)
2. something that is not necessary (with *not have to*)
3. advice (with *should* or *ought to*)

C Complete the chart with information from the text in exercise **A**. Discuss your answers with a partner.

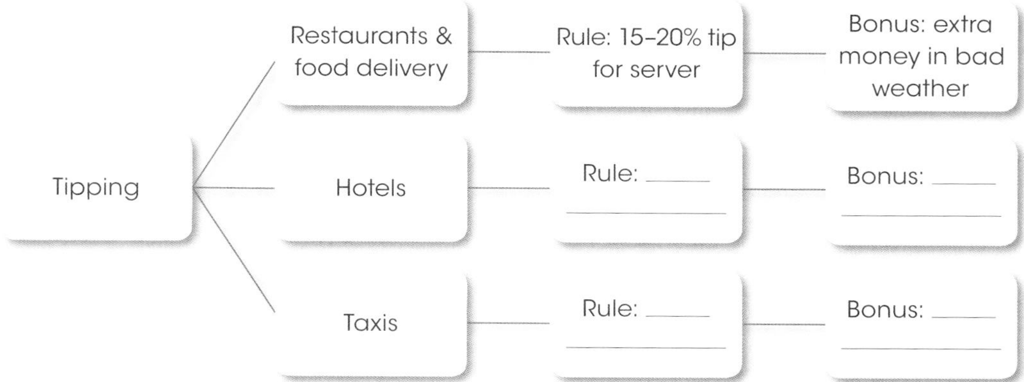

2 BEFORE YOU WRITE.

A Work with a partner. Brainstorm customs that visitors often find confusing when they visit your country, such as tipping, giving gifts, greeting people, arriving on time, and so on.

B Choose one custom from your list in exercise **A**. Then in your notebook, make a chart like the one in exercise **1C**. Write the basic "rules" for the custom.

3 WRITE two to three paragraphs explaining the custom to a visitor to your country. Use your chart from exercise **2B** and the text in help **1A** to guide you.

WRITING FOCUS Using Bullets to Organize Points

Notice how bullets are used in the text in exercise **1A**. In this text, after each bullet, the author uses a word in **bold** followed by a colon (:) to introduce a topic.

- **Restaurants:** When you eat in a restaurant . . .

4 SELF ASSESS. Underline the modals and modal-like expressions in your paragraphs. Then use the checklist to assess your work.

☐ I used *not have to* correctly. [7.1]
☐ I used *be supposed to* correctly. [7.2]
☐ I used *should* and *ought to* correctly. [7.6]
☐ I used the same pattern and punctuation after each bullet in my text. [WRITING FOCUS]

UNIT 8 Our Mysterious World

Modals: Part 2

▶ Giant statues on Mount Nemrut in Turkey show King Antiochus I, Theos of Commagene, lions, eagles, and gods.

EXPLORE

CD2-29

1 READ the conversation about a mysterious weather event. What is unusual about this kind of weather?

The Weather That Nobody Forecast

Krista: Hey, Gino. You're not going to believe the article I just read on the Internet. It's called *The Weather That Nobody Forecast*. Listen to this:

"Brignoles, France . . . London, England . . . Naphlion, Greece . . . Odzaci, Serbia . . . Kansas City, United States. What do these towns and cities have in common? They have all been the scene of a mysterious weather event. In all these locations, people have reported at one time or another that they saw frogs coming down like rain from the sky."

Gino: That **can't be** true!

Krista: Well, the article says that a lot of climate scientists have tried to come up with an explanation. That **must mean** they take the reports seriously, right?

Gino: I guess so. Have they figured out[1] why? What **could** possibly **be causing** frogs to fall from the sky?

Krista: Well, according to some scientists, it **could be** waterspouts.

Gino: What's a waterspout?

Krista: It's a tornado[2] that forms over water and travels over land. Sometimes a waterspout picks up animals and objects and carries them over long distances. So this is what **might be happening** to the frogs. According to the theory, the strong winds pick up the frogs and carry them along until they finally drop to the ground.

Gino: Incredible!

Krista: I know, but not everyone agrees with the waterspout theory. That **may not be** the right explanation. The cause **might be** a powerful flow of air called an updraft, which can lift small things such as frogs into the sky. However, no one has been able to prove either theory, so frog rainfall is still a bit of a mystery.

[1] **figure out:** to solve, understand
[2] **tornado:** a violent wind storm with a tall column of air that spins very fast

2 CHECK. Correct the error in each sentence according to the information in the conversation.

1. Many people said that they saw ~~lizards~~ frogs fall from the sky.
2. Some biologists have tried to explain frog rain.
3. A snowstorm is a possible reason for frog rain.
4. Strong winds can transport frogs short distances.
5. Scientists agree about the causes of frog rainfall.

3 DISCOVER. Complete the exercises to learn about the grammar in this lesson.

A Find these sentences in the conversation from exercise **1**. Write the missing words. Then circle the modals.

1. That ___can't be___ true!
2. That ______________ they take the reports seriously, right?
3. Well, according to some scientists, it ______________ waterspouts.
4. That ______________ the right explanation.
5. The cause ______________ a powerful flow of air. . .

B Look at the modals in exercise **A** again. What do they mean in this context? Write each modal in the correct column.

Very Certain	Not Certain
can't	

LEARN

8.1 Possibility: Present and Future

	Not Certain about Present or Future Events
Could/May (Not)/Might (Not)	The exam **could last** two hours. I'm not sure. It **may rain**. The sky looks a bit gray. Let's take an umbrella just in case. You **might have to** wait until the fall to take Chinese. Ask the professor. He **might not be** well today, so he **may not** come.
	Very Certain about Present or Future Events
Couldn't/Can't	That **couldn't be** Bill over there. Bill is much shorter. That **can't be** Mary. Mary isn't that tall.

1. Modals can be used to express possibility about something happening now or at some future time. a. *Could, may,* and *might* express the possibility that something will happen or that something is true. b. *May not* and *might not* express the possibility that something will not happen or is not true. c. *Couldn't* and *can't* express certainty that something is not possible or true.	 a. The hurricane **may change** its path. It **might go** south, not east. b. He **may not come** to work today. I hear he's having car trouble. c. It **couldn't be** a bird. It doesn't have feathers. He won the lottery? You **can't be** serious!
2. Do not use contractions for *may not* or *might not.*	✓ I may not finish my paper on time. ✗ I mayn't finish my paper on time.
3. Use *could* to ask questions about possibility. Do not use *may* or *might.*	Where **could** my wallet **be**? It's not in my bag.

4 Rewrite the statements. Use *may (not), might (not), could(n't),* or *can't* and the words in parentheses. More than one answer is sometimes possible.

1. It's possible that next summer will be hotter than usual.
   Next summer _might be/may be/could be_ (be) hotter than usual.
2. The paper says it's 120 degrees outside, but I don't believe it.
   It ______________ (be) that hot outside.
3. There's a 50 percent chance that it will snow tomorrow.
   It ______________ (snow) tomorrow.
4. There's a chance that you will see red rain someday, but it's not likely.
   You ______________ (see) red rain someday.
5. It's snowing very hard, so it's possible that we won't have class this afternoon.
   We ______________ (have) class this afternoon

6. Marc isn't here.

Where ______________ he ______________ (be)?

7. I really don't think that animal is a frog. It has a tail.

That animal ______________________ (be) a frog.

8.2 Logical Conclusions: Present and Future

	Almost Certain about Present or Future Events
Must (Not)/Has (Got To)	She just got a promotion at work. She **must be** happy. He **must not know** the address. That's why he's checking online. That **has (got) to be** a letter from Claire. I recognize her handwriting.

1. A logical conclusion is a judgment that we come to based on knowledge or evidence. We are almost 100 percent certain that the statement is true.	Robin lost her wallet. She **must be** upset.
2. Use *must, have to,* and *have got to* in affirmative statements that are logical conclusions.	My keys **must be** in my backpack. I saw them there last night. My wallet **has to be** somewhere in the house. I'm sure I left it there. The bill **has got to be** wrong. There **is** no way we used this much electricity.
3. Use *must not* for negative statements that are logical conclusions. Do not use *have to* or *have got to* with *not.*	She **must not be** his sister. They don't look anything alike.
4. Do not use a modal of logical conclusion when you state a fact. Instead, use a simple present or future form of the verb (*will, be going to*).	The store is closed. The sign says so. He'**ll be** here later. He called to let me know.

5 Complete the exercises.

A Read each statement about honeybees. Then complete each logical conclusion. Use *must* or *must not.*

1. These honeybees aren't moving.

   They ____must____ be dead.

2. Many honeybees are flying away from their hives and dying.

   There ______________ be a reason for this behavior.

3. It's a mystery why so many bee colonies are dying.

   Scientists ______________ know the reason.

4. The research on bees is taking a long time.

   It ______________ require a lot of work.

5. Fruit farmers depend on bees to pollinate their crops.

   The fact that there are fewer bees ________________ worry farmers.

6. Scientists still have a lot of questions about the situation.

   The scientists ________________________ be able to give fruit farmers much information.

7. Some beekeepers have lost up to 90 percent of their bees.

   The beekeepers ____________________________ be happy.

8. There will be less honey available for sale.

   That ____________________ mean that the price of honey will increase.

B **SPEAK.** Work with a partner. Find the sentences in exercise **A** in which *must* can be replaced by *have to* and *have got to*.

They must be dead.
They have to be dead.
They have got to be dead.

6 **ANALYZE THE GRAMMAR.** Read the sentences about bee research. Decide how *must* and *must not* are used in each sentence. Write **LC** for *logical conclusion*, **O** for *obligation*, or **P** for *prohibition*.

> **REAL ENGLISH**
>
> *Must* has three different uses. Its meaning depends on the context of the sentence.
>
> *You look pale. You* ***must*** *be sick.* (conclusion)
> *You* ***must*** *take your medication.* (obligation)
> *You* ***must not*** *smoke here.* (prohibition)

__O__ 1. The researchers must observe the bees carefully. If they don't, they might make mistakes in their research.

_____ 2. Other people must not go near the bees. Bees are dangerous.

_____ 3. The researchers always look calm. They must not be afraid of bees.

_____ 4. They must write down all their observations. That's an important part of the work.

_____ 5. They must not talk to anybody about their findings until their study is complete.

_____ 6. Some of their observation notes are missing. The researchers must not be happy.

_____ 7. The bees are leaving. There must be a problem.

_____ 8. The researchers must think that something in the environment is harming the bees.

8.3 Possibility and Logical Conclusions: Progressive

Modal (*Not*) + *Be* + Verb + *-ing*	
	Not Certain about Present or Future Events
May (Not)/Might (Not)/ Could	Professor Wang **may be giving** a lecture now. He's in the lecture hall. Sam **might be meeting** with his study group. It sometimes meets on Mondays. Lisa **could be coming** by taxi. She often takes one when she's late for class.
	Very Certain about Present or Future Events
Can't/Couldn't/Must (Not)	The teacher **can't be holding** office hours. His door is locked. They **couldn't be taking** an exam now. The class ended 15 minutes ago. Jen **must be studying**. She picked up her laptop and went to the library.

1. To express a possible continuing action in the present or future, use modal + *be* + verb + *-ing*.	Jay **might be talking** to Professor Angad in the lab. I saw them in there a minute ago. Suki's team **may be playing** basketball tonight. She was wearing her uniform when she left.
2. *May/Might/Could* + *be* + verb + *-ing* can be used to talk about possible future plans.	I **may be moving** in six months. I'm waiting to hear about the job I applied for. I **might not be taking** math next semester.
3. *Must* + *be* + verb + *-ing* can be used to talk about something that is very likely in the present or in the future.	The team **must be feeling** great. They just won the championship. Alan **must be graduating** next month. He has finished his coursework and passed his exams.
4. *Can't/Couldn't* + *be* + verb + *-ing* are used to express certainty that an action is not taking place.	Ben **can't be driving** to work. His car is in the driveway.

7 Complete each conversation. Use the modal and the progressive form of the verb in parentheses.

1. **A:** What do you think those researchers are doing here?
   B: They ___must be studying___ (must / study) the 17-year cicadas. These insects come out of the ground every 17 years, and this is the year.
2. **A:** Why are those people talking to the scientist?
   B: They ________________ (may / describe) the cicadas they saw.
3. **A:** One woman looks angry. She's pointing at all the cicadas in her garden.
   B: She ________________ (might / complain) about them.
4. **A:** What is that researcher doing with the audio equipment?
   B: He ________________ (could / record) the sound of the cicadas.
5. **A:** Wow! Listen to that noise.
   B: I know. It ________________ (must / keep) people up at night.

◄ A 17-year cicada

6. **A:** Look at the cicadas on that man's arm. He's just standing there calmly.
   B: I see. The cicadas ______________________ (must not / bother) him.

7. **A:** The researchers look like they're counting the cicadas. Are they?
   B: No, they ______________________ them (could not / count). There are too many to count—probably billions this year.

8. **A:** Why are there so few cars on the road tonight?
   B: I'm not sure, but people ______________________ (might not / drive) because it's dangerous. When cicadas fly into car windshields, it's difficult to see.

PRACTICE

8 Circle the correct modals to complete the paragraph.

Can Plants Hear?

According to a recent study, plants (1) **have got to / might** be able to "listen to" other nearby plants. You might think this theory is impossible and (2) **can't / might not** be true. However, the study suggests that some plants—such as basil—are good neighbors. Researchers think that they (3) **may / must** be helping other plants grow better. This (4) **could / must** be because the plants are communicating through sound vibrations (movements), but there will need to be more research before we know for sure. It (5) **must / can't** be difficult to get money for research, though, because the researchers say they have very little money left to continue their plant study. If they do not get more funding, they (6) **may not / must not** be able to continue their work. This would be a shame because the research is important. The results of these studies (7) **could / must** help humans in the future. For example, farmers (8) **could / have to** use sound to encourage or discourage the growth of certain plants. Just imagine, one day a farmer might even use music to help crops grow. It (9) **must not / may not** happen anytime soon, but it's possible.

9 Read the headlines. Then complete the statements about them. Use *might, may not, must,* or *can't* and the correct form of the verbs in parentheses. Add *not* where necessary. More than one answer is sometimes possible.

Residents Want to Stop New Building Near Bat Cave

1. "The residents _____must like_____ (like) bats and, and they _____must not think_____ (think) the new building is a good idea."

Plants Unhappy Without Other Plants Nearby

2. "Plants don't have feelings. The writer ______________________ (joke)."

Shark Seen on Subway Car in New York City

3. "That ______________________ (be) true. There are no sharks in the city."

Goats Replace Gardeners in Washington, DC, Cemetery

4. "Hmm. That ______________________ (be) a good idea for a lot of parks. Goats could control the number of weeds and keep down costs."

Study Suggests That Dogs Respond to Owners' Emotions

5. "So that ______________________ (explain) why my dog usually yawns when I yawn."

Bear Walks into Hotel in Juneau, Alaska; Eats Candy in Lobby

6. "Bears ______________________ (love) candy."

10 LISTEN & SPEAK.

CD2-30

A Listen to each group of sounds. Take notes in your notebook about what you think you hear.

B Work with a partner. Compare and discuss your notes. Use *may, might, could,* or *must*. Then share your ideas with the class.

A: *The first one must be a scary place. It could be an old house in a horror movie.*
B: *Yeah, it sounds really creepy. Did you hear the footsteps? It could be a ghost!*

11 APPLY.

A The photo shows an unusual relationship. In your notebook, answer the questions below. Use *may (not), might (not), could (not), can't,* or *must (not)*.

What kind of animals are in the picture?
Is the small animal afraid of the big animal?
Is the large animal asleep or awake?
Do you think the big animal will hurt the small animal?
What do you think the relationship between these two animals is?

B Work in groups. Discuss your answers. Give reasons for what you wrote.

The large animal can't be a tiger because tigers have stripes . . .

EXPLORE

CD2-31

1 READ the article about an archaeological discovery of a strange army. What questions did the discovery raise?

The Emperor's Terra Cotta Army

Near the city of Xian, China, in 1974, two farmers found a piece of terra cotta[1] that looked like a human head. Archaeologists began digging at the site, and they soon realized that the head belonged to a clay soldier. Over time, the archaeologists uncovered an entire army of such soldiers . . . over 6000 of them. These soldiers and their weapons[2] were found near the tomb of China's first emperor, Qin Shi Huang Di. Qin **must have wanted** the clay army to protect him in the afterlife.

Creating the soldiers **must have been** extremely challenging. The craftsmen[3] first had to find clay that was strong enough to shape into huge figures. Each soldier is about six feet tall (1.8 meters) and weighs over 600 pounds (272.2 kilograms). The most surprising finding was that each figure is unique—no two are exactly alike. How **could** the craftsmen **have produced** this collection? It's a mystery.

According to some sources, the workers **may have used** molds.[4] Molds allow for mass production because they produce objects that are the same. However, with molds it isn't possible to make individual features. That's why some scholars now believe that the craftsmen **must have added** details to the molded pieces by hand. They **might have wanted** the figures to look like people in the emperor's service, but no one knows for sure.

Archaeologists have explored only a fraction of the emperor's burial ground so far. In the coming years, they hope to learn even more about his unusual army, created over 2000 years ago.

[1] **terra cotta:** brownish-red clay that has been baked and is used for making things
[2] **weapon:** a tool used to harm or kill
[3] **craftsman:** a man who is skilled at making things with his hands
[4] **mold:** a form with an empty space inside into which materials are put to shape objects

2 CHECK. Read the statements. Circle **T** for *true* or **F** for *false*.

1. Archaeologists found a village made out of clay. **T** **F**
2. Experts believe that the emperor was worried about his safety after he died. **T** **F**
3. Each figure weighs about the same as an average human. **T** **F**
4. The figures were completely made by molds. **T** **F**
5. Archaeologists have completed their work at the site of Qin's tomb. **T** **F**

3 DISCOVER. Complete the exercises to learn about the grammar in this lesson.

A Find these sentences in the article from exercise **1**. Write the missing words.

1. Qin must have wanted the clay army to protect him in the afterlife.
2. Creating the soldiers ________________ extremely challenging.
3. How ________ the craftsmen ________ this collection?
4. According to some sources, the workers ________________ molds.
5. . . . the craftsmen ________________ details to the molded pieces by hand.
6. They ________________ the figures to look like people in the emperor's service, but no one knows for sure.

B Look at the sentences in exercise **A**. Write the number of each sentence next to the correct statement.

1. The writer is very certain that this is true. ________
2. The writer thinks this is possible, but is not certain. ________

LEARN

8.4 Possibility: Past

	Modal + (*Not*) + *Have* + Past Participle
May (Not)	Charlie **may have done** the painting, but I'm not sure. Pat **may not have gone** to bed yet. It's only 9:30 p.m.
Might (Not)	Pam **might have been** sick. I know she went home early. They **might not have wanted** to go to the party.
Could/ Couldn't	We **could have crashed**. We were lucky you saw the other car coming. Alex **couldn't have stolen** the money. He was at work at the time of the robbery.

1. To express possibility in the past, use a modal + *have* + the past participle of a verb. a. Use *may (not) have, might (not) have,* or *could have* when it's possible that something happened. b. *Could have* is also used to express something that was possible but did not happen.	a. He **may have gotten** lost. Give him a call. The mail **might not have come** yet. I'll check. b. He **could have dropped** the class, but he decided not to.
2. **Be careful!** *Couldn't have* is used when the speaker or writer believes the past action was not possible.	Her computer crashed while she was working, so she **couldn't have finished** the research. (It was impossible for her to have finished the research.)
3. Use *could have* to ask questions about possibility. *May have* is not used to ask about possibility. *Might have* is rarely used.	✓ **Could** I **have signed up** for the wrong class? ✗ May I have signed up for the wrong class?

4 Complete the exercises.

A Complete the conversation about the terra cotta warriors. Use the words in parentheses and the correct form of the verbs.

Guide: Notice how realistic the faces of the warriors are.

Rita: How (1) _could the ancient artists have created_ (the ancient artists / could / create) such realistic faces?

Guide: I don't know, but (2) ______________________ (they / could / ask) people to pose for them while they carved the statues, just like artists do today.

Felix: And why is there one soldier with a green face?

Guide: Some experts think (3) ______________________ (the artist / could / not do) that on purpose. They think the artist made a mistake.

Felix: (4) ______________________ (the artist / could / be) color blind?

Guide: Yes, maybe, but there's another possible explanation. The color green was a symbol of youth and energy in ancient China. (5) ______________________ (the artist / could / paint) the soldier's face green to show his bravery.

▲ A terra cotta warrior

Ryan: It's amazing that the tombs weren't discovered until the 1970s. How (6) ____________________ (people / could / not know) about the tombs for such a long time?

Guide: Before the discovery, the figures were under a beach. (7) ____________________ (no one / could / notice) that the figures were there. Remember, the villagers had to dig down over 16 feet before they found the tomb with the soldiers.

Cara: I understand that archaeologists also found models of horses and carriages in the tombs.

Guide: Yes, that's true. It's not entirely clear why they were built . . . but (8) ____________________ (the emperor / could / want) them for his travels during the afterlife.

B **ANALYZE THE GRAMMAR.** Work with a partner. Role-play the conversation in exercise **A**. Replace *could* with *may* or *might* in each sentence where possible. When it is not possible to replace it, discuss the reason.

5 Complete each conversation with *might not have* or *couldn't have* and the past participle of the verb(s) in parentheses.

1. **A:** The craftsmen probably needed a month or so to create each statue.
   B: No, they <u>couldn't have made</u> (make) the statues that quickly. It was a lot of work.

2. **A:** The guide didn't answer my question about the weapons.
   B: She ____________________ (hear) the question.

3. **A:** Why did Frank leave the tour early?

   B: I don't know. He ______________________ (like) it.

4. **A:** Uh oh. I think I left my camera at the hotel this morning.

   B: You ______________________ (leave) it there. You had it this afternoon.

   A: Then maybe I left it on the tour bus.

   B: Let's hurry. You can check with the driver. He ______________________ (leave) the parking area yet. Let's hope he hasn't.

5. **A:** You know, it's too bad we didn't get to the museum earlier this morning.

   B: But we ______________________ (see) the exhibit any earlier. The place doesn't open until 8:00 a.m.

8.5 Logical Conclusions: Past

Subject + *Must* (+ *Not*) + *Have* + Past Participle
She **must have loved** art. She collected paintings and sculptures. He **must not have heard** the question. He didn't answer it.

1. Use *must* or *must not* + *have* + the past participle of a verb to express a logical conclusion about something in the past. The conclusion is based on knowledge or evidence.	I **must have left** my laptop at home. It's not in my backpack.
2. *Had to have* + past participle can also be used to express a logical conclusion about the past.	Those statues **had to have been** very difficult to make.

6 Complete the exercises.

A Complete each logical conclusion with *must have* or *must not have* and the verb in parentheses.

1. Hannah works on archaeological digs in Rome. She _must have studied_ (study) archaeology in school.
2. She can't find her hand shovel. That's strange. She ______________________ (leave) it at the work site yesterday.
3. Glen didn't find any stone cooking tools at the site. The ancient Romans ______________________ (prepare) food there.
4. He spent a lot of time in the lab last year. He ______________________ (spend) much time digging outside at the work site.
5. Sam's team won an award for their work. They ______________________ (make) an unusual discovery.

6. The team leader has Cathy's report. She ______________________ (complete) it last night.

7. Ruth's team worked in the hot sun for ten or more hours every day.

   They ______________________ (be) exhausted when they got home.

8. They gave up after a year of disappointing archaeological research.

   They ______________________ (discover) anything interesting at the site.

9. Megan almost fainted from the heat the other day, and she had to lie down.

   She ______________________ (drink) enough water.

10. Victor's team finally left the site. They ______________________ (decide) there was nothing interesting to find there.

7 Complete the conversation with the words in parentheses. Use *must have* for logical conclusions. Use *had to* for obligations.

REAL ENGLISH

Use *had to*, not *must have*, for past obligations.

*They **had to take** a test yesterday.*
***Did you have to revise** your essay?*

Andy: So, Cara, you used to be an archaeologist, right?
(1) ___Your job must have been___ (your job / be) very interesting.

Cara: Yes, it was.

Ben: (2) ______________________ (you / go) to college to become an archaeologist?

Cara: Yes, and I went to graduate school, too. (3) ______________________ (I / not have) a master's degree, but I wanted to get one, anyway.

Dan: (4) ______________________ (you / work) on a lot of digs?

Cara: I did early in my career. It was fun, but it was tough at times, because I didn't get to see my husband very often.

Ben: (5) ______________________ (it / be) hard to spend all that time away from him.

Cara: Yes, it was. That's why I switched to working in the lab after a few years. During my career (6) ______________________ (I / spend) thousands of hours analyzing material in the lab, though of course, I never kept track of the time. Sometimes, (7) ______________________ (I / analyze) things that the police found underground. They always needed the information quickly.

Ben: That (8) ______________________ (work / be) fascinating.

8.6 Possibility and Logical Conclusions: Progressive

Modal (+ *Not*) + *Have Been* + Verb + *-ing*	
	Not Certain about Past Events
Could/May (Not)/ Might (Not)	We **could have been experiencing** a small earthquake. I felt the ground move. Stress at work **might have been contributing** to his health problems.
	Certain about Past Events
Couldn't/Must (Not)	She **couldn't have been lying**. She always tells the truth. He **must not have been taking** calls. I kept getting his voicemail.

To draw conclusions about a continuing action in the past, use a modal (+ *not*) + *have been* + verb + *-ing*.	Rena **might have been studying** in the library last night. I know she likes the peace and quiet there. Katie's hair is wet. She **must have been swimming**.

8 Use the words in parentheses to write an answer for each question.

1. How could the archaeological site have been robbed? It was closed to visitors at 5:00 p.m. yesterday, right?

   Yes, no one could have been touring the site after 5:00.

   (no one / could / tour / the site after 5:00)

2. The looters were familiar with the tour schedule. How is that possible?

   ____

   (they / must / watch / the site / for several days)

3. It's strange that the guard didn't hear anything when the looters arrived.

   ____

   (he / might not / pay / attention)

4. The looters knew exactly what they were doing. Why were they so successful?

   ____

   (they / could / plan / the theft / for months)

5. It's strange that the looters took only coins. Why didn't they take anything else?

   ____

   (they / might / plan / to return / for more things later)

6. It took a long time for the police to arrive at the site.

   ____

   (they / must / have / trouble finding the site)

7. The police searched the site, but they didn't find anyone. Why not?

____

(the looters / may / hide in a secret cave)

8. The police finally caught the looters this morning. The police looked really tired. Why?

____

(they / must / wait / all night for the looters to come out)

PRACTICE

9 READ & WRITE.

A Look at the photograph and read the paragraph. Who painted the mural?

> This photo shows the Palazzo Vecchio in Florence, Italy. Leonardo da Vinci made a famous painting in this room in 1505. Later, another painter, Vasari, painted the mural that we now see in the photograph. Some people believe that Leonardo da Vinci's missing painting is under Vasari's mural. They think it is possible that Vasari protected Da Vinci's painting by building a wall over it and then painting his own mural on the new wall.

▼ Palazzo Vecchio, Florence, Italy

B Complete the sentences about the painting in exercise **A**. Use *may, might, could,* or *must.* Add *not* where necessary. More than one answer is sometimes possible.

1. It's possible that someone destroyed *The Battle of Anghiari* years ago.

   Someone ___may OR might OR could have destroyed___ the painting.

2. It wasn't possible for Vasari to remove Leonardo's painting from the hall.

   Vasari ______________________________ Leonardo's painting from the hall.

3. It's possible that Vasari painted over Leonardo's painting.

   Vasari ______________________________ over Leonardo's painting.

4. It's almost certain that Vasari wanted to save Leonardo's painting.

   Vasari ______________________________ to save Leonardo's painting.

5. It's possible that Vasari built a second wall to protect Leonardo's painting.

   Vasari ______________________________ a second wall to protect the painting.

6. It was impossible for Leonardo's assistants to steal Leonardo's painting.

   Vasari's assistants ______________________________ Leonardo's painting.

7. At first, the Italian government tried to look beneath Vasari's mural. I'm sure they wanted to search for Leonardo's painting there.

   They ______________________________ to search for Leonardo's painting beneath Vasari's.

8. The Italian government decided to leave the paintings alone. I think that they left the paintings alone because they didn't want to damage them.

   They ______________________________ to damage either of the paintings.

10 **PRONUNCIATION.** Read the chart and listen to the examples. Then complete the exercises.

CD2-32

PRONUNCIATION **Reduced Past Modals**

The *have* in modals of past possibility and logical conclusion is often pronounced like the word *of.*

Examples:	**Full Pronunciation**	**Reduced Pronunciation**
	They may have left the house.	They *may of* left the house.
	It might have happened fast.	It *might of* happened fast.
	I could have screamed.	I *could of* screamed.
	She must have known the truth.	She *must of* known the truth.
	You might not have known that.	You *might not of* known that.
	He could not have called my number.	He *couldn't of* called my number.

In informal conversation, some people say *mighta, coulda,* and *musta* instead of *might of, could of,* and *must of.*

	It might have happened fast.	It *mighta* happened fast.

CD2-33

A Listen to the sentences. Write the full form of the missing words.

1. We ___may have___ forgotten to lock the door.
2. Everybody ________________ been at the game that night.
3. You ________________ dropped your keys on the way home.
4. Max ________________ noticed the footprints in the yard.
5. You ________________ left the window open.
6. We ________________ checked the security system last night.
7. You ________________ heard the footsteps outside.
8. It ________________ happened yesterday.

B Complete each sentence with your own ideas. Then read the sentences aloud to a partner. Practice the reduced pronunciation of the modals.

1. I could have ________________ yesterday, but I didn't.
2. My grandparents might have ________________, but I don't know for sure.
3. My parents must have ________________ when I ________________ ________________.
4. Our English teacher must not have ________________ when ________________ ________________.
5. In the past, people might not have ________________.

11 **EDIT.** Read the text about a strange robbery. Find and correct six more errors with modals.

It was a strange crime. One night, a man climbed into a 5000-gallon fish tank. He must have ~~be~~ been crazy! The fish were halibut, and he wanted to steal them. He must not have know how to catch fish properly because he attacked them with a heavy piece of metal. The tank became a mess. The man must not cleaned up the area because he left a trail of evidence that led the police to his house. The police were looking for the most important fish that was stolen—a 50-pound halibut. She may been a well-loved fish because everyone called her "Big Mamma." Unfortunately, the police never found Big Mamma because she had been eaten at a dinner party at the man's house. The people at the party were shocked. They could not have know that they were eating Big Mamma at the time. Those guests must been very angry because they spoke against the man at his court trial. The court gave the man a sentence of four years in prison. He offered to catch a new halibut to replace Big Mamma. He was a diver and surfer, so it's possible he could had caught another big fish. The court said thanks, but no thanks.

12 SPEAK & WRITE.

A Look at the time line about Roanoke, an English colony that mysteriously disappeared from North America in 1590. Work with a partner. Answer the questions.

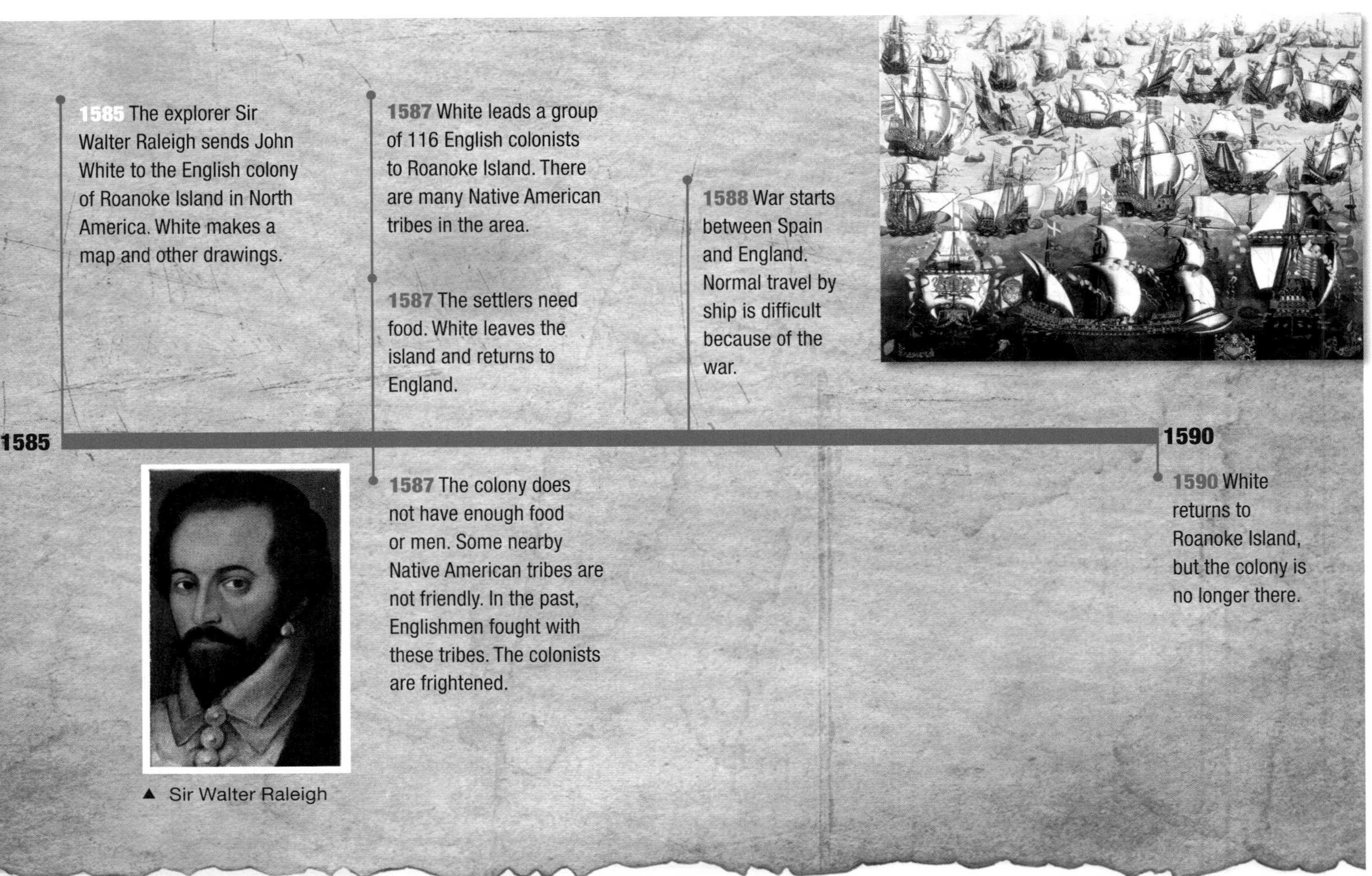

1585
1585 The explorer Sir Walter Raleigh sends John White to the English colony of Roanoke Island in North America. White makes a map and other drawings.
1587 White leads a group of 116 English colonists to Roanoke Island. There are many Native American tribes in the area.
1587 The settlers need food. White leaves the island and returns to England.
1587 The colony does not have enough food or men. Some nearby Native American tribes are not friendly. In the past, Englishmen fought with these tribes. The colonists are frightened.
1588 War starts between Spain and England. Normal travel by ship is difficult because of the war.
1590
1590 White returns to Roanoke Island, but the colony is no longer there.

▲ Sir Walter Raleigh

1. Who do you think John White was?

   A: *John White might have been a leader in a town in England.*

   B: *Or he could have been an explorer.*

2. Why do you think John White decided to travel to Roanoke Island?
3. What did he make drawings of?
4. Why did he return to England shortly after he brought the colonists to Roanoke?
5. Why didn't White return to Roanoke Island for three years?
6. When White returned to Roanoke Island, why didn't he find the colony?

B Write your answers to the questions in your notebook. Use *may, might, could,* and *must.* Add *not* where necessary.

John White might have been a leader in a town in England.

CD2-34

13 Listen to some popular theories about what happened to the settlers on Roanoke Island. Then choose the correct way to complete each theory.

1. According to Theory 1, Native Americans _____ killed the colonists.

   a. must not have (b.) may have

2. According to Theory 2, the colonists _____ died from a disease.

   a. may have b. couldn't have

3. According to Theory 3, the fence shows that a storm _____ destroyed the Roanoke colony.

   a. might have b. couldn't have

4. According to Theory 4, the colonists and the Croatoan Native American tribe _____.

   a. could have lived together

   b. could have had a big fight

5. According to Theory 5, the colonists _____.

   a. could have built a fort 70 miles away

   b. must not have moved to a different place

▼ Hand-colored woodcut showing John White's return to Roanoke Island in 1590

14 APPLY.

A Work with a partner. Complete the sentence based on the information in exercises **12** and **13**.

Roanoke Island must have gotten its nickname "The Lost Colony" because . . .

B Work in a group. Look at the list of unusual place names listed. Suggest reasons for the names. Write a sentence for each place name. Use *may have, might have, could have,* or *must have* + past participle.

Seven Sisters (Alberta, Canada)
Burnt Hill (Berkshire, England)
Cape Farewell (South Island, New Zealand)
Crazy Corner (County Westmeath, Ireland)
Disappointment Islands (South Pacific)
Moneygold (County Sligo, Ireland)
Nowhere Else (Tasmania, Australia)
Bearskin Neck (Massachusetts, USA)

Seven sisters may have discovered the town of Seven Sisters.

C Share your group's sentences with the class.

Charts 8.1–8.5

1 Complete the sentences about Nik Wallenda's tightrope walk. Use *may/might/could/must (not) or can't* and the verbs in parentheses. More than one answer is sometimes possible.

1. When people learned of Wallenda's plan to walk above the Grand Canyon on a wire, they thought, "He ___must be___ (be) crazy."
2. One tourist watching Wallenda said, "It's so dangerous. He ______________ (fall). I hope he doesn't."
3. The wind started blowing and Wallenda stopped twice. The wind ______________ (bother) him.
4. His family looked nervous. They ______________ (be) worried.
5. Of course, Wallenda had practiced. He ______________ (do) it without a lot of training.
6. Wallenda successfully crossed the Grand Canyon. He ______________ (succeed) without luck, skill, and self-confidence.

▲ Nik Wallenda crossing the Grand Canyon

2 Read the sentences. Then rewrite the second sentence. Replace the underlined words with appropriate modals. Do not change the meaning of the sentence.

1. I can't find my ring. <u>It's probably</u> on my bedside table.

   It ___must be___ on my bedside table.

2. Matilda was late for work yesterday. <u>Maybe she got</u> stuck in traffic.

   She ______________ stuck in traffic.

3. Paul lost his job. <u>I'm sure</u> he's upset.

   He ______________ upset.

4. Kendra studied for weeks, but she failed the exam. How <u>was it possible for her to fail</u>?

   How ______________ ?

5. I called Ana's name, but she didn't look up. She <u>probably didn't hear</u> me.

   She ______________ me.

6. Henry didn't steal the car. It <u>was impossible for him to have stolen</u> it because he was at work.

   He ______________ it because he was at work.

Charts 8.1, 8.2, 8.4, 8.5

3 LISTEN.

CD2-35

A Listen to the report about a surprising archaeological discovery. Before the discovery, what did many people believe about the Maya?

CD2-35

B Listen again. Mark the statements **T** for *true* or **F** for *false* according to the information in the report.

___F___ 1. The Maya must have predicted 2012 as the end of the world.

______ 2. The room that was discovered must have been the workroom of a Maya king.

______ 3. Kings may have wanted scribes to tell them what was going to happen in the future.

______ 4. Scribes may have used past events and complex arithmetic to predict the future.

______ 5. Archaeologists think they might understand everything about the murals soon.

______ 6. The Maya must have been afraid that their world was going to end.

Charts 8.1, 8.2, 8.4, 8.5

4 EDIT. Read the text. Find and correct six more errors with modals.

People sometimes believe in strange things. Some people believed that the Maya predicted the end of the world in 2012. They must ~~be~~ have been surprised when the world did not end. In fact, the Maya never made such a prediction. Other people used to believe in the existence of the Loch Ness Monster. They may have saw a photo once of an odd creature in the water. The picture, taken many years ago, looked real, so they thought the monster must existed. But there must not be another explanation. In fact, the Scottish doctor who took the famous photo of the creature said that it wasn't a monster. It was just an animal he didn't recognize. Now some people have a new theory: the Loch Ness Monster may have die because of global warming!

Some people also believe in crop circles. They think the circles may contain messages from aliens. The circles first appeared in England in the 1970s. In 1991, two Englishmen announced that they had made some of the circles. However, that announcement didn't stop people from believing that aliens had made them. The believers say that the men maybe have made the crop circles in England, but they could not made all the other circles in Europe, Australia, North America, and Japan.

So, the mystery is not why strange events happen. The mystery is really why people believe that such events happen, even when there is evidence that they didn't.

▲ Crop circles

Charts 8.1–8.6

5 SPEAK. Work in groups. Discuss your opinions about the headlines. Use modals of possibility and logical conclusion.

Spaceship Flies Over London
Mother Finds Son on Social Media Site After 22 Years
Man Has Heart Attack While Driving, Gets 3 Tickets
Bear with Head in Jar Rescued
Ghost Saves Man's Life
Bank Employee Drops 90,000 Euros in River

It couldn't have been a spaceship. It must have been an airplane or a star.

Connect the Grammar to Writing

1 READ & NOTICE THE GRAMMAR.

A Who is the most interesting or mysterious person in your family? Think about what you know and don't know about this person. Tell a partner. Then read the article.

Family Exploration

You never know what you might find out about your family. I must have been about ten years old when I first discovered that I had a distant relative who had been an explorer. I loved to go exploring myself. One day I went on an "expedition," and I must have forgotten to tell my grandmother. I couldn't have been away for more than three hours, but she was worried. "Pedro!" she said angrily when I came back, "Something could have happened to you. Next time, tell me where you're going. You must have some of my great-uncle's blood in you!"

This is how I discovered that I am distantly related to a man called Bruno, who knew the famous Brazilian explorer, Cândido Rondon. In fact, Bruno was one of the members of the famous expedition in Mato Grasso in 1909. They ran out of supplies on the long journey, and they almost didn't survive.

Bruno never married, and he died young. I don't know much about him. He must have been very brave. He couldn't have been much older than I am now when he went on his first expedition in the Amazon. I'm not sure, but he may have gone on ten different expeditions in that area. He might have seen tribes that had never met outsiders before.

Bruno had to have been one of the most adventurous people in Brazil at that time. I'm proud that he was part of my family.

▲ Cândido Rondon

GRAMMAR FOCUS

In the article in exercise **A**, the writer uses the following modals:

must have **+ past participle**	• to express a logical conclusion about the past *(He* ***must have been*** *very brave.)*
might/may have **+ past participle**	• to express possibility in the past *(. . . he* ***may have gone*** *on ten different . . .)*
could not have **+ past participle**	• to express that the past action was not possible *(I* ***couldn't have been*** *away for more than . . .)*

B Read the article in exercise **A** again. Find and underline other examples of logical conclusions, possibilities, and impossibilities about the past.

C Complete the chart with information from the article in exercise **A**. Discuss your answers with a partner.

What the author knows for sure	What the author guesses
He has a distant relative who was an explorer.	Bruno must have been very brave.

2 BEFORE YOU WRITE.

A Draw a family tree going as far back as you possibly can. What do you know about your relatives who lived a long time ago? Share your family tree with a partner.

B Choose one family member to write about. Make a chart like the one in exercise **1C**. Write logical conclusions or possibilities about the past in the right-hand column.

3 WRITE two or three paragraphs about a distant relative or ancestor. Give information you know about him or her. Then discuss what may or must have happened in his or her life. Use your chart from exercise **2B** and the article in exercise **1A** to help you.

WRITING FOCUS Using *In Fact* to Emphasize an Interesting Idea

In fact is used to introduce and add emphasis to an interesting idea that builds on information in the previous sentence.

This is how I discovered that I am distantly related to a man called Bruno, who knew the famous Brazilian explorer, Cândido Rondon. ***In fact****, Bruno was one of the members of the famous expedition in Mato Grasso in 1909.*

4 SELF ASSESS. Underline the verb forms in your paragraphs. Then use the checklist to assess your work.

- ☐ I used modals of possibility and logical conclusion about the present correctly. [8.1, 8.2]
- ☐ I used modals of possibility about the past correctly. [8.4]
- ☐ I used modals of logical conclusion about the past correctly. [8.5]
- ☐ I used *In fact* to emphasize an interesting idea. [WRITING FOCUS]

1 Stative Verbs

Description	Feelings	Desires	Measurements	Mental States	Possession	Senses
appear*	appreciate	hope	cost	agree	belong	feel
be	care	need	measure	believe	contain	hear
consist of	dislike	prefer	weigh	concern	have	hurt
look	forgive	want		disagree	own	notice
look like	hate	wish		doubt	possess	see
resemble	like			forget		smell
seem	love			guess		sound
	mind			know		taste
	miss			imagine		
				mean		
				recognize		
				remember		
				suppose		
				surprise		
				think		
				understand		

*Verbs in blue have both a stative and active meaning

2 Spelling Rules for the *-ed* Form of Verbs

1. Add *-ed* to the base form of most verbs that end in a consonant.	start-start**ed** talk-talk**ed**
2. Add *-d* if the base form of the verb ends in *-e*.	dance-danc**ed** live-liv**ed**
3. For one-syllable verbs that end in a consonant + a vowel + a consonant (CVC), double the final consonant and add *-ed*.	stop-stop**ped** rob-rob**bed**
Do not double the last consonant of verbs that end in *-w*, *-x*, or *-y*.	follow-follow**ed** fix-fix**ed** play-play**ed**
4. When the base form of the verb ends in a consonant + *-y*, change the *-y* to *-i* and add *–ed*.	cry-cr**ied** worry-worr**ied**
Do not change the *-y* to *-i* when the verb ends in a vowel + *-y*.	stay-stay**ed**
5. For two-syllable verbs that end in CVC and have stress on the first syllable, add *-ed*. Do not double the final consonant.	ORder-order**ed** HAPpen-HAPpen**ed**
For two-syllable verbs that end in CVC and have stress on the last syllable, double the final consonant and add *-ed*.	ocCUR-occur**red** preFER-prefer**red**

3 Spelling Rules for the *-ing* Form of Verbs

1. Add *-ing* to the base form of most verbs.	eat-eat**ing** do-do**ing** speak-speak**ing** carry-carry**ing**
2. For one-syllable verbs that end in a consonant + a vowel + a consonant (CVC), double the final consonant and add *-ing.* Do not double the final consonant for verbs that end in CVC when the final consonant is *-w, -x,* or *-y.*	stop-sto**pping** sit-si**tting** show-show**ing** fix-fix**ing** stay-stay**ing**
3. When the verb ends in a consonant + *-e,* drop the *-e* and add *-ing.*	ride-rid**ing** write-writ**ing**
4. For two-syllable verbs that end in CVC and have stress on the first syllable, add *-ing.* Do not double the final consonant. For two-syllable verbs that end in CVC and have stress on the last syllable, double the final consonant and add *-ing.*	ENter-enter**ing** LISTen-listen**ing** beGIN-begi**nning** ocCUR-occu**rring**

4 Spelling Rules for Regular Plural Nouns

1. Add *-s* to most nouns.	student-student**s** teacher-teacher**s** pen-pen**s**
2. Add *-es* to nouns that end in *-ch, -s, -sh,* and *-x.*	watch-watch**es** class-class**es** dish-dish**es** box-box**es**
3. Add *-s* to nouns that end in a vowel + *-y.*	boy-boy**s** day-day**s**
4. Change the *-y* to *-i* and add *-es* to nouns that end in a consonant + *-y.*	city-cit**ies** country-countr**ies**
5. Add *-s* to nouns that end in a vowel + *-o.*	video-video**s** radio-radio**s**
6. Add *-es* to nouns that end in a consonant + *-o.* Exceptions: photo → photos piano → pianos	potato-potato**es** tomato-tomato**es**

5 Common Irregular Verb Forms

Base Form	Simple Past	Past Participle
be	was, were	been
beat	beat	beaten
become	became	become
begin	began	begun
bend	bent	bent
bite	bit	bitten
blow	blew	blown
break	broke	broken
bring	brought	brought
build	built	built
buy	bought	bought
catch	caught	caught
choose	chose	chosen
come	came	come
cost	cost	cost
cut	cut	cut
dig	dug	dug
dive	dived/dove	dived
do	did	done
draw	drew	drawn
drink	drank	drunk
drive	drove	driven
eat	ate	eaten
fall	fell	fallen
feed	fed	fed
feel	felt	felt
fight	fought	fought
find	found	found
fit	fit	fit/fitted
fly	flew	flown
forget	forgot	forgotten
forgive	forgave	forgiven
freeze	froze	frozen
get	got	got/gotten
give	gave	given
go	went	gone
grow	grew	grown
hang	hung	hung
have	had	had
hear	heard	heard
hide	hid	hidden
hit	hit	hit
hold	held	held
hurt	hurt	hurt
keep	kept	kept
know	knew	known

Base Form	Simple Past	Past Participle
lay	laid	laid
lead	led	led
leave	left	left
lend	lent	lent
let	let	let
lie	lay	lain
light	lit/lighted	lit/lighted
lose	lost	lost
make	made	made
mean	meant	meant
meet	met	met
pay	paid	paid
prove	proved	proved/proven
put	put	put
quit	quit	quit
read	read	read
ride	rode	ridden
ring	rang	rung
rise	rose	risen
run	ran	run
say	said	said
sit	sat	sat
sleep	slept	slept
slide	slid	slid
speak	spoke	spoken
spend	spent	spent
spread	spread	spread
stand	stood	stood
steal	stole	stolen
stick	stuck	stuck
strike	struck	struck
swear	swore	sworn
sweep	swept	swept
swim	swam	swum
take	took	taken
teach	taught	taught
tear	tore	torn
tell	told	told
think	thought	thought
throw	threw	thrown
understand	understood	understood
upset	upset	upset
wake	woke	woken
wear	wore	worn
win	won	won
write	wrote	written

6 Patterns with Gerunds

Verb + Gerund			
They ***enjoy dancing****.* *She* ***delayed going*** *to the doctor.*			
admit	detest	miss	resent
advise	discuss	permit	resist
anticipate	dislike	postpone	risk
appreciate	enjoy	practice	stop
avoid	finish	put off	suggest
can't help	forbid	quit	tolerate
complete	imagine	recall	understand
consider	keep	recommend	
delay	mention	regret	
deny	mind	remember	

Verb + Preposition + Gerund			
He ***succeeded in winning*** *the prize.* *Are you* ***thinking about taking*** *another course?*			
apologize for	concentrate on	object to	thank (someone) for
argue about	dream about/of	plan on/for	think about
believe in	insist on	succeed in	warn (someone) about
complain about	keep on	talk about	worry about

Noun + Preposition + Gerund		
What's the ***purpose of doing*** *this exercise?* *I don't know his* ***reason for being*** *late.*		
benefit of	interest in	purpose of
cause of	problem with	reason for

Adjective + Preposition + Gerund			
I'm ***excited about studying*** *abroad.* *Are you* ***interested in going****?*			
accustomed to	excited about	nervous about	tired of
afraid of	famous for	responsible for	upset about/with
bad/good at	(in)capable of	sick of	used to
concerned about	interested in	sorry about/for	worried about

7 Patterns with Infinitives

Verb + Infinitive			
They ***need to leave****.* *I* ***am learning to speak*** *English.*			
agree	claim	know how	seem
appear	consent	learn	swear
arrange	decide	manage	tend
ask	demand	need	threaten
attempt	deserve	offer	try
be able	expect	plan	volunteer
beg	fail	prepare	want
can afford	forget	pretend	wish
care	hope	promise	would like
choose	intend	refuse	

Verb + Object + Infinitive			
I ***want you to leave****.* *He* ***expects me to call*** *him.*			
advise	convince	hire	require
allow	dare	instruct	select
appoint	enable	invite	teach
ask*	encourage	need*	tell
beg*	expect*	order	urge
cause	forbid	pay*	want*
challenge	force	permit	warn
choose*	get	persuade	would like*
command	help**	remind	

*These verbs can be either with or without an object. (*I* ***want [you] to go****.*)

After *help*, *to* is often omitted. (*He* ***helped me move**.*)

8 Adjectives Followed by Infinitives

afraid	embarrassed	lucky	sad
ashamed	excited	necessary	shocked
careful	glad	pleased	sorry
certain	good	proud	stupid
challenging	happy	ready	surprised
determined	hard	relieved	upset
difficult	important	reluctant	useful
disappointed	impossible	rewarding	willing
easy	likely	right	wrong

9 Transitive Verbs

arrest	control	found	observe	refuse	steal
avoid	cost	generate	offer	regard	take
attract	create	get	order	release	threaten
bother	damage	give	owe	remove	throw
bring	destroy	harm	pass	repair	train
buy	discover	hurt	plant	report	trap
call	disturb	identify	pollute	rescue	use
catch	do	kill	post	save	want
chase	estimate	lend	prepare	say	wash
complete	expect	limit	produce	see	tell
conserve	feed	locate	propose	send	surround
consider	find	lock	protect	shape	
consume	follow	make	provide	show	
contact	force	name	put	solve	

Intransitive Verbs

appear	exist	occur	stay
arrive	fall	rain	survive
be	fly	rise	take place
come	go	run	talk
cough	happen	sit	wait
cry	laugh	sleep	walk
die	live	smile	
disappear	look	snow	
dry (up)	matter	stand	

Verbs That Are Transitive and Intransitive

answer	increase	promise	teach
bite	know	read	think
clean (up)	leave	sell	try
eat	lose	serve	visit
finish	move	sign	walk
flood	pay	sing	write
hunt	play	start	

10 Phrasal Verbs and Their Meanings

Transitive Phrasal Verbs (Separable)		
(s.o. = someone s.t. = something)		
Phrasal Verb	**Meaning**	**Example Sentence**
blow (s.t.)* up	cause something to explode	*The workers **blew** the bridge **up**.*
bring (s.t.) back	return	*She **brought** the shirt **back** to the store.*
bring (s.t.) up	1. raise from childhood 2. introduce a topic to discuss	*1. My grandmother **brought** me **up**.* *2. Don't **bring up** that subject.*
call (s.o.)** back	return a telephone call	*I **called** Rajil **back** but there was no answer.*
call (s.t.) off	cancel	*They **called** the wedding **off** after their fight.*
call (s.t.) out	say something loudly	*He stood up when someone **called** his name **out**.*
check (s.t.) out	find out information	*I **checked** several places **out** before making a decision.*
cheer (s.o.) up	make someone feel happier	*Her visit to the hospital **cheered** the patients **up**.*
clear (s.o.) up	clarify, explain	*She **cleared** the problem **up**.*
cut (s.t.) down	cut through the trunk of a tree so that it falls down	*The town **cut** many trees **down** to make room for new roads.*
do (s.t.) over	do again	*His teacher asked him to **do** the essay **over**.*
figure (s.t.) out	solve, understand	*The student **figured** the problem **out**.*
fill (s.t.) in	complete information on a form	*I **filled** the blanks **in** on a hob application.*
fill (s.t.) out	complete an application or form	*I had to **fill** many forms **out** at the doctor's office.*
find (s.t.) out	learn, uncover	*Did you **find** anything **out** about the new plans?*
get (s.t.) across	succeed in making people understand an idea	*Leo **gets** his ideas **across** with pictures.*
give (s.t.) away	offer something freely	*They are **giving** prizes **away** at the store.*
give (s.t.) back	return	*The boy **gave** the pen **back** to the teacher.*
give (s.t.) up	stop doing	*I **gave up** sugar last year. Will you **give** it **up**?*
help (s.o.) out	aid, support someone	*I often **help** my older neighbors **out**.*
lay (s.o.) off	dismiss workers from their jobs	*My company **laid** 200 workers **off** last year.*
leave (s.t.) on	allow a machine to continue working	*I **left** the lights **on** all night.*
let (s.o./s.t.) in	allow someone or something to enter	*She opened a window to **let** some fresh air **in**.*
look (s.t.) over	examine	*We **looked** the contract **over** before signing it.*
look (s.t.) up	find information by looking in something like a reference book or list	*I **looked** the word **up** in the dictionary.*
make (s.o./s.t.) into	change someone or something to become someone or something else	*They **made** the book **into** a movie.*
make (s.t.) out of	produce something from a material or existing object	*Lily **made** the costume **out of** old clothes.*
make (s.t.) up	say something untrue or fictional (a story, a lie)	*The child **made** the story **up**. It wasn't true at all.*
pay (s.o./s.t.) back	return money, repay a loan	*I **paid** my friend **back**. I owed him $10.*
pick (s.o./s.t.) up	1. get someone or something 2. lift 3. acquire a skill over time without a lot of effort	*1. He **picked up** his date at her house.* *2. I **picked** the ball **up** and threw it.* *3. Joe **picked** the language **up** just by talking to people*
point (s.t.) out	tell someone about a fact or mistake	*I **pointed** the problem **out** right away.*
put (s.t.) aside	keep something to be dealt with or used at a later time	*Let's **put** the list of names **aside** until we need them.*
put (s.t) away	put something in the place where it is normally kept when it is not used	*Please **put** your books **away** before we start the test.*

Transitive Phrasal Verbs (Separable) *(Continued)*		
put (s.t.) off	delay, postpone	*Don't **put** your homework **off** until tomorrow.*
put (s.t.) on	place clothing or makeup on your body in order to wear it	*Emma **put** her coat **on** and left.*
put (s.t.) out	1. take outside 2. extinguish	*1. He **put** the trash **out**.* *2. Firefighters **put out** the fire.*
set (s.t.) up	1. arrange 2. start something	*1. She **set** the tables **up** for the party.* *2. They **set up** the project.*
show (s.t) off	make something obvious to a lot of people because you are proud of it	*Tom's mother **showed** his award **off** to everyone.*
shut (s.t.) off	1. stop something from working 2. stop the power	*1. Can you **shut** the water **off**?* *2. I **shut** the oven **off**.*
slip (s.t.) off	remove clothing quickly	*They **slip** their shoes **off** when they enter a room.*
sort (s.t.) out	make sense of something	*We have to **sort** this problem **out**.*
straighten (s.t.) up	make neat and orderly	*I **straightened** the living room **up**. It was a mess.*
take (s.t.) back	own again	*He **took** his tools **back** that he loaned me.*
take (s.t.) out	remove	*I **take** the trash **out** on Mondays.*
talk (s.t.) over	discuss a topic until it is completely understood	*Let's **talk** this plan **ove**r before we do anything.*
think (s.t.) over	reflect, ponder	*She **thought** the job offer **over** carefully.*
throw (s.t.) away/ throw (s.t.) out	get rid of something, discard	*He **threw** the old newspapers **away**. I **threw out** the old milk in the fridge.*
try (s.t.) on	put on clothing to see if it fits	*He **tried** the shoes **on** but didn't buy them.*
turn (s.o./s.t.) down	refuse	*His manager **turned** his proposal **down**.*
turn (s.o.) off	disgust or offend	*People who brag **turn** me **off**.*
turn (s.t.) off	stop something from working	*Can you **turn** the TV **off**, please?*
turn (s.t.) on	switch on, operate	*I **turned** the lights **on** in the dark room.*
turn (s.t.) up	increase the volume	***Turn** the radio **up** so we can hear the news.*
wake (s.o.) up	stop sleeping	*The noise **woke** the baby **up**.*
write (s.t.) down	write on paper	*I **wrote** the information **down**.*

*s.t. = something **s.o. = someone

Transitive Phrasal Verbs (Inseparable)		
*We'll **look into** the problem.*		
Phrasal Verb	**Meaning**	**Example Sentence**
account for (s.t.)	explain or give the necessary information about something	*What **accounts for** Ned's problems in school?*
come across (s.t.)	find something accidentally	*I **came across** a very old family photo.*
come from (somewhere)	be a native or resident of	*She **comes from** London.*
come up with (s.t.)	invent	*Let's **come up with** a new game.*
count on (s.o/s.t.)	depend on	*You can always **count on** good friends to help you.*
drop out of (s.t.)	quit	*Jin **dropped out of** the study group.*
fall for (s.o.)	be strongly attracted to someone and to start loving the person	*Chris fell for **her** the moment he saw her.*
follow through with (s.t.)	complete	*You must **follow through with** your promises.*
get off (s.t.)	leave (a bus/a train)	*I forgot to **get off** the bus at my stop.*
get on (s.t.)	board (a car/a train)	*I **got on** the plane last.*

Transitive Phrasal Verbs (Inseparable) *(Continued)*		
get out of (s.t.)	1. leave (a car/a taxi) 2. avoid	*1. I **got out of** the car.* *2. She **got out of** doing her chores.*
get together with (s.o.)	meet	*I **got together with** Ana on Saturday.*
get over (s.t.)	return to a normal state	*I just **got over** a bad cold. I feel much better now!*
go over (s.t.)	review	*Let's **go over** our notes before the exam.*
keep up with (s.o./s.t.)	move at the same speed or progress at the same rate	*Slow down. I can't **keep up with** you.*
look after (s.o./s.t.)	take care of	*He has to **look after** his sister. His parents are out.*
look for (s.o./s.t.)	try to find someone or something that you want or need	*I'm **looking for** someone who can help me.*
look into (s.t.)	investigate	*The police **looked into** the crime and solved it.*
pass by (s.o./s.t.)	go past a person, place, etc., on your way to another place	*If you **pass by** the house, call first.*
put up with (s.t.)	tolerate or accept something even though you find it unpleasant	*We have to **put up with** a lot of noise in this building.*
run into (s.o.)	meet accidentally	*She **ran into** Mai on campus.*
turn into (s.t.)	become something different	*The trip **turned into** a nightmare.*
turn to (s.o.)	ask someone for help or advice	*I **turn to** my parents when I need advice.*
take up (s.t.)	use an amount of time, space, or effort	*The table **takes up** too much space.*

Intransitive Phrasal Verbs (Inseparable)		
*My car **broke down** again!*		
Phrasal Verb	**Meaning**	**Example Sentence**
add up	make sense	*What he says does not **add up**.*
break down	stop working	*This machine **breaks down** all the time.*
break up	separate	*Their marriage **broke up** after a year.*
catch up	reach the same level as others in a group	*You can **catch up** with the others in the class, but you have to work hard.*
check out	pay the bill and leave a hotel	*We have to **check out** by noon.*
come back	return	*I'll **come back** soon.*
come on	(of a machine) start working	*It takes a few minutes for the copier to **come on**.*
come out	reach a result	*The meeting **came out** well. We were all satisfied.*
cry out	make a loud sound because you are frightened, unhappy, or in pain	*When the children saw the bear, they **cried out**.*
die out	become less and less common and eventually disappear completely	*Many languages have **died out**.*
dress up	put on more formal clothes	*He **dressed up** in his best suit to attend the wedding.*
drop in	visit without an appointment	***Drop in** when you can.*
drop out	leave or stop	*She **dropped out** of school very young.*
eat out	eat in a restaurant	*She hates to cook so she **eats out** frequently.*
end up	come finally to a particular place or position	*We couldn't decide where to eat. We **ended up** at a pizza place.*
fall down	fall accidentally	*I wasn't looking and **fell down**.*
fool around	play with	*He **fools around** with old cars for fun.*
get ahead	succeed, improve oneself	*Now that she has a new job, she is **getting ahead**.*
get along	have a friendly relationship	*My coworkers and I **get along** well together.*

Intransitive Phrasal Verbs (Inseparable) *(Continued)*		
get around	go from one place to another in a certain way	*I **get around** by bike.*
get up	awaken, arise	*I **got up** late this morning.*
give up	stop trying	*I played the piano for seven years but then **gave up**.*
go ahead	begin or continue to do	*You can **go ahead**. We'll wait for Jane.*
go away	leave, depart	*The rabbits in the garden finally **went away**.*
go down	decrease	*Prices of cars have **gone down** recently.*
go on	continue	*How long do you think this speech will **go on**?*
go out	1. leave one's home 2. have a romantic relationship with someone	*1. Jon has **gone out**. He should return soon.* *2. Lee and Sam have been **going out** for a year.*
go up	rise, go higher	*The price of gasoline has **gone up**.*
grow up	become and adult	*Our daughter has **grown up** now.*
hang on	wait	***Hang on** while I change my shoes.*
hang out	spend time with others informally	*My friends and I like to **hang out** on Friday nights.*
hold on	1. struggle against difficulty 2. keep your hand on or around something	*1. **Hold on** just a little longer. It's almost over.* *2. **Hold on** so that you don't fall.*
look around	examine an area	*We **looked around** before choosing a place to camp.*
look out	be careful	***Look out**! You'll fall!*
loosen up	become more relaxed	*My boss used to be very tense, but she has **loosened up** over the years.*
make up	agree to be friends again	*They had a fight, but soon **made up**.*
move in	start to live in	*We **moved in** last week. We love the area!*
move out	leave a place permanently	*When is your roommate **moving out**?*
pass away	die	*My father **passed away** last year.*
run out	use all of something	*Is there more of paper for the printer? We **ran out**.*
set out	start a journey	*We're going to **set out** at 6 a.m.*
show up	arrive (sometimes unexpectedly or late)	*They **showed up** after the train left.*
sign up	join, agree to do something	*The course looked interesting, so I **signed up**.*
sit down	seat oneself	*I **sat down** on a bench in the park.*
speak up	talk louder	*Will you **speak up**? I can't hear you?*
stand out	be very noticeable	*Can you make his face **stand out** more so that everyone can see him?*
stand up	get on one's feet	*The teacher asked the students to **stand up**.*
stay on	remain somewhere after other people have left or after when you were going to leave	*We haven't seen everything, so we'll **stay on** another day.*
stay up	keep awake	*The student **stayed up** all night to study.*
take off	1. leave the ground and start flying 2. increase quickly	*1. After a long wait, the airplane finally **took off**.* *2. Sales of the new product have **taken off**.*
turn out	happen in a particular way or have a particular result	*I hope everything **turns out** well.*
watch out	be careful	***Watch out!** There's a lot of ice on this road.*
work out	exercise	*The football player **works out** three times a week.*

11 Guide to Pronunciation Symbols

Vowels

Symbol	Key Word	Pronunciation
/a/	hot	/hat/
	far	/far/
/æ/	cat	/kæt/
/aɪ/	fine	/faɪn/
/aʊ/	house	/haʊs/
/ɛ/	bed	/bɛd/
/eɪ/	name	/neɪm/
/i/	need	/nid/
/ɪ/	sit	/sɪt/
/oʊ/	go	/goʊ/
/ʊ/	book	/bʊk/
/u/	boot	/but/
/ɔ/	dog	/dɔg/
	four	/fɔr/
/ɔɪ/	toy	/tɔɪ/
/ʌ/	cup	/kʌp/
/ɛr/	bird	/bɛrd/
/ə/	about	/əˈbaʊt/
	after	/ˈæftər/

Consonants

Symbol	Key Word	Pronunciation
/b/	boy	/bɔɪ/
/d/	day	/deɪ/
/dʒ/	just	/dʒʌst/
/f/	face	/feɪs/
/g/	get	/gɛt/
/h/	hat	/hæt/
/k/	car	/kar/
/l/	light	/laɪt/
/m/	my	/maɪ/
/n/	nine	/naɪn/
/ŋ/	sing	/sɪŋ/
/p/	pen	/pɛn/
/r/	right	/raɪt/
/s/	see	/si/
/t/	tea	/ti/
/tʃ/	cheap	/tʃip/
/v/	vote	/voʊt/
/w/	west	/wɛst/
/y/	yes	/yɛs/
/z/	zoo	/zu/
/ð/	they	/ðeɪ/
/θ/	think	/θɪŋk/
/ʃ/	shoe	/ʃu/
/ʒ/	vision	/ˈvɪʒən/

Source: The *Newbury House Dictionary plus Grammar Reference, Fifth Edition*, National Geographic Learning/Cengage Learning, 2014

GLOSSARY OF GRAMMAR TERMS

action verb: a verb that shows an action.

➢ *He **drives** every day.*

➢ *They **left** yesterday morning.*

active voice: a sentence in which the subject performs the action of the verb. (See *passive.*)

➢ *Michael ate the hamburger.*

adjective: a word that describes or modifies a noun or pronoun.

➢ *She is **friendly**.*

➢ *Brazil is a **huge** country.*

adjective clause: (See *relative clause.*)

adverb: a word that describes or modifies a verb, an adjective, or another adverb.

➢ *He eats **quickly**.*

➢ *She drives **carefully**.*

adverb clause: a kind of dependent clause. Like single adverbs, they can show time, reason, purpose, and condition.

➢ ***When the party was over**, everyone left.*

adverb of frequency: (See *frequency adverb.*)

adverb of manner: an adverb that describes the action of the verb. Many adverbs of manner are formed by adding *-ly* to the adjective.

➢ *You sing **beautifully**.*

➢ *He speaks **slowly**.*

affirmative statement: a statement that does not have a verb in the negative form.

➢ *My uncle lives in Portland.*

article: a word used before a noun; *a, an, the.*

➢ *I looked up at **the** moon.*

➢ *Lucy had **a** sandwich and **an** apple for lunch.*

auxiliary verb: (Also called *helping verb.*) a verb used with the main verb. *Be, do, have,* and *will* are common auxiliary verbs when they are followed by another verb. Modals are also auxiliary verbs.

➢ *I **am** working.*

➢ *He **won't** be in class tomorrow.*

➢ *She **can** speak Korean.*

base form: the form of the verb without *to* or any endings such as *-ing, -s,* or *-ed.*

➢ *eat, sleep, go, walk*

capital letter: an uppercase letter.

➢ *New York, Mr. Franklin, Japan*

clause: a group of words with a subject and a verb. (See *dependent clause* and *main clause.*)

➢ *We watched the game.* (one clause)

➢ *We watched the game after we ate dinner.* (two clauses)

comma: a punctuation mark that separates parts of a sentence.

➢ *After he left work**,** he went to the gym.*

➢ *I can't speak Russian**,** but my sister can.*

common noun: a noun that does not name a specific person, place, thing, or idea.

➢ *man, country, book, help*

comparative: the form of an adjective used to talk about the difference between two people, places, or things.

➢ *I'm **taller** than my mother.*

➢ *That book is **more interesting** than this one.*

conditional: a structure used to express an activity or event that depends on something else.

➢ ***If the weather is nice on Sunday**, we'll go to the beach.*

conjunction: a word used to connect information or ideas. *And, but, or,* and *because* are conjunctions.

➢ *He put cheese **and** onions on his sandwich.*

➢ *I wanted to go, **but** I had too much homework.*

➢ *We were confused **because** we didn't listen.*

consonant: a sound represented by the following letters and combinations of the letters:

➢ *b, c, d, f, g, h, j, k, l, m, n, p, q, r, s, t, v, w, x, y, z.*

contraction: two words combined into a shorter form.

➢ *did not* → ***didn't***

➢ *I am* → ***I'm***

➢ *she is* → ***she's***

➢ *we will* → ***we'll***

count noun: a noun that names something you can count. They are singular or plural.

➢ *I ate an **egg** for breakfast.*

➢ *I have **six apples** in my bag.*

definite article: the article *the*. It is used when you are referring to a specific, person, place, or thing.

➢ *I found it on **the** Internet.*

➢ ***The** children are sleeping.*

demonstrative pronoun: a pronoun that identifies a person or thing.

➢ ***This** is my sister, Kate.*

➢ ***Those** are Jamal's books.*

dependent clause: a clause that cannot stand alone as a sentence. It must be used with a main clause.

➢ *I went for a walk **before I ate breakfast**.*

direct object: a noun or pronoun that receives the action of the verb.

➢ *Aldo asked a **question**.*

➢ *Karen helped **me**.*

direct quote: a statement of a speaker's exact words using quotation marks.

➢ *Our teacher said, **"Do exercises 5 and 6 for homework."***

exclamation point: a punctuation mark that shows emotion (anger, surprise, excitement, etc.) or emphasis

➢ *We won the game**!***

➢ *It's snowing**!***

formal: describes language used in academic writing or speaking, or in polite or official situations rather than in everyday speech or writing.

➢ *Please do not take photographs inside the museum.*

➢ *May I leave early today?*

frequency adverb: an adverb that tells how often something happens. Some common adverbs of frequency are *never, rarely, sometimes, often, usually*, and *always*.

➢ *I **always** drink coffee in the morning.*

➢ *He **usually** leaves work at six.*

frequency expression: an expression that tells how often something happens.

➢ *We go to the grocery store **every Saturday**.*

➢ *He plays tennis **twice a week**.*

future: a form of a verb that expresses an action or situation that has not happened yet. *Will, be going to*, present progressive, and simple present are used to express the future.

➢ *I **will call** you later.*

➢ *We**'re going** to the movies tomorrow.*

➢ *I**'m taking** French next semester.*

➢ *The show **starts** after dinner.*

future conditional: expresses something that we believe will happen in the future based on certain conditions; the *if* clause + simple present gives the condition, and *will* or *be going to* + the base form of the verb gives the result.

➢ *If you don't go to practice, the coach will not let you play in the game.*

future perfect: a verb form used to talk about an action or event that will happen before a certain time in the future.

➢ *I**'ll have finished** the work by the time you return.*

generic noun: a noun that refers to people, places, and things in general

➢ ***Hospitals** are for sick **people**.*

➢ *I like **music**.*

gerund: an *-ing* verb form that is used as a noun. It can be the subject of a sentence, or the object of a verb or preposition. (See page A4 for lists of common verbs followed by gerunds.)

➢ ***Surfing** is a popular sport.*

➢ *We enjoy **swimming**.*

➢ *The boy is interested in **running**.*

gerund phrase: an *-ing* verb form + an object or a prepositional phrase. It can be the subject of a sentence, or the object of a verb or preposition.

➢ ***Swimming in the ocean** is fun.*

➢ *I love **eating chocolate**.*

➢ *We are thinking about **watching the new TV show**.*

helping verb: (See *auxiliary verb.*)

***if* clause:** a clause that begins with *if* that expresses a condition.

➢ ***If you drive too fast,** you will get a ticket.*

imperative: a sentence that gives an instruction or command.

➢ ***Turn** left at the light.*

➢ ***Don't use** the elevator.*

indefinite article: *a* and *an*, articles used when you are not referring to a specific person, place, or thing. They are used before singular count nouns.

➢ *We have **a** test today.*

➢ *She's **an** engineer.*

indefinite pronoun: a pronoun used to refer to people or things that are not specific or not known. *Someone, something, everyone, everything, no one, nothing*, and *nowhere* are common indefinite pronouns.

➢ ***Everyone** is here today.*

➢ ***No one** is absent.*

➢ *Would you like **something** to eat?*

independent clause: a clause that can stand alone as a complete sentence. It has a subject and a verb.

➢ ***I went for a walk** before breakfast.*

infinitive: *to* + the base form of a verb.

➢ *He wants **to see** the new movie.*

infinitive of purpose: *to* + the base form of the verb used to express purpose or to answer the question *Why?* (also *in order to)*

➢ *Scientists studied the water **in order to learn** about the disease.*

➢ *We went to the store **to buy** milk.*

informal: language used in casual, everyday conversation and writing.

- ➢ *Who are you talking to?*
- ➢ *We'll be there at eight.*

information question: (See *Wh-* question.)

inseparable phrasal verb: a phrasal verb that cannot have an noun or pronoun between its two parts (verb + particle). The verb and the particle always stay together.

- ➢ *I **ran into** a friend in the library.*
- ➢ *Do you and your coworkers **get along**?*

intonation: the rise or fall of a person's voice. For example, rising intonation is often used to ask a question.

intransitive verb: a verb that cannot be followed by a direct object.

- ➢ *We didn't **agree**.*
- ➢ *The students **smiled** and **laughed**.*

irregular adjective: an adjective that does not change form in the usual way.

- ➢ *good ⟶ better*
- ➢ *bad ⟶ worse*

irregular adverb: an adverb that does not change form in the usual way.

- ➢ *well ⟶ better*
- ➢ *badly ⟶ worse*

irregular verb: a verb with forms that do not follow the rules for regular verbs.

- ➢ *swim ⟶ swam*
- ➢ *have ⟶ had*

main clause: a clause that can stand alone as a sentence. It has a subject and a verb. (See *independent clause.)*

- ➢ ***I heard the news** when I was driving home.*

main verb: the verb that is the main clause.

- ➢ *We **drove** home after we had dinner.*

measurement word: a word used to talk about a specific amount or quantity of a non-count noun.

- ➢ *We need to buy a **box** of pasta and a **gallon** of milk.*

modal: an auxiliary verb that adds a degree of certainty, possibility, or time to a verb. *May, might, can, could, will, would,* and *should* are common modals.

- ➢ *You **should** eat more vegetables.*
- ➢ *Julie **can** speak three languages.*

negative statement: a statement that has a verb in the negative form.

- ➢ *I don't have any sisters.*
- ➢ *She doesn't drink coffee.*

non-count noun: a noun that names something that cannot be counted.

- ➢ *Carlos drinks a lot of **coffee**.*
- ➢ *I need some **salt** for the **recipe**.*

non-identifying relative clause: a relative clause that gives extra information about the noun it is describing. The information is not necessary to understand who or what the noun refers to.

- ➢ *Nelson Mandela, **who was a great leader**, died in 2013.*

noun: a word that names a person, place, or thing.

- ➢ *They're **students**.*
- ➢ *He's a **teacher**.*

noun clause: a kind of dependent clause. A noun clause can be used in place of a noun, a noun phrase or a pronoun.

- ➢ *Could you tell me **where the bank is**?*

object: a noun or pronoun that receives the action of the verb.

- ➢ *Mechanics fix **cars**.*

object pronoun: takes the place of a noun as the object of the sentence; *me, you, him, her, it, us, them.*

- ➢ *Rita is my neighbor. I see **her** every day.*
- ➢ *Can you help **us**?*

passive: a verb form that expresses who or what receives the action of the verb, not who or what performs the action

- ➢ *My wallet **has been stolen**.*

past perfect: a verb form used to talk about an action that happened before another action or time in the past.

- ➢ *They **had met** in school, but then they didn't see each other again for many years.*

past perfect progressive: a verb form used for an action or event that was happening until or just before another action, event, or time.

- ➢ *He**'d been driving** for twelve hours when they ran out of gas.*

past progressive: a verb form used to talk about an action that was in progress in the past.

- ➢ *He **was watching** TV when the phone rang.*

period: a punctuation mark used at the end of a statement.

- ➢ *She lives in Moscow.*

phrasal verb: a two-word or three-word verb. The phrasal verb means something different from the two or three words separately. (See pages A7–A9 for lists of common phrasal verbs.)

- ➢ ***Turn off** the light when you leave.*
- ➢ *She**'s come up with** an interesting idea.*

phrase: a group of words that go together; not a complete sentence (i.e., does not have both a subject and a verb).

➢ *He lives* ***near the train station****.*

plural noun: the form of a noun that indicates more than one person, place, or thing.

➢ *He put three* ***boxes*** *on the table.*

➢ *Argentina and Mexico are* ***countries****.*

possessive adjective: an adjective that shows ownership or a relationship: *my, your, his, her, its, our, their.*

➢ ***My*** *car is green.*

➢ ***Your*** *keys are on the table.*

possessive noun: a noun that shows ownership or a relationship. To make most singular nouns possessive, use an apostrophe (') + -*s*. To make plural nouns possessive, add an apostrophe.

➢ ***Leo's*** *apartment is large.*

➢ *The* ***girls'*** *books are on the table.*

possessive pronoun: a pronoun that shows ownership or a relationship: *mine, yours, his, hers, ours, theirs*. Possessive pronouns are used in place of a possessive adjective + noun.

➢ *My sister's eyes are blue.* ***Mine*** *are brown. What color are* ***yours****?*

preposition: a word that describes the relationships between nouns; prepositions show space, time, direction, cause, and effect. Often they occur together with certain verbs or adjectives.

➢ *I live* ***on*** *Center Street.*

➢ *We left* ***at*** *noon.*

➢ *I'm worried* ***about*** *the test.*

present continuous: (See *present progressive.*)

present perfect: a verb form that connects the past to the present.

➢ *Julia* ***has lived*** *in London for 10 years.*

➢ *Monika* ***has broken*** *the world record.*

➢ *Zack and Dan* ***have never been*** *to Germany.*

present perfect progressive: a verb form used for ongoing actions that began in the past and continue up to the present.

➢ *You****'ve been working*** *too hard.*

present progressive: (also called *present continuous*) a verb form used to talk about an action or event that is in progress at the moment of speaking; the form can also refer to a planned event in the future.

➢ *That car* ***is speeding****.*

➢ *I* ***am taking*** *three classes this semester.*

➢ *We* ***are eating*** *at that new restaurant Friday night.*

pronoun: a word that takes the place of a noun or refers to a noun.

➢ *The teacher is sick today.* ***He*** *has a cold.*

proper noun: a noun that names a specific person, place, or thing.

➢ ***Maggie*** *lives in a town near* ***Dallas****.*

punctuation: a mark that makes ideas in writing clear. Common punctuation marks include the comma (,), period (.), exclamation point (!), and question mark (?).

➢ *John plays soccer****,*** *but I don't.*

➢ *She's from Japan****.***

➢ *That's amazing****!***

➢ *Where are you from****?***

quantifier: a word used to describe the amount of a noun.

➢ *We need* ***some*** *potatoes for the recipe.*

➢ *I usually put* ***a little*** *milk in my coffee.*

question mark: a punctuation mark used at the end of a question.

➢ *Are you a student****?***

regular: a noun, verb, adjective, or adverb that changes form according to standard rules.

➢ *apple → apple****s***

➢ *talk → talk****ed****/talk****ing***

➢ *small → small****er***

➢ *slow → slow****ly***

reported speech: part of a sentence (a noun clause or infinitive phrase) that reports what someone has said.

➢ *They said* ***they would be late****.*

➢ *They told* ***us not to wait****.*

sentence: a thought that is expressed in words, usually with a subject and verb. A sentence begins with a capital letter and ends with a period, exclamation point, or question mark.

➢ *The bell rang loudly.*

➢ *Don't eat that!*

separable phrasal verb: a phrasal verb that can have a noun or a pronoun (object) between its two parts (verb + particle).

➢ ***Turn*** *the light* ***off****.*

➢ ***Turn off*** *the light.*

short answer: a common spoken answer to a question that is not always a complete sentence.

➢ *A: Did you do the homework?*

➢ *B:* ***Yes, I did./No, I didn't.***

➢ *A: Where are you going?*

➢ *B:* ***To the store.***

simple past: a verb form used to talk about completed actions.

➢ *Last night we* ***ate*** *dinner at home.*

➢ *I* ***visited*** *my parents last weekend.*

simple present: a verb form used to talk about habits or routines, schedules, and facts.

- ➢ *He **likes** apples and oranges.*
- ➢ *Toronto **gets** a lot of snow in the winter.*

singular noun: a noun that names only one person, place, or thing.

- ➢ *They have **a son** and **a daughter**.*

statement: a sentence that gives information.

- ➢ *My house has five rooms.*
- ➢ *He doesn't have a car.*

stative verb: a verb that does not describe an action. Non-action verbs indicate states, sense, feelings, or ownership. They are not common in the progressive.

- ➢ *I **love** my grandparents.*
- ➢ *I **see** Marta. She's across the street.*
- ➢ *They **have** a new car.*

stress: to say a syllable or a word with more volume or emphasis.

subject: the noun or pronoun that is the topic of the sentence.

- ➢ ***Patricia** is a doctor.*
- ➢ ***They** are from Iceland.*

subject pronoun: a pronoun that is the subject of a sentence: *I, you, he, she, it*, and *they*.

- ➢ ***I** have one brother.*
- ➢ ***He** lives in Miami.*

superlative: the form of an adjective or adverb used to compare three or more people, places, or things.

- ➢ *Mount Everest is **the highest** mountain in the world.*
- ➢ *Evgeny is **the youngest** student in our class.*

syllable: a part of a word that contains a single vowel sound and is pronounced as a unit.

- ➢ *The word **pen** has one syllable.*
- ➢ *The word **pencil** has two syllables (pen-cil).*

tense: the form of the verb that shows the time of the action.

- ➢ *They **sell** apples.* (simple present)
- ➢ *They **sold** cars.* (simple past)

third-person singular: in the simple present, the third-person singular ends in *–s* or *–es*. Singular nouns and the pronouns *he, she, it,* take the third-person singular form.

- ➢ *She **plays** the piano.*
- ➢ *Mr. Smith **teaches** her.*

time clause: a clause that tells when an action or event happened or will happen. Time clauses are introduced by conjunctions, such as *when, after, before, while,* and *since*.

- ➢ *I have lived here **since I was a child**.*
- ➢ ***While I was walking home,** it began to rain.*
- ➢ *I'm going to call my parents **after I eat dinner**.*

time expression: a phrase that tells when something happened or will happen. Time expressions usually go at the end or the beginning of sentence.

- ➢ ***Last week** I went hiking.*
- ➢ *She's moving **next month**.*

transitive verb: a verb that is followed by a direct object.

- ➢ *We **took** an umbrella.*

transition word: a word or phrase that connects ideas between sentences.

- ➢ *I'd like to go. **However,** I have too much work to do.*

unreal: used to describe situations that are contrary-to-fact, impossible, or unlikely to happen.

- ➢ *If I **weren't learning** English, I **would have** more free time.*
- ➢ *I **wish I had** a million dollars.*

verb: a word that shows action, gives a state, or shows possession.

- ➢ Tori **skated** across the ice.
- ➢ She **is** an excellent athlete.
- ➢ She **has** many medals.

voiced: a sound that is spoken with the vibration of the vocal cords. The consonants *b, d, g, j, l, m, n, r, th* (as in *then*), *v, w, z,* and all vowels are typically voiced.

voiceless: a sound that is spoken without the vibration of the vocal cords. The consonants *k, p, s, t,* and *ch,* sh, *th* (as in thing) are voiceless.

vowel: a sound represented in English by the letters: *a, e, i, o, u*, and sometimes *y*.

***Wh-* question:** a question that asks for specific information, not *"Yes"* or *"No."* (See *Wh- word.*)

- ➢ ***Where do they live?***
- ➢ ***What do you usually do on weeeknds?***

***Wh-* word:** a word such as *who, what, when, where, why,* or *how* that is used to begin a *Wh-* question.

***Yes/No* question:** a question that can be answered by *"Yes"* or *"No."*

- ➢ ***Do you live in Dublin?** Yes, I do./No I don't.*
- ➢ ***Can you ski?** Yes, I can./No, I can't.*

INDEX

Note: All page references in blue are in Split Edition B.

J

L

M

N

O

P

Q

R

W

Y

Text and Listening

4: Exercise 1. Source: National Geographic Magazine, January 2008. **64:** Exercise 1: National Geographic Magazine, August 2011. **12:** Exercise 1. Source: National Geographic Magazine, September 2011. **18:** Exercise 1. Source: National Geographic Magazine, January 2012. **32:** Exercise 1. Source: http://events.nationalgeographic.com/events/exhibits/polar-obsession. **41:** Exercise 1. Source: http://www.historylink.org/index.cfm?DisplayPage=output.cfm&file_id=9851. **46:** Exercise 1. Source: http://www.nationalgeographic.com/explorers/bios/barton-seaver. **48:** Exercise 1. Source: http://adventureblog.nationalgeographic.com/tag/alex-honnold. **59:** Exercise 3. Sources: http://scienceblogs.com/usasciencefestival/2012/11/08/women-who-changed-the-world-through-science-engineering-liu-yang-astronaut; http://www.huffingtonpost.com/2012/06/15/liu-yang-china-female-astronaut_n_1601063.html. **71:** Exercise 1. Source: http://natgeotv.com.au/videos/future-matters/clever-clothes 1707C4C2.aspx **78:** Exercise 1. Sources: http://environment.nationalgeographic.com/environment/sustainable-earth/11-of-the-fastest-growing-green-jobs/#/rio-20-green-jobs-roof-top-garden_55050_600x450.jpg; http://news.nationalgeographic.com/news/2012/07/pictures/120730-future-floating-cities-science-green-environment. **92:** Exercise 1. Sources: http://video.nationalgeographic.com/video/news/140402-mars-utah-vin; http://newswatch.nationalgeographic.com/2014/03/25/first-person-what-im-learning-on-a-simulated-mars-mission. **98:** Exercise 7C. Source: http://news.nationalgeographic.com/news/2007/09/070927-polynesians-sailors.html. **101:** Exercise 1. Source: http://www.nationalgeographic.com/adventure/0602/features/north-pole-expedition.html. **109:** Exercise 1. Sources: http://www.nationalgeographic.com/explorers/bios/albert-lin; http://www.nationalgeographic.com/explorers/projects/valley-khans-project. **120:** Exercise 1. Source: http://news.nationalgeographic.com/news/2005/03/0321_050321_babies.html. **124:** Exercise 1. Source: http://ngm.nationalgeographic.com/2011/10/teenage-brains/dobbs-text. **130:** Exercise 9. Source: http://www.mnn.com/lifestyle/eco-tourism/stories/5-teens-who-have-sailed-around-the-world-solo. **131:** Exercise 1. Source: http://news.nationalgeographic.com/news/2010/07/100701-boston-university-health-genes-live-100-longevity-genetic-science. **136:** Exercise 8. Source: assets.aarp.org/rgcenter/general/exercise-bulletin-survey.pdf. **139:** Exercise 3. Source: http://www.firstpeople.us/FP-Html-Legends/TheWonderfulTurtle-Lakota.html. **144:** Exercise 1. Sources: http://ngm.nationalgeographic.com/print/2010/05/sleep/max-text; http://www.npr.org/templates/story/story.php?storyId=4955790. **152:** Exercise 1. Sources: http://video.nationalgeographic.com/video/places/regions-places/south-america/paraguay_paraguayshaman; http://www.nature.org/ourinitiatives/urgentissues/rainforests/rainforests-facts.xml; http://www.sfgate.com/science/article/Amazon-deforestation-grows-outside-Brazil-3832770.php; http://www.wltus.org/shocking-deforestation-in-paraguay; http://rainforests.mongabay.com/1007.htm; http://www.rain-tree.com/article4.htm; http://news.nationalgeographic.com/news/2003/06/0626_030626_tvparaguaymedicine_2.html. **158:** Exercise 9. Source: National Geographic Magazine, February 2013. **161:** Exercise 1. Sources: http://www.looktothestars.org/news/7936-feliciano-dos-santos-says-lets-wash-our-hands; Milson, Andrew J. *Health*. National Geographic Global series. 2014; www.pbs.org/frontlineworld/stories/mozambique704/video/video index.html. **166:** Exercise 8. Sources: http://www.nationalgeographic.com/explorers/bios/hayat-sindi; http://education.nationalgeographic.com/education/news/real-world-geography-dr-hayat-sindi/?ar_a=1. **169:** Exercise 8. Source: http://www.nationmultimedia.com/opinion/Healthcare-in-Thailand-a-story-to-inspire-confiden-30180854.html. **170:** Exercise 2. Source: http://news.nationalgeographic.com/news/2013/06/130628-richard-louv-nature-deficit-disorder-health-environment. **184:** Exercise 1. Sources: http://www.youtube.com/watch?v=CRT4dU6r-KQ; http://www.jul.com; http://www.tripadvisor.com/Hotel_Review-g2237714-d1591061-Reviews-Khao_Sok_Nature_Resort-Phanom_Surat_Thani_Province.html; http://www.khaosoknatureresort.com. **208:** Exercise 1. Source: http://education.nationalgeographic.com/education/media/strange-rains/?ar_a=1. **212:** Exercise 5. Source: http://news.nationalgeographic.com/news/2007/02/070223-bees.html. **214:** Exercise 8. Source: http://news.nationalgeographic.com/news/2013/13/130507-talking-chili-plant-communication-science. **223:** Exercise 9. Source: http://news.nationalgeographic.com/news/2012/03/120312-leonardo-da-vinci-mural-lost-painting-florence-science-world. **216:** Exercise 1. Sources: http://ngm.nationalgeographic.com/2012/06/terra-cotta-warriors/larmer-text; http://science.nationalgeographic.com/science/archaeology/emperor-qin; http://www.livescience.com/25510-terracotta-warriors.html. **227:** Exercise 13. Source: http://news.nationalgeographic.com/news/2013/12/131208-roanoke-lost-colony-discovery-history-raleigh. **229:** Exercise 1. Source: http://www.globalpost.com/dispatch/news/regions/americas/united-states/130623/famed-tightrope-daredevil-nik-wallenda-cross-gra. **230:** Exercise 3. Source: http://news.nationalgeographic.com/news/2012/05/120510-maya-2012-doomsday-calendar-end-of-world-science.

Definitions for glossed words: Sources: *The Newbury House Dictionary plus Grammar Reference,* Fifth Edition, National Geographic Learning/Cengage Learning, 2014; *Collins Cobuild Illuminated Basic Dictionary of American English,* Cengage Learning 2010, Collings Cobuild/Harper Collins Publishers, First Edition, 2010; *Collins Cobuild School Dictionary of American English,* Cengage Learning 2009, Collins Cobuild/Harper Collins Publishers, 2008; Collins Cobuild Advanced Learner's Dictionary, 5th Edition, Harper Collins Publishers, 2006.

Photo Credits:

Inside Front Cover, left column: ©Cristina Mittermeier/National Geographic Creative, Courtesy of The Thayer Collection, Reprinted with permission of Barton Seaver, photo by Katie Stoops, ©Calit2, Erik Jepsen, ©Vander Meulen, Rebecca J/National Geographic Creative; right column: ©Cengage/National Geographic Creative, ©Tyrone Turner/National Geographic Creative, ©Cengage/National Geographic Creative, ©Rebecca Hale/National Geographic Creative, ©Jay Ullal/Black Star/Newscom.

2-3: ©Design Pics Inc/National Geographic Creative; **4, 5:** ©Michael Nichols/National Geographic Creative; **9:** ©Makoto Fujio/Getty Images; **12:** ©Echo/Getty Images; **13:** ©Genevieve Naylor/Corbis; **17:** ©KeithSzafranski/iStockphoto; **18:** ©National Geographic Image Collection/Alamy; **19:** ©Jodi Cobb/National Geographic/SuperStock, **22:** ©alkir/iStockphoto; **24:** ©INTERFOTO/Alamy; **28:** ©Catchlight Visual Services/Alamy; **30-31:** ©Jimmy Chin and Lynsey Dyer/National Geographic Creative; **32, 33**: ©Paul Nicklen/National Geographic Creative; **38:** ©Joel Sartore/National Geographic Creative; **39 top:** © Jeff Compasso/Alamy, **bottom:** ©Diane Cook and Len Jenshel/National Geographic Creative; **41 top:** Courtesy of the Thayer Collection, **bottom:** ©David Pluth/National Geographic Creative; **42:** ©David Pluth/National Geographic Creative; **46:** Reprinted with permission of Barton Seaver, photo by Katie Stoops; **48-49:** ©Jimmy Chin/National Geographic Creative, **55:** ©Hulton Archive/Getty Images; **56:** ©Bill Hatcher/National Geographic Creative; **57:** ©www.sand3r.com/Getty Images; **58:** ©Frans Lanting/National Geographic Creative; **59:** ©Lui Siu Wai/Xinhua/Photoshot/Newscom; **60:** ©Christopher Futcher/iStockphoto; **62-63:** ©southeast asia/Alamy; **64:** ©Koichi Kamoshida/Getty Images; **65:** ©Yoshikazu Tsuno/AFP/Getty Images; **71 top:** ©Gry Karin Stimo/SINTEF, **bottom:** © Danita Delimont/Getty Images; **72:** ©Yoshikazu Tsuno/AFP/Getty Images; **78, 79:** ©Rex Features via AP Images; **84, 88:** ©Bloomberg via Getty Images; **90-91:** ©Piriya Photography/Getty Images; **92-93:** ©Image Asset Management Ltd./Alamy; **94:** ©European Space Agency/NASA; **96-97:** ©JPL-Caltech/NASA; **99:** ©Blaine Harrington III/Alamy; **100 left to right:** ©Matthew Jacques/Shutterstock, ©Top Photo Corporation/Thinkstock, © CatchaSnap/Shutterstock; **101 background:** ©Julia Ivantsova/Shutterstock; **101 both, 102:** ©Borge Ousland/National Geographic Creative; **105:** ©David Liittschwager/National Geographic Creative; **106:** ©Raymond Gehman/National Geographic Creative; **107:** ©Bobby Model/National Geographic Creative; **109:** ©Calit2, Erik Jepsen; **110:** ©James Stanfield/National Geographic Creative; **112 background:** ©Miro Novak/Shutterstock; **114-115:** ©Alison Wright/National Geographic Creative; **116-117:** ©Jon Bower at Apexphotos/Getty Images; **116:** ©Edmund Lowe/Alamy; **122:** Photo by Draycat; **123:** ©katorisi; **124-125:** ©Michael Nichols/National Geographic Creative; **129:** ©epa european pressphoto agency b.v./Alamy; **131, 132:** ©David McLain/National Geographic Creative; **135 background:** ©Odua Images/Shutterstock; **136 background:** ©Feng Yu/Shutterstock; **138:** ©Aaron Juey/National Geographic Creative; **140:** ©Rachid Dahnoun/Getty Images; **142-143:** ©Shah Marai/AFP/Getty Images; **144-145:** ©Bill Hatcher/National Geographic Creative; **148:** ©Dan Kitwood/Getty Images; **149:** ©Silvia Reiche/Minden Pictures/Getty Images**; 152:** ©Wade Davis/Getty Images; **153:** © blickwinkel/Alamy; **158:** ©wacpan/Shutterstock; **161, 162:** ©Feliciano dos Santos/National Geographic Creative; **166:** ©Cengage/National Geographic Creative; **168:** ©ZUMA Press, Inc./Alamy; **172:** ©Fitbit, Inc.; **174-175:** ©Frans Lanting/National Geographic Creative; **176-177:** ©Tim Laman/National Geographic Creative; **176:** ©Paul Sutherland/National Geographic Creative; **179:** ©LOOK-foto/SuperStock; **184-185:** ©Iakov Kalinin/Shutterstock; **184:** ©Gary Dublanko/Alamy; **185:** ©LOOK Die Bildagentur der Fotografen GmbH/Alamy; **187:** ©Hemis/Alamy; **189:** ©Jon Arnold Images Ltd/Alamy; **191:** ©Fred Tanneau/Getty Images; **192:** ©ImageBROKER/Glow Images; **194:** © Frans Lemmens/Getty Images; **198:** ©Michele Falzone/Getty Images; **201:** ©DINODIA/age fotostock; **204:** ©Anna Hoychuk/Shutterstock; **206-207:** © funkyfood London—Paul Williams/Alamy; **208-209:** © Rui Almeida Fotografia/Getty Images; **209 clockwise from the left:** ©Smit/Shutterstock, ©Krishnadas/Shutterstock, ©Mirek Kijewski/Shutterstock; **213:** ©Hannele Lahti/National Geographic Creative; **215:** ©Barcroft Media/Getty Images; **216-217:** ©John Henshall/Alamy; **219:** © O. Louis Mazzatenta/National Geographic Creative; **223:** ©Vandeville Eric/Abaca/Newscom; **226 background:** ©Seregam/Shutterstock**, left:** ©Culture Club/Getty Images, **right:** ©UniversalImagesGroup/Getty Images; **227:** ©North Wind Picture Archives/Alamy; **229:** ©Mike Blake/Reuters; **231:** ©Patrickm/Reporters/Redux.

MAP

4, 12, 23, 32, 48, 92, 98, 109, 183: National Geographic Maps

ILLUSTRATION

10, 23, 53, 61, 83, 89, 113, 124, 136, 173, 182, 202, 205: Cenveo Publisher Services